ESSENTIAL SOLDIERS

## BLACK POWER SERIES

General Editors: Ibram X. Kendi and Ashley D. Farmer

# Essential Soldiers

*Women Activists and*
*Black Power Movement Leadership*

Kenja McCray

NEW YORK UNIVERSITY PRESS

New York

NEW YORK UNIVERSITY PRESS
New York
www.nyupress.org

Library of Congress Cataloging-in-Publication Data
Names: McCray, Kenja, author.
Title: Essential soldiers : women activists and Black Power Movement Leadership /
Kenja McCray.
Other titles: Black power series.
Description: New York : New York University Press, 2025. | Series: Black power series |
Includes bibliographical references and index.
Identifiers: LCCN 2024041634 (print) | LCCN 2024041635 (ebook) |
ISBN 9781479833047 (hardback) | ISBN 9781479833061 (ebook) |
ISBN 9781479833078 (ebook other)
Subjects: LCSH: African American women political activists. | Pan-Africanism—History. |
Black nationalism—United States—History.
Classification: LCC E185.615 .M36 2025 (print) | LCC E185.615 (ebook) |
DDC 323.119607309046—dc23/eng/20240905
LC record available at https://lccn.loc.gov/2024041634
LC ebook record available at https://lccn.loc.gov/2024041635

This book is printed on acid-free paper, and its binding materials are chosen for strength and durability. We strive to use environmentally responsible suppliers and materials to the greatest extent possible in publishing our books.

The manufacturer's authorized representative in the EU for product safety is Mare Nostrum Group B.V., Mauritskade 21D, 1091 GC Amsterdam, The Netherlands. Email: gpsr@mare-nostrum.co.uk.

Manufactured in the United States of America

10 9 8 7 6 5 4 3 2 1

Also available as an ebook

# CONTENTS

PREFACE

My interest in 1960s Black women activists' stories began with attempts to make sense of the incredible personal transformation happening in my late teens and early twenties. Like writer Ta-Nehisi Coates, I was one of the many young people whose awareness about the conditions of my existence developed amid early 1990s Afrocentricity.[1] "In this blooming consciousness, in this period of intense questioning, I was not alone," Coates wrote in *Between the World and Me*.[2] I intimately knew how the author's coming-of-age experience was not isolated when I read that passage. Many of my peers and I were with Coates, at least in spirit, opening our supple minds to kernels of knowledge planted during preceding decades.

For me, the 1990s involved newfound Kwanzaa celebrations and conferences keynoted by battle-weary but determined Black Power movement veterans when I was a student at Spelman, a historically Black women's college in Atlanta, Georgia. My evenings and weekends were filled with politicized poetry slams, "conscious" rap music performances, and meetings packed with folks trying to change the world in youthful bursts of exuberance. I also spent a lot of time at the African American book and media stores that functioned as hubs for such activities. Coates vividly described the times, musing that "seeds planted in the 1960s forgotten by so many, sprung up from the ground and bore fruit" during the era. Rappers transmitted the words and images of Black nationalist leaders in their lyrics, beat breaks, and videos. Coates described playing taped Black Power media purchased at African American bookstores on his boombox, much as I did.[3]

Coates's book contemplated aspects of Black masculinity as guidance to his son. Like so many authors who have penned reflections on Black nationalism, Black Power, and Black consciousness, he focused on the contours of African American manhood. Conceptions of my sense of Black femininity, however, shaped my experiences as a United States-born southerner descended from enslaved Africans. I joined a sisterhood called Auset (AST) in the 1990s and participated in a process called the "Journey to African Womanhood." Not limited to being men's helpmates, my peers and I were primed for leadership by an elders' council. In turn, we boldly committed ourselves to occupying positions at the forefront of the struggle against sexism, racism, and classism.[4] Little did I know at the time, "African womanhood" was a Black nationalist designation with a decades-long history. My AST sisters and I thought we were inventing the proverbial wheel. I had no knowledge of the Committee for a Unified Newark (CFUN) Mumininas' primer on Black nationalist womanhood from two decades earlier. Although our contemporary version of African womanhood was different from theirs, the booklet was filled with instructive information that AST could have used for our journey.

After I officially declared a history major at Spelman, I learned about delving into bodies of literature and mining primary sources. Texts and documents on Black nationalism revealed that the active and outspoken women who indirectly influenced my activism and writing had not received the same level of attention as the men, and cultural nationalist women were particularly marginalized. Their shrouded existence in the literature belied all the work they performed in service of the Black freedom struggle. I chose to write about the female cultural nationalist activists who were instrumental in shaping African womanhood because the ideology is worth examining in historical context.

This book is particularly for my daughters and other young people who are protesting, organizing, institution building, and consciousness raising in the world today. They should not have to reinvent the wheel. My aim is to provide them with the core aspects of *kazi* leadership, the work-centered, group-centered, and African-centered form of servant leadership exhibited by Pan-African cultural nationalist women. In the process, my goal is to explore some of the trials and triumphs of cultural nationalist advocates and institutions. I am also writing this book to honor the tenacious, astute women Pan-African cultural nationalists who committed themselves to the protracted, often thankless struggle for Black freedom, empowerment, and equality. I especially endeavor to communicate the stories of the activists who shared their experiences for this project to new and broader audiences in ways that inspire novel understandings and forge new connections between the past, present, and future.

# ABBREVIATIONS

ACBPA    Allegheny County Black Political Assembly
AFS    African Free School
ALD    African Liberation Day
ALSC    African Liberation Support Committee
ASA    African American Students Association
ASCRIA    African Society for Cultural Relations with Independent Africa
AST    Auset, an African Sisterhood
ATA    African American Teachers Association
BPP    Black Panther Party
BWG    Black Women's Group (also Black Woman's Group)
BWUF    Black Women's United Front
CAP    Congress of African People
CDF    Children's Defense Fund
CFUN    Committee for a Unified Newark (also Committee for Unified Newark)
COINTELPRO    Counterintelligence Program
CORE    Congress of Racial Equality
CUNY    City University of New York
FBI    Federal Bureau of Investigation
HBCU    historically Black colleges and universities
IBI    independent Black institution
IPE    Institute for Positive Education
LAUSD    Los Angeles Unified School District
LRS    League of Revolutionary Struggle
M-L-M    Marxism-Leninism-Mao Zedong thought (also Marxism-Leninism-Maoism)
MMBI    Mary McLeod Bethune Institute
NAACP    National Association for the Advancement of Colored People
NBA    National Black Assembly

NBPC  National Black Political Convention
NBUF  National Black United Front
NCNW  National Council of Negro Women
NOI  Nation of Islam
PRIDE  Promotion of Racial Identity, Dignity, and Equality
SNCC  Student Nonviolent Coordinating Committee (also Student National Coordinating Committee)
UCLA  University of California Los Angeles
UFT  United Federation of Teachers
USTI  Urban Survival Training Institute
WATU  Working Always Through Unity

# Introduction

During the late 1960s, advocates of the Los Angeles-based Us Organization could leaf through a one-dollar booklet to read the pronouncements of the group's chairman, Maulana Karenga. The quotes covered topics ranging from the fundamental nature of "Blackness" to the importance of family in the struggle for African American liberation. Karenga's ideas about gender were included in the booklet and stressed that "a man has to be a leader." The woman's limited roles focused on "inspir[ing] her man" and "educat[ing] their children." According to the *Quotable Karenga*, which was published in 1967, gender equality "is false; it's the devil's concept. Our concept is complimentary [*sic*]. Complimentary means you complete or make perfect that which is imperfect." During the Us Organization's early years, ideas that emphasized female subordination formed the bedrock of the group's guiding doctrine, which was called Kawaida.

Notions of gender inequality, however, would not go uncontested.[1] Women advocates particularly challenged such philosophies as Kawaida doctrine matured, expanded, and impacted other nationalist ideologies during the Black Power era. Kawaida became a guiding influence for activists in groups from New Jersey and New York City to St. Louis and New Orleans. Women were central to the functioning of the organizations, particularly when male members were under siege due to intergroup conflict and state efforts to neutralize their activism. Women were also key actors in food cooperatives, educational and training programs, mass communication pursuits, community enterprises, and political organizing. As women grappled with sexism in Black nationalist groups and participated in the larger Black freedom struggle, they developed literature, activities, and organizations to address their issues and to broaden the overall Black cultural nationalist vision for ending oppression. Women particularly helped reformulate and modernize Kawaida-influenced Pan-African cultural nationalism by "renegotiating" restrictive gender roles.[2]

1

By the early 1980s, people who picked up a copy of *Kawaida Theory* could learn that, in addition to complementarity, Karenga now asserted the importance of a "nonsexist" egalitarianism focused on accepting "the equal human and social worth and right" of both men and women.[3] Readers could also obtain *Working Together, We Can Make a Change*, a booklet by a woman advocate in the Kawaida-influenced Ahidiana organization. In *Working Together*, Tayari kwa Salaam declared that women were "essential soldiers" in the fight for both Black freedom and women's liberation.[4]

Despite such changes in the literature over the years between 1967 and the 1980s, pioneering Black feminist scholars Johnetta B. Cole and Beverly Guy-Sheftall argued two decades later that "Kawaida theory" was "an unmistakable articulation of male supremacy."[5] Notably, the scholars' 2003 study did not give much voice to women affiliated with Kawaida-influenced cultural nationalist organizations, despite the activists' history of resisting male chauvinism and the changes that they helped engender in Kawaida-influenced ideology and organizational policy. Although Cole and Guy-Sheftall acknowledged that Karenga's views had evolved over time, they gave little attention to the women who influenced such changes in his thinking. As historian Ashley D. Farmer has pointed out, scholars tend to overlook women's essential roles in refashioning gender constructs in Kawaida-influenced organizations because of the doctrine's patriarchal reputation.[6]

In this book, I center the women who made up a substantial part of the membership of these organizations. The stories collected here contribute to recent histories that recover the ideas, motivations, backgrounds, and work of the women who helped shape Kawaida-influenced Pan-African cultural nationalism by redefining their prescribed roles. Women often embodied *kazi* as a rationale for broadening their positions within cultural nationalism. *Kazi* is a Swahili word for "work," and a Kawaida principle calling for sustained, vigorous personal effort in support of nation building. Women activists in Kawaida-influenced organizations engaged in a specific form of service leadership that I call "*kazi* leadership." Somewhat like Robert Greenleaf's servant leaders, female advocates in Kawaida-influenced organizations focused on collectivity. Members of their communities often deemed the women leaders because of the service they performed. Their specific calling to nation build in service of the struggle for Black liberation, and their particular use of critical and cultural consciousness, made *kazi* leaders unique as servant leaders.[7] *Kazi* leadership involved women's employment of the concept that the Black liberation movement required everyone to work wherever they were capable and needed, even in capacities that breached gender norms and reconfigured restrictive roles for women within Kawaida-influenced organizations.[8]

\* \* \*

The activists in this book hailed from diverse backgrounds, held a myriad of varying affinities, and voiced different perspectives on the meanings of freedom as well as the methods of obtaining equality across time, space, and circumstance. They nevertheless espoused what can be termed Black cultural nationalism at some point in time. Black nationalism, much like other ideologies, is complex, adaptable, and manifold, and has been configured and expressed in several distinct forms.[9] Black cultural nationalism, broadly defined, is the belief that African Americans have a unique aesthetic, distinct values, and a sense of communalism emerging from their African heritage and diasporic folkways.[10] African American studies experts Akinyele Umoja and Charles Jones described cultural nationalism as "an ideological orientation and practice that emphasizes identity, philosophy, customs, . . . folklore, holidays, art (e.g., visual, music, and literature), aesthetics, language, and family and community building as a primary vehicle of asserting the integrity and self-determination of a people." According to Umoja and Jones, Kawaida's adherents were among the foremost advocates of the idea that cultural transformation was a necessary precursor to achieving Black political power and social change.[11]

Kawaida philosophy was a specific cultural nationalist form, which Ron Everett (later Maulana Karenga) began developing in the 1960s to build an African-centered cultural framework that African Americans could utilize in liberating themselves from oppression. Karenga interpreted the East African Swahili word *kawaida* to mean "tradition and reason."[12] However, it literally means "usual thing or customary."[13] Historian Russell Rickford presents a more critical definition of Kawaida, stating that the doctrine was, on the surface, a product of painstakingly culled African traditions and analyses of African American realities; however, it was more a set of quasi-religious principles claiming to show the path to a better way of life. An organizational handbook for workers at The East, a Brooklyn-based cooperative-business, cultural, and educational center, described Kawaida as "an Ideology, a total value system which interprets Life," and "a framework in which to place all ideas & problems dealing with the community of Black people." In other places throughout the manual, East workers were called "advocates of Kawaida."[14]

Kawaida was meant to support organizing efforts during the Black liberation struggles of the 1960s. The philosophy emphasized the use of an African-derived ritual, language, and logic to raise awareness and transform and support advocates in the process of challenging European American and capitalist hegemony. Resistance to "sexual domination" later emerged as a Kawaida goal.[15] Seven ideas called the Nguzo Saba, or the Seven Principles of Blackness, comprise the philosophy's core. They are unity, self-determination, collective work and responsibility, cooperative economics, purpose, creativity, and faith. Its most widely known derivative is the annual, late-December celebration known as Kwanzaa.

This book traces women in four Kawaida-influenced Pan-African cultural nationalist organizations: Us; Committee for [a] Unified Newark (CFUN), and the Congress of African People; The East; and Ahidiana.[16] The broad designation "Pan-African" describes advocates' common "commitment to linking struggles for freedom and dignity throughout the African continent and diaspora."[17] Additional information about each group appears in table 1.1.

"Kawaida-influenced" Pan-African cultural nationalism is a contested category. In the booklet *Kwanzaa: Origin, Concepts, Practice*, Maulana Karenga established that, among others, the four groups included in this study were institutions subscribing to "Kawaida views and values" at some point. In fact, he gave special recognition to what he called "the most viable and durable nationalist organizations shaped in the Kawaida mold." The East in New York City and Ahidiana in New Orleans were two such groups. These organizations, Karenga wrote, were instrumental in perpetuating and expanding Kwanzaa via large annual celebrations in their cities, literary production, and institution-building practices that included Kawaida principles.[18]

TABLE I.1. Kawaida-Influenced Organizations

| Organization Name(s) | Years of Operation | Main Branch | Description |
|---|---|---|---|
| Us Organization (later New Afroamerican Movement, Kawaida Groundwork Committee, Organization Us, and Us) | 1965–present | Los Angeles | The vanguard Black Power-era Kawaida organization; aim was developing a philosophy for self-determined, liberative organizing; name meant "us" (Black people) as opposed to "them" (white people)[a] |
| Spirit House, Committee for [a] Unified Newark (CFUN), the Congress of African People (CAP) | 1967–1976 | Newark | Community theater and branch Kawaida temple; political action group; united front organization with such affiliates as Pittsburgh CAP, USTI (Philadelphia), and WATU (St. Louis) |
| The East Organization | 1969–1986 | New York | Cultural and educational center, bookstore, and health food co-op; also housed the Uhuru Sasa School |
| Ahidiana | 1972–1987 | New Orleans | Bookstore, community center, printing press, school, and study group |

a Scot Brown, Fighting for US, 161; Scot Brown, "The US Organization, Black Power Vanguard Politics, and the United Front Ideal."

There is no universally accepted definition of a Kawaida-influenced organization. Although some activists disagreed with the idea that Ahidiana was Kawaida-influenced, other Ahidiana advocates asserted that it was. For instance, former member Michael McMillan wrote, "Ahidiana was guided by the Kawaida philosophy of Maulana Karenga, founder of Us Organization, and creator of the holiday Kwanzaa." McMillan noted that Karenga's *Kawaida Theory* was sold in Ahidiana's bookstore, and reading it inspired him to pursue a psychology degree despite previously dropping out of college.[19]

Several East members also saw their organization as Kawaida-inspired. Martha Bright said, "The East is a Kawaida organization . . . just like [the Committee for a Unified Newark], . . . just like Karenga's Us Organization, . . . and there were other organizations in Chicago and Detroit and in the South that were Kawaida organizations. . . . The East was absolutely one of the original [groups]."[20] Steven "Akili" Walker affiliated with The East through its Uhuru Sasa School during his teen years. He wrote in his autobiography that he received the name Akili Hakima at The East, where advocates "practiced the doctrine of

Kawaida." Like Martha Bright, he saw The East's work as part of a broader movement, noting that "there were many other organizations around the country following this doctrine."[21] Statements written in The East *Worker's Manual* confirm Bright's and Walker's assertions about the group's Kawaida focus. The manual states, "Mashariki (East) is a cultural organization based on Seven (7) Principles. . . . We of Mashariki are members of the Kawaida faith. . . . Kawaida is the alternative value system which can free Black people from the materialistic, White, European system of values."[22]

The "Kawaida-influenced" designation does not negate the groups' unique qualities or divergences in philosophy and practice. "[There] was a lot of cooperation," Bright remembered, and "there were many commonalities." At the same time, there were "inter- and intra-organizational rivalries. . . . The way we do things here in Brooklyn was not necessarily the way things were done in Jersey and Chicago and Louisiana and California."[23]

Just as they differed on the question of Kawaida's influence on Pan-African organizations, women activists varied in their self-definition within the categories of women's rights activism, feminism, and womanism. Some advocates defined themselves as feminists, at times further describing themselves with such identifiers as "Black" and "Third World." Others rejected feminism as the domain of White women.[24] Many women activists in the organizations preferred to be called womanists. In her essay collection *In Search of Our Mothers' Gardens*, Alice Walker defined womanism as a shade of Black or non-White feminism particularly committed to the survival of an entire people, no matter their gender. Additionally, others embraced differing womanisms such as Clenora Hudson-Weems's Africana womanism. Hudson-Weems's theory is rooted in Black nationalism and emphasizes gender compatibility, respect for elders, mothering, nurturing, and spirituality.[25] Presenting various womanisms and feminisms as specific categories accommodates multiple paradigms and acknowledges the importance of self-determined naming.

These feminist and womanist activists are situated within the Black freedom struggle, a long process composed of distinct but overlapping movements. This definition acknowledges the idea that the Black freedom struggle is a centuries-long series of endeavors that began with the fight for manumission from chattel bondage in the British North American colonies; however, it also accounts for other characterizations, which point out that the struggle has been a movement of movements. That is, several movements have ebbed and flowed within the larger framework of the Black freedom struggle, which included the Black Power movement of the late 1960s and 1970s as well as the reverberations of the movement's grassroots institutions and activism lasting into the 1980s and beyond.

* * *

Who was a *kazi* leader? Many became activists for similar reasons as their predecessors and contemporary activists involved in other movements within the Black freedom struggle. The tumultuous circumstances of their era shaped and catalyzed these baby boomers' advocacies for Black Power cultural nationalism. Their environment also fostered a cosmopolitan outlook, which they often channeled into Pan-Africanism. Pan-African cultural nationalist women were products of the Black campus movement, taking its core tenets and implementing them across the country by helping establish institutions such as bookstores, presses, and educational programs in neighborhoods beset by urban crisis.

What did *kazi* leaders do? In Kawaida-influenced cultural nationalist organizations, as in other nationalist expressions, women's work often emphasized birthing and nurturing extended families as the cornerstone of nation-building efforts. Women organized and directed other, less-feminized activities like media operations, voter registration drives, political campaigns, fundraising, boycotts, and pickets. Even while engaging in activities typically associated with femininity, they were key to the process of actualizing cultural nationalist concepts like *taifa saa* (nation time) and *ujamaa* (cooperative economics) through enterprise development focused on clothing sales and production, health and nutrition, and food preparation and activism. They also helped organize cooperative businesses, as well as political conferences and study groups aimed at consciousness raising. The women's peers often informally acknowledged their leadership roles. Peer designation as leaders, however, did not always correlate with official leadership titles.[26]

Independent and supplementary Black educational programs were some of the most significant cultural nationalist community ventures. CFUN's Kawaida-influenced "African woman" Pan-African cultural nationalist gender ideal was initially based on an ideology that circumscribed female advocates' roles while also elevating them as parents and teachers. Movement schools nevertheless had become important venues for women's political theorizing and activism by the early 1970s. The role these women played in the Black Power movement may be likened to that of "republican mothers" during the early national period in the early nineteenth-century United States. In similar ways, determined Pan-African community "mamas" would employ Black nationalist ideals to lead organizations, develop programs, and advance their education and training.[27] At times, cultural nationalist women advanced Black Power masculinism while working within traditional roles. On other occasions, they sidestepped, openly critiqued, and vigorously resisted patriarchal practices. Their theorizing helped produce more modern and progressive gender ideals and policies within cultural nationalist organizations. In this way, women's roles in cultural nationalism evolved from a singular focus on complementarity to incorporate and express *kazi* leadership.

There were three basic characteristics of *kazi* leadership:

1. A primary dedication to performing the difficult, sustained work of nation building among African and African-descended people, rather than a desire to be "in charge."[28]
2. A commitment to collectivity and cooperation, or the belief that there must be multiple program administrators, institution developers, and group leaders within the freedom struggle. Those occupying such positions must be from various walks of life, especially in terms of gender and age.[29]
3. A focus on developing consciousness derived from meaningful and critical knowledge of the cultures, heritage, and struggles of African and African-descended peoples.[30]

Labeling the women's efforts *kazi* leadership is not meant to suggest a qualified kind of leadership. The term articulates a specific type of leadership emerging among women in Pan-African cultural nationalist organizations of the Black Power era. This type developed in the process of studying women, but *kazi* leadership is not inherently gendered.

*Kazi* reflects a more collective, grassroots kind of leadership that arose from Pan-African cultural nationalist formations. It stands in contrast to other leadership models. For example, Maulana Karenga and Amiri Baraka, both prominent leaders of Pan-African nationalist organizations, faced accusations of allowing a cult of personality to flourish within the groups they led.[31] Moreover, much of the literature about Kawaida-influenced organizations focuses on the best-known leaders. *Kazi* instead aligns with the idea that it is a fallacy to believe that one leader, organization, or ideology has the blueprint for Black empowerment. East leader Jitu Weusi emphasized the importance of "collective leadership" to the Black freedom struggle. He defined the term as meaningful and critical consciousness of the cultures, heritage, and struggles of African and African-descended peoples. Weusi wrote that collective leadership is important, because no individual can develop and sustain an institution alone. Sincere leaders must be willing to lead and follow, he insisted, and "hard work and respect for good work" produce results. Weusi's reflections encompass the basic characteristics of *kazi* leadership. The experience of female members in Kawaida-influenced organizations reinforces Weusi's observations, pointing to the necessity of understanding collective leadership.[32]

\* \* \*

Over the past forty years, a body of literature on Kawaida-influenced organizations has developed, and it reflects the complexity of women's roles therein. The first published history of a Kawaida organization, a piece about the Congress of African People (CAP), appeared in the 1980s.[33] A certain segment of the literature treats Pan-African cultural nationalist women's activities as a part of larger organizational histories or of men's narratives. My work expands on such historiography, because subsuming women's images and experiences within more general histories does not shed enough light on women advocates' impact on the Kawaida-influenced Pan-African cultural nationalist aspect of the long Black freedom struggle. *The Autobiography of Leroi*

*Jones* (1984), by Amiri Baraka; *A Nation within a Nation: Amiri Baraka (LeRoi Jones) and Black Power Politics* (1999), by Komozi Woodard; *Fighting for US: Maulana Karenga, the US Organization, and Black Cultural Nationalism* (2003), by Scot Brown; *A View from The East: Black Cultural Nationalism and Education in New York City* (2009), by Kwasi Konadu; *Amiri Baraka and the Congress of African People: History and Memory* (2015), by Michael Simanga; and *We Are an African People: Independent Education, Black Power, and the Radical Imagination* (2016), by Russell Rickford, all include reflections on women advocates. The authors, however, consider Pan-African cultural nationalist women as backdrops to autobiographies or biographies of prominent male Kawaida leaders, or in writing about broader organizational and movement histories. In *Remaking Black Power: How Black Women Transformed an Era* (2017), Ashley D. Farmer features two chapters on women in the Us Organization, CFUN/CAP, and The East, explaining how they helped shaped the Black Power era by redefining concepts of "the African woman" and "the Pan-African woman." Farmer's work is an intellectual history drawing mainly from textual archival materials. *Essential Soldiers* employs a different methodological focus in its emphasis on oral history and memory. All the authors rightfully call attention to the nature of masculine, cult-of-personality leadership. None, however, defines and codifies the leadership that women exhibited in their associations with Kawaida-influenced Pan-African cultural nationalist organizations.

Building on these previous efforts, *Essential Soldiers* highlights women's images and roles in Pan-African cultural nationalism, tying together several organizations with the connecting thread of Kawaida influence. This book contributes to the discussion of women's roles within the Black Power movement and the long Black freedom struggle by broadening the literature to address radical women who (a) were associated with organizations beyond the better-known Black Panther Party (BPP), the Student Nonviolent Coordinating Committee (SNCC), or SNCC-derived groups such as the Third World Women's Alliance; and (b) were integral to the functioning of key Black Power-era organizations and to the broadening of Kawaida philosophy's scope, but who may not have achieved iconic status as Black Power revolutionaries.[34] This book also foregrounds women's recollections with womanist methods in mind. Men's remembrances are therefore included, but the book more fully explores women's roles across the various organizations to develop a clearer picture of the ways the philosophy shaped their experiences, how the women molded the philosophy, and the roles that women played as activists and leaders in Kawaida-influenced organizations.[35]

It is worth mentioning that there are no archives specifically focused on sources concerned with women's experiences in Kawaida-influenced organizations, a fact that underscores the importance of this study. Archival sources are scarce, and *What We Stood For: The Story of a Revolutionary Black Woman*, by Deborah Jones with the assistance of Thandisizwe Chimurenga, is the only published autobiography of a woman involved in a Kawaida organization at this time. There does, however, exist a growing list of secondary sources on women in such organizations, as discussed on the previous pages. Despite recent scholars' efforts to present new information about African American women's influence on the Black Power movement, still more research is needed to deepen our knowledge of female advocates who were in the various organizations that incorporated some form of Kawaida philosophy as a guiding philosophy. This work is by no means an attempt to erase male chauvinism from the history of Kawaida-influenced cultural nationalism. Its purpose is to present a fuller picture, underlining women's demonstration of a unique, work-centered, people-centered, and African-centered form of service leadership in Kawaida-influenced groups.[36] To accomplish this, I primarily use oral history methods, focusing on women affiliated with Us, CAP, Ahidiana, and The East, and treating their advocacy in multiple realms, from the press to educational programs. The aim is to illuminate the memories and motivations of women in Kawaida-influenced Pan-African cultural nationalist organizations and chart their work as service leaders.

\* \* \*

*Essential Soldiers* is rooted in memory and oral history methods. The chapters are, therefore, organized thematically and unfold around topics that emerged from women Pan-African nationalist advocates' own words. The activists' ideas generally are put in a sort of "conversation" around common themes and occasionally are grouped according to organizational affiliations. The major exception is chapter 4, which has content that significantly lends itself to institutional groupings. Chapter 1, "'Nobody Knows Our Names': Motivations and Origins," discusses Pan-African cultural nationalist women's motivations for joining the Black freedom struggle and explores some of their similarities with other activists involved in various aspects of the struggle. Female activists in Kawaida-influenced organizations descended from many impulses within the struggle for Black freedom, from classical nationalism to radical ideologies. The women were not anomalous for participating in Pan-African cultural nationalist organizations. Their motivations arose from their origins in vindicationist ideological traditions and from sentiments nurtured within family households influenced by the likes of labor movement organizers and Garveyites. This chapter also addresses the ways the political and social climate in 1960s America shaped the worldview of women who would eventually join Kawaida-influenced Pan-African cultural nationalist organizations. Their perspectives fell on a continuum with earlier versions of modern Black nationalism and civil rights movement protests. Born during the years between World War II and the Cuban Revolution, the women discussed coming of age in an era of rapid change. They were moved by the spirit of the times, and their sensibilities about being in the world were transformed as they came to identify with global politics, adopt African-influenced aesthetics and modes of self-definition, and develop a swaggering sense of Black pride.

Chapter 2, "'Agitate. Educate. Organize': Women in Kawaida-Influenced Neighborhood Organizations, the Press, and Protest Politics," chronicles women who affiliated with Kawaida-influenced organizations through their involvement in neighborhood programs and protests. The section is focused on female advocates' efforts via political organizing, consciousness raising, direct action, education, print media, and nation building by way of public institutions and household development. Various elements, including the concept of *kazi*, or vigorous, sustained work, influenced their approaches to activism. Some female activists became involved in the Black freedom struggle seeking to take responsibility for the well-being of their communities in the context of urban crisis. Many of the women eventually lodged challenges to gender-based restrictions both inside and outside cultural nationalist organizations. As a result of their work within Black nationalist organizations, women developed valuable leadership skills and abilities.

The oral narratives collected for this book reflected the women's essential roles in nation building, from the earliest stages of planning and development to the routine sustaining of establishments and programs. Chapter 3, "'*Taifa Saa* Means Nation Time': Women, Institution Building, and Program Development," highlights the importance of the advocates' efforts while discussing instances of how women in Kawaida-influenced organizations often worked within standard gender roles. Additionally, accounts such as those of the advocates involved in Ahidiana's sisterhood gatherings reflected the idea that certain female cultural nationalists actively reshaped gendered notions about nation building to support the work that they saw as integral to community welfare and important to what they viewed as African Americans' shared fate.

Chapter 4, "'To Build Our Nation . . . Teach Our Children!': Women's Gender Roles in Independent and Supplementary Black Educational Programs," focuses on the daycare centers, schools, and adult education, after-school, and weekend programs of Us, Committee for a Unified Newark and the Congress of African People, The East, and Ahidiana. These organizations originally rested on a philosophy that constrained women's gender roles to home, education, and the support of men's agendas. As a result, educational institutions served as vital sites for women's political work within such a context. Although advocates often envisioned womanhood within Kawaida-influenced groups as a specifically African diasporic identity, Pan-African cultural nationalist beliefs about women's gender roles also resembled mainstream American early national period republican motherhood ideology. The majority-female body of teachers in Kawaida-influenced independent Black institutions (IBIs) was central to the process of developing citizens in the incipient nation, much like republican mothers. Additionally, Pan-African cultural nationalist women leveraged their access to education, training, and leadership opportunities to transcend their designated gender roles. The women employed key Kawaida values, like service as educators, to organize programs such as communal child-care. Doing so aided advocates in conducting political work beyond the bounds of their domestic duties. Finally, the epilogue grapples with important lessons of the past, including an overview of the pitfalls and promises of Kawaida-influenced Pan-African cultural nationalism as well as the ongoing necessity of *kazi* leadership.

# 1

## "Nobody Knows Our Names"

### *Motivations and Origins*

On a balmy summer day in Newark, New Jersey, Amina Baraka sat on the stoop of her home recounting days spent as an activist and organizer during the Black Power movement. As the mild breeze tousled her silvery-gray hair, she discussed her time in the Committee for a Unified Newark (CFUN) and the Congress of African People (CAP). She spoke confidently and positively for the most part, remembering those days with fondness. Occasionally, however, disappointment tinged her story. The dismay was sometimes subtle. At other times, it blared louder than the sirens whizzing by the tree-lined street where she lived. Recalling details of the work that she and other women performed to help organize the 1972 National Black Political Convention (NBPC), she punctuated her list with the following statement, "We were there. But nobody—like Jimmy Baldwin's book—nobody knows our names. . . . That is haunting me and [is] the reason I'm giving this interview."[1]

Telling the stories of the female activists who were in Kawaida-influenced Pan-African cultural nationalist organizations—making their names known—is what propels this book. This chapter uncovers some of their motivations for joining the fight for freedom and equality and highlights the idea that their similarities with earlier activists place them on a continuum within the long Black freedom struggle. While popular accounts see them as exceptionally oppressed within a hyper-masculine Black Power movement, illuminating their motivations and influences reveals a more complicated picture. Although male chauvinism did impact these women, they were people of complex character who cannot be reduced to objects of oppression.[2]

Saying their names and listening to their voices, as acts of seeing and hearing Pan-African cultural nationalist women, we see that they were not chronological anomalies or fringe elements in a movement that "seemed to come out of nowhere." Instead, they were multifaceted people who were similar to their predecessors in many ways.[3] The women's organizational and ideological connections to pioneering activists like Queen Mother Audley Moore and Fannie Lou Hamer, as well as to theories like "race first," race vindication, efficient womanhood, and community feminism, stimulated their activist tendencies.[4] These connections also demonstrated that they descended from multiple strains of the Black freedom struggle—from classical Black nationalism to civil rights, labor organizing, and radical movements.[5]

Yet it must be emphasized that, though the women remembered and understood their own activism within the frameworks of anteceding struggles such as the Old Left, many Cold War-era ideological shifts influenced the tenor of their activism.[6] The Black Left feminists of the 1920s and 1930s, for example, affected the Black feminists and the "new communist movement" of the 1970s. Radical influence was, however, minimized during the interim period of Cold War repression, and civil rights organizing escalated to Black Power stridency in the face of intractable and nebulous forms of oppression. Although there were underlying continuities between the phases of the long Black freedom struggle, cultural nationalist activists of the Black Power era did not join a unified and cohesive movement for Black freedom. They joined groups like the Us Organization, Committee for a Unified Newark, The East, and Ahidiana during a period that was distinct in its characteristics and inspiration in many ways. The attitudes and actions of Pan-African cultural nationalist women were shaped by a growing consciousness of Black Power and identity, which was manifested in the 1960s domestically in the ongoing civil rights struggle and growing cultural independence from White norms, and internationally in Pan-African liberation movements. The women's narratives reflect their involvement in these events and the impact on their own developing sense of identity and belonging in the long Black freedom struggle.

### "Black Consciousness . . . Rolled Strong": Influences of the 1960s Political and Social Climate

On June 17, 1966, almost a year after an explosive uprising against persistent inequality and police brutality rocked the Black neighborhood of

Watts in Los Angeles, hundreds of peaceful protestors in the Meredith March Against Fear entered the Delta town of Greenwood en route to Jackson, Mississippi from Memphis, Tennessee. Late in the day, Stokely Carmichael, SNCC chairman and one of several march leaders, was arrested for the twenty-seventh time. After his release that evening, Carmichael addressed the large group of people who gathered to take a stand against pervasive White supremacist violence and encourage Black citizens to register and vote. He declared, "I ain't going to jail no more," frustrated with the petty harassment meant to cause attrition within the movement. "The only way we gonna stop them white men from whuppin' us . . . is to take over! We been sayin' 'Freedom Now' for six years and we ain't got nothing. What we gonna start sayin' now is *Black Power!*'" Several times, he raised the cry, "What do we want?" The crowd roared back each time, "*Black Power!!!*"[7] Although this was neither the first nor the only time the words had been uttered, the news media in attendance that scorching evening captured the highly charged call to action, signaling to the entire nation that "Black Power" had arrived. Both the uprising and the march represented turning points in the long struggle for freedom. The climate in Black America had changed.[8] The 1960s produced this atmosphere, which also shaped the unique worldview of the women who became cultural nationalists during the era.

Two powerful factors persisted in post–World War II America: disfranchisement and racial violence (both physical and passive).[9] The strident Black response was a justifiable reaction to the United States' ongoing oppression of African Americans despite a long history of nonviolent social protest.[10] While those who joined cultural nationalist groups during the Black Power era had commonalities with activists from previous waves of the long Black freedom struggle, their involvement emerged at a distinctive turning point, producing different outcomes.[11] Black Power was a period of the struggle that produced more militant leaders; goals that included community control, self-respect, self-defense, and self-determination; and new symbols such as the raised fist and the black panther. Many advocates sympathized with, supported, or had previously been involved with the nonviolent civil rights movement. Yet, when a new wave of activists like Carmichael challenged nonviolent tactics and integrationist goals, some of the women who previously connected with the expressions of the Black freedom struggle either changed or broadened their ideologies or affiliations.

Several of the women attested to the fact that the spirit of the times—a rising tide of expectations in the wake of civil rights gains, evaporating hopes as the movement reached its limitations, a flood of civil unrest, and the resulting conservative backlash—shaped their outlook as young African Americans and molded the cultural nationalist movement's character. Former Pittsburgh CAP member Tamanika Howze (Bruwana Mundi) recalled her increasing affinity for the perspectives of Black Power activists like Carmichael during the late 1960s. Her interest in advocating for Black political, economic, and psychological self-determination grew. Simultaneously, her faith in the old approach waned when the proposition of an interracial beloved community never materialized in her neighborhood.[12] Howze (then Donna McMicheaux) had high regard for the civil rights movement's success in challenging legal segregation, but she communicated a nagging sense of the movement's limitations in terms of addressing the continued economic inequality, ghettoization, and cultural subordination she experienced growing up in Pittsburgh's Hill District.

In addition to a new generation of outspoken leaders like Carmichael, the Nation of Islam (NOI) and its dynamic minister Malcolm X stood in apparent contrast to the civil rights message of racial inclusiveness.[13] Several women, including Amina Baraka, Maisha Sullivan Ongoza (Philadelphia CAP), and Nana Anoa Nantambu (Ahidiana, New Orleans), cited the Nation's influence on their generation of activists. Baraka described the Nation's ubiquity around her home on the notoriously fierce Howard Street in Newark.[14] NOI member Shirley 7X was Ongoza's older sibling and guardian. Shirley's positive lifestyle changes regarding discipline, maturity, and diet guided young Maisha's childhood development. Both Ongoza and Nantambu also recalled the influence of NOI newspapers and books, which touted Black separatism and were readily available in the women's homes and communities.[15]

While the NOI was influential as a mass organization, its best-known minister, Malcolm X (Omowale Malik Shabazz or El Hajj Malik El Shabazz), distinctively set the tone for Black Power and cultural nationalism more than any other individual.[16] Just as the NOI was different from movements within the Black freedom struggle that fought for African

Americans' equal rights via litigation, political action, and nonviolent social protest, scholars have also pointed out that the Islam-oriented NOI was part of an older, "fundamental" Black nationalist tradition focused more on anti-White rhetoric and self-help than direct action. Thus, Malcolm's expanding role as a Black liberation leader intent on more insurgent forms of political action and his position as an NOI minister eventually became incompatible.

Likewise, according to some of the women's narratives, many young nationalists searched for Black liberation ideologies that supported more political engagement and expanded spiritual practices beyond or in addition to the NOI. After Malcolm X's break with the Nation of Islam, the influential leader initiated new models for Black nationalism. Key characteristics of these models provided impetus for a number of 1960s Black Power activists to join the movement or change activist affiliations, thus shaping their values and organizing methods.[17] The popularity of such models partially grew out of the fact that Malcolm transformed into a symbol that was imprinted on activists' memories as a reference point or an archetype of the new Black Power militancy after his assassination on February 21, 1965.[18]

Pan-African cultural nationalist women's narratives reflect several themes related to Malcolm's appeal and ideals, including his resonance with urban dwellers, celebration of continental African cultures, naming practices and self-reinvention, affirmation of Black beauty, advocacy for liberative education, and Black nationalism. The women also highlighted influences from anticolonial liberation movements around the world, a topic that was important to Malcolm X. The way that he inspired Pan-African cultural nationalist women's sense of advocacy as well as their *kazi* leadership demonstrates that they were not completely marginalized or operating solely within a male-dominated context. When they joined the movement, they became part of the larger body of male and female advocates who carried on Malcolm's work, promoted his memory, and spread his ideology among a new wave of activists after his assassination.[19]

In addition to African American nationalist influences, several broad elements of the 1960s and 1970s shaped Black Power-era cultural nationalist women. The turbulent times impacted many Americans' approaches to matters of race and identity. The civil rights movement's successes especially buoyed African Americans' hopes for change, transforming their perceptions of themselves and altering the ways they expected others to see them.[20] Newly delivered civil rights laws could not, however, be a cure-all for the country's racism, which Martin Luther King Jr. referred to as "a cancerous social illness" that continued to plague America.[21] Many of the nation's young people who were turning toward Black Power ideology evidently agreed. Charles Evers, Mississippi NAACP field secretary and brother of slain freedom fighter Medgar Evers, captured the younger activists' more militant beliefs when he said, "There are many Negroes who now feel the only time we are going to get a response and action is when we start shooting whites, and many of them are ready to do it now."[22]

Young Black Americans' feverish sentiments must have been palpable to Evers, not least because he was living amid the "Long Hot Summers." This era, which lasted from 1964 through 1967, saw a series of urban rebellions in cities across the country during the scorching summer months. Some of the worst urban uprisings in US history were among the scores of spontaneous events in the 1960s. From Harlem, Rochester, and Jersey City in 1964, to Atlanta, Cleveland, and Chicago in 1966, and Newark, Cincinnati, Detroit, and Philadelphia in 1967, the 233 total rebellions over the four-year period resulted in 131 deaths, 5,454 injuries, and 29,254 arrests. These expressions of exasperation and anger witnessed occupants of urban areas hurling rocks and bottles at those considered outsiders or oppressors, expropriating goods from various stores and warehouses, or torching the vehicles and businesses of perceived offenders. The rebellions reached epidemic levels during the Black Power era, spilling beyond the Long Hot Summers and into the spring of 1968, when Martin Luther King Jr. was assassinated. The uprisings would not subside until 1971. Seven hundred and fifty-two urban rebellions broke out during the entire eight-year period, with more than a hundred occurring in the aftermath of King's assassination in 1968, the peak period of frustration and unrest during this era. That year, 289 total eruptions occurred, sixty-six people were killed, and over five thousand were injured.[23]

Future *kazi* leaders like St. Louis CAP's Jamala Rogers recalled the rebellions of the Long Hot Summers as important events in their lives. Like other young African Americans at the time, Rogers oriented herself toward cultural nationalism in the aftermath of the 1960s and 1970s uprisings.[24] While Rogers witnessed upheaval in her hometown of Kansas City, Missouri, after King's 1968 assassination, two of the most intense urban rebellions took place in Watts (1965) and Newark (1967). Historians have documented the uprisings' significance in stimulating Maulana Karenga's and Amiri Baraka's entry into political activism and their eventual development of the Us Organization and Committee for a Unified Newark, yet few have explored the effect on the female cultural nationalists who filled those groups' ranks. The rebellions of the Long Hot Summers served as catalysts for many of the women who became *kazi* leaders in Pan-African cultural nationalist organizations. The fierce racial conflict of the 1960s was one force spurring women toward more radical modes of thought and action. Another was an increasing sense of distinct Black identity, revolving around cultural matters such as dress and hairstyle.

## The Radicalization of a Generation

In October 1966, mere months after the Meredith March, throngs of students descended on Howard University's Cramton Auditorium to elect Robin Gregory as their homecoming queen. In certain ways, this was like preceding homecoming affairs. But the event was also extraordinary because it featured a unique underdog candidate. Campaigning on a platform of Black pride, Gregory did not process her tresses like the other candidates and the scores of campus queens preceding her. She wore her tightly coiled, dark hair in a cropped "Afro." The auditorium erupted with the onlookers' cheers in what Gregory characterized as a moment of African American "self-acceptance" after years of "self-abnegation" and shame about their natural appearances. Bursting into chants of "Black Power," the students rang out the opening salvo of the campus movement.[25] Their robust response reflected "the radicalization of a generation." The students' attitudes contrasted with the reaction of top university administrator James Nabrit, who broke the long tradition of presidents confirming homecoming queens by his refusal to crown a woman with an African-inspired hairstyle.[26]

Such was the spirit of these times, which forged the generation coming of age during the 1960s. While these young people had much in common with their predecessors, they also differed in important ways. Many older African Americans like Nabrit deemed the new, counter-cultural, natural (and long) hair trends and radical politics unacceptable and embarrassing. Nonetheless, the fact that Howard's outgoing homecoming queen, Charlotte Fleming, eventually crowned Gregory signaled that many young people of the era supported their peers' new, radical stances.[27]

With the radicalization of the generation coming of age in the 1960s, a new kind of female model emerged, inspiring politically motivated forms of aesthetic activism related to self-image and representation.[28] While cultural nationalist women like Martha Bright, Shukuru Sanders, Subira Kifano, Vera Warren-Williams, Tamanika Howze, and Amina Baraka shared certain traits with civil rights advocates of previous phases of the freedom struggle, nationally known activists such as Angela Davis and Kathleen Cleaver, local Pittsburgh playwright Robert Lee "Rob" Penny, and groups such as the Grandassa Models—all of whom departed from traditional patterns—influenced the new generation's self-image, activism, and leadership.[29]

East organization member Tamisha Wendie Peterson highlighted the influence of Grandassa, a group that showcased a natural Black beauty aesthetic and African-inspired clothing. She specifically cited "Black Rose," who was Grandassa model and hairstylist Rose Nelmes. Commenting on the popularity of Afro hairstyles, Peterson explained, "All of the women who wore naturals . . . knew Black Rose. Everybody knew Black Rose. That's where you'd go to get your hair cut nice and neatly."[30] Peterson stressed that many popular hairstyles were "just the Afro . . . in different shapes."[31]

Another cultural nationalist woman, Imani Omotayo of the Us Organization in Los Angeles, crafted a self-narrative that constructed her ethnicity as essentially "African." Omotayo discussed feeling pressured in mainstream spaces to straighten her hair and to generally adopt European-centered beauty standards. She declared, "We're African people. . . . Why should we try to look that way [i.e., European]? . . . That's not the way we're born. Why can't we be proud of the way we look?"[32]

Oral narratives like Peterson's and Omotayo's prompt alternative readings of textual sources. Their recollections make an advertisement for Black Rose's services more legible in terms of what it might have meant to Black women with natural hairstyles. The ad appeared in *Black News* and showcased the politically charged meaning of hair at the time. "We are Afrikan peoples," it read. "Our hair is partial proof of our nationality. Project that image with creative hair styles fashioned to your particular face and personality."[33] At the very least, the statements on the promotional announcement reflected a viewpoint attractive to Black Rose's target clientele—that Afros and braids were political expressions. Yet, given Rose's activities in connection with Grandassa, it is likely that the write-up revealed the stylist's sentiments about natural hair as more than pure aesthetics. It was also reflective of the wearer's personal identity. The statements additionally reflected the connection between style and a larger Pan-African nationalist paradigm.

Black Rose's ad was not the only piece about natural hair in *Black News*. "The Mwanamke Weusi" (Black Woman) column sometimes provided hair care tips, further underscoring the connection between women's particular approaches to Pan-African cultural nationalist activism, hair, and personal politics as well as the ways female advocates exercised *kazi* leadership by creating and maintaining spaces for expressing their ideas about the links between style, politics, culture, and identity. Writers of the column focused on connections between unprocessed hair, physical health, and psychological well-being. Such media items reveal not only the prevailing cultural nationalist hair politics but also the ways beauty culture was a form of activism that catalyzed advocates and was used in service of self-definition, self-determination, self-esteem, racial pride, dignity, and activist entrepreneurship, particularly for Black women.[34] The women's oral narratives as well as textual archives reveal the importance of proud African-identified self-representation within the climate of the Long 1960s. The radicalization of this generation of Black women had origins outside the American context as well. Global events of the post–World War II era further disturbed the waters of those turbulent times and induced cultural nationalist women to broaden their views on Black identity and leadership.

"I Could Not Sit Back . . . and Opt Out": Pan-African Cultural
Nationalist Women's Black Freedom Struggle Narratives and
Ways of Being in the World

Many women Pan-African cultural nationalists involved in Kawaida-
influenced organizations were born during the decades between the end
of World War II and the Cuban Revolution (1944–1959). Their world
was rapidly changing. In addition to the exigencies of the political climate in the United States, global events also molded their Pan-African
cultural nationalist leadership sensibilities. Their narratives confirm that
Long 1960s phenomena, from the growth of the NOI to the Long Hot
Summers, influenced these budding activists, students, and Black Power
advocates. Moreover, at the time, a new generation of Black leaders who
grew up amid creeping urban blight came to associate the destiny of
the Black freedom struggle with the outcomes of nationalist movements
in Fidel Castro's Cuba, Mao Zedong's China, and Patrice Lumumba's
Congo. Black Power-era cultural nationalists came of age in an environment of crumbling colonial empires, their world a sphere divided
into two opposing Cold War positions, east and west. A rising Third
World South challenged the legitimacy of this bipolar construct. World
events such as the Vietnam conflict, the Cuban Revolution, and the
South African apartheid struggle figure prominently in the influences
cited by Pan-African cultural nationalist activists. Thus, both national
events and global affairs molded this group. Along with personal contact
with international students, cross-cultural exchanges, and transnational
experiences across the African diaspora, these contributed to forming
their personal politics as well as the movement they helped shape.[35]

Martha Bright, an East member, discussed her motivation for joining
the struggle. Born in Brooklyn in 1948, she grew up as a Jehovah's Wit-
ness, part of a religious group that eschewed political involvement. As a
teen during the politically charged 1960s, Bright recalled seeing global
events on television and desiring to get involved to help make a change.
She recalled leaving the Jehovah's Witnesses to engage what she saw as a
global freedom struggle: "I left because I wanted to be involved. I could
not sit back and watch all that was going on in the world and opt out."
Another East activist, Mtamanika Beatty, confirmed that the expanding
"cultural consciousness" in the country and the world raised her own

level of awareness. Like their male counterparts, women who would become cultural nationalists in the 1960s and 1970s watched global events
unfold as they matured, and these events were catalysts for their budding activism.[36]

Their engagement with the Chinese Revolution and Maoism is one
example of how the advocates' ways of being in the world contoured
their politics. In October 1949, the People's Republic of China came
into existence as Mao Zedong's victorious troops pushed the opposing
Kuomintang off the mainland and onto the island of Taiwan. John O.
Killens, a notable Black Arts Movement writer, summed up the event's
significance to the Black freedom struggle, remarking, "If [the Chinese]
could come, from the very lower depths, come so far so fast then why not
African-Americans? Why not us?"[37] Additionally, Black radicals viewed
the Chinese as people of color who would lead the socialist revolution
for all the darker-skinned and Third World peoples around the globe.[38]

Communist China's influence on cultural nationalist women's outlook and activism was especially evident in ideas about gender roles.
Theories from the Chinese Revolution became particularly attractive to
female activists because they addressed "the woman question" during
this period of increasingly masculinist liberation expressions. Killens
wrote that women were required to sit at the rear of the metaphorical
bus in certain factions of the Black cultural revolution. In contrast, he
added, the Chinese emphasized the significance of the adage "Women
hold up one-half of the world."[39]

Maoist reforms relating to women's status in communist China affected female Pan-African cultural nationalists' actual and perceived
roles in the Black freedom struggle. An example of the use of Maoism to
augment Black cultural nationalism can be found in Ahidiana's movement work. An Africanized version of the Chinese saying "Our women
keep our skies from falling" was emblazoned on the cover of an essay
series. A graphic of feminine figures clothed in wrap skirts called *lapas*
framed the words. The ladies seemingly supported the African diaspora
section of the Atlantic world and stood beneath a figure resembling an
Egyptian goddess.[40]

Another example of communist China's influence is evident in a 2003
dissertation by Tayari kwa Salaam of Ahidiana, in which she wrote about
organizing a party of African American independent school educators

and administrators traveling to China for eighteen days.[41] Articles published about the 1970s expedition included Maulana Karenga and Kalamu ya Salaam among tour group members but do not mention any female travelers. Despite such omissions, the Salaams' daughter, Kiini Ibura, emphasized her mother, Tayari's, China tour as important in her own recollections. As a girl growing up in Ahidiana, Kiini recalled being exposed to internationalist ideas and networks. As an adult, the internationalist perspective she gained through Ahidiana was foundational to her thinking about gender and to her career as a global traveler, visual artist, and published author.[42]

Teachers at the Kawaida-influenced Ahidiana Work/Study Center exhibited *kazi* leadership in their use of Chinese pictures and literature to reinforce the significance of gender neutrality in the freedom struggle. "We had all these drawings from books from communist China and . . . the women and the men used one uniform," Kiini recalled. Although Ahidiana did not espouse communism, Kiini explained that the Work/Study Center's instructors selectively used images from communist China to bolster the idea that the roles of great leader, freedom fighter, and nationalist were gender-neutral.[43]

Ahidiana's mid- to late 1970s practice of using Maoist uniforms to teach a new generation about gender neutrality reflected changing ideologies over time and was not necessarily the stance of cultural nationalists in all Kawaida-influenced organizations. On the contrary, the practice reflected Ahidiana members' specific brand of egalitarianism and their syncretic use of Kawaida doctrine—that is, their incorporation of various practices and ideologies, such as Maoism and Pan-Africanism, as their organizations evolved. This contrasted with early Kawaida doctrine and practices emanating from the Us Organization, which rested on the idea of inherent differences between the sexes via complementarity and played out in gendered prescriptions for dress, grooming, and behavior.[44]

A socialist since the 1970s, Amina Baraka reflected on how Maoism influenced her activism. She observed that Mao Zedong's communist doctrines especially molded her thinking about "the larger woman question." She surmised that many Pan-African cultural nationalists were initially more concerned with fighting racism than with achieving gender equity. With few other examples of freedom fighters to offer alternative gender models, they drew on religiously based patriarchal examples from the Nation of Islam as well as Christian notions from the civil rights movement. Baraka speculated that early Kawaida-based organizational male chauvinism might have been unintentional. She went on to explain that, as more female CAP members studied Marxism-Leninism and Maoism, they began to challenge their second-class status as cultural nationalist women.[45] This reality was reflected in the Black Women's United Front (BWUF) "Woman Question" essay. Referring to CAP's earlier beliefs about the women's rights movement, the essay stated, "When the question of women's liberation came up, this was rejected immediately as middle class and white. We never did see our liberation coming separate from that of Black people (and we still hold this view)." The authors said, "We did not have Marxism-Leninism-Mao Tse Tung Thought (M-L-M) to guide our analysis so we could not see women's oppression as a part of the development of Capitalism [sic]," highlighting the importance of socialism in the evolution of CAP's activist stance on women's issues.[46]

Amina Baraka also indicated that studying African liberation struggles spurred some women to push against restrictive cultural nationalist gender roles. She explained that reading about women's changing roles in African liberation struggles, from frontline soldier to unit commander, raised consciousness about the limitations of CAP's stance on gender in the movement.[47] Black nationalist women sought more influence in the movement by embracing a modern perspective on gender roles as projected by African women. Amina related that some of the women believed that adopting gender roles more typically associated with power and leadership in certain African liberation struggles would convince cultural nationalist men of female equality. She went on to explain that, since earlier cultural nationalist gender roles were often discussed in the context of "African culture," women who desired more equality believed that introducing a broader range of possibilities would persuade men to adopt more progressive views. "We figured," she said, "when they read about Josina Machel, Samora Machel's wife, they'll change their minds."[48]

Samora Machel was the guerilla front commander of the Mozambique Liberation Front (FRELIMO), which resisted the better resourced and outfitted Portuguese from 1964 to 1974 and became the first president of the People's Republic of Mozambique. His first wife, Josina, was an armed FRELIMO soldier, a community organizer, and the head of the country's Department of International Relations women's section. Her staunch advocacy for full female inclusion in all areas of the liberation struggle represented a departure from standard beliefs about women's roles in "traditional African" society. In many ways her stance reflected FRELIMO's overall commitment to equality, which was part of the independence movement's efforts to attack both "the racist and sexist practices of Portuguese colonial authorities" and African practices that "curtailed the power and status of women."[49]

Amina Baraka and fellow cultural nationalist women advocates also looked for inspiration in freedom fighter Winnie Madikizela-Mandela, the first Black medical social worker in South Africa and the political colleague and second wife of African National Congress leader Nelson Mandela. The couple married in 1958 and remained separated due to Nelson Mandela's frequent detainments and ultimate twenty-six-year prison term for his connection with the civil disobedience campaigns of the same decade. Forced into single motherhood, Madikizela-Mandela carried on the anti-apartheid struggle as one of the movement's best-known spokespersons and leaders, facing imprisonment and risking her life for equality in her country. During the Black consciousness era (1968–1977), Winnie Mandela founded the Black Women's Federation, an organ for helping ordinary women to assert themselves in "vocal" and "self-confident" political roles.[50]

Amina Baraka concluded that the efforts of Pan-African cultural nationalist women to secure more egalitarian gender roles by providing examples of revolutionary African women such as Josina Machel and Winnie Mandela produced mixed results. Some men changed their beliefs about male dominance, while others did not. One of those who did was Sababa Akili, a member of the Cleveland cultural nationalist group Afro Set. He remembered how women, including Amina Baraka, posed forceful challenges to chauvinistic perspectives on women's gender roles and polygamous practices. He also described having a personal epiphany after several interactions with them, ultimately deeming beliefs and practices reinforcing female inequality to be incorrect political positions.[51]

The importance of transnational or cross-cultural exchange throughout the African diaspora was not limited to gender ideologies on the African continent. Travel was an especially important expression of cultural nationalist women's Pan-Africanist consciousness. Their activities abroad encompassed what they viewed as an effort to assist with post-colonial independence projects as well as to bolster African American self-determination through land acquisition and organization creation. For instance, The East organization conducted seasonal visits to the Republic of Guyana. Members of the organization initially traveled in 1970 to the South American nation when it was in the throes of gaining full independence from Britain.[52] The country won political sovereignty in 1966 and established the Cooperative Republic of Guyana during the same year as The East's initial visit. At the time, the country's leadership struggled with developing a stable and self-determined government to serve the needs of all its constituents. Guyanese administrators faced the responsibility of achieving these goals amid racial strife between an East Indian-descended majority (52 percent) and an African-descended minority (42 percent).[53]

The broad goal for The East's involvement in Guyana was institutional development and nation building both for the Guyanese population and for the African American nationalists. The specific purpose of their 1970 visit was attending a meeting of Pan-Africanists and Black revolutionary nationalists that the African Society for Cultural Relations with Independent Africa (ASCRIA) assembled.[54] ASCRIA founder and socialist political figure Eusi Kwayana (formerly Sidney King) arranged the conference along with Ann King, née Cook (later Tchaiko Kwayana). A radical thinker in her own right, Cook grew up in rural Buena Vista, Georgia, but traveled to various countries in Africa and Latin America. Recognizing the common forms of oppression that African-descended people faced, she emphasized the importance of global Black solidarity in her writing. While working in New York as an educator at City College, she connected East members with Eusi Kwayana, the influential Guyanese Pan-Africanist whom she later married. Eusi Kwayana's motivation for connecting with East members was to build solidarity with oppressed American minorities and thereby attract the Guyanese government's support via its prime minister, Forbes Burnham. Burnham wanted to encourage African American and Afro-Caribbean settlement in the sparsely populated hinterlands of the country. This was reportedly an effort to thwart land grabbing and augment his own Black voting base by using Kwayana's connections to attract settlers.[55]

Further substantiating the idea that the times she lived in would not allow her to opt out of world affairs, Martha Bright's narrative highlighted the Guyana travels of East-affiliated cultural nationalist women. Along the way, they gained experience and nurtured relationships through transnational, Pan-Africanist networks. *Kazi* was important to East advocates and has been cited as a critical component in shaping Pan-African nationalist notions of masculinity.[56] Additionally, East women explicitly employed the Kawaida-influenced concept of *kazi* in recounting their stories about the gendered significance of their travels abroad. In their narratives, Bright and another Brooklyn-based East advocate, Shukuru Sanders, described how The East Sisterhood, a Kawaida-based group oriented toward women's training and development, made an excursion to Guyana lasting about two weeks. "The sisterhood went on the Guyana project in 1971," Bright said. "We worked on the . . . road project when Guyana was a newly independent nation from England. [A] whole contingent of East sisters went . . . and we worked. We did physical work out there on that project."[57] Her statements suggested the importance of applying *kazi* to the women's mission of assisting in any necessary way with projects they considered to be postcolonial development and in emphasizing the nation-building work that female advocates performed as significant.

Women in CFUN expressed ideas similar to those articulated by East women regarding how *kazi* elicited a kind of leadership that cut against notions of limited, domestic feminine roles:

> Black women will have to learn and develop whatever is needed by the nation. . . . The necessary roles will change as the needs of the nation change. . . . It might be "nice" (but harmful) to think that women should just sit at home—sewing cooking, taking care of the house and children but we have to deal with reality, that WE ARE A BLACK AND POWERLESS PEOPLE and will have to do all that we can to gain power—self-determination, self-respect, self-defense.[58]

Although the Mumininas wrote that women were inherently submissive, they also discussed the importance of nation building by any means necessary.

Like Bright, Shukuru Sanders would not "opt out" of world affairs. She shared similar recollections of Guyana, although her itinerary took her to ASCRIA meetings and on tours rather than to the road project. Sanders's development of transnational ties shaped her future activism and career. Her Guyana trip helped her develop affiliations that led her back to the South American country in 1977. Having completed nursing studies at Harlem Hospital, she served three and a half years as a midwife in Guyana. Describing the relationship between transnational migrants, Black Power political exiles seeking refuge in the country, and the Guyanese government as "complicated," Sanders outlined the increasingly corrupt environment emanating from the Burnham regime's effort to retain political and economic dominance until the 1980s. She recalled returning to the United States in 1980 after a car explosion killed Walter Rodney, a notable Guyanese academic and prominent leader of the Working People's Alliance, which opposed the prevailing regime.[59]

Shukuru Sanders's narrative confirmed that global independence struggles awakened the women's interest in the fate of the world's people of color. Moreover, the roles that women all over the world played in various social movements stimulated some female cultural nationalists to exhibit leadership in challenging their own status in the Black freedom struggle. Concerns for global social movements that were fostered within cultural nationalist circles encouraged the women to involve themselves in cross-cultural experiences, which included supporting postcolonial development projects and forming transnational networks. Although cultural nationalist women's sense of *kazi* leadership was initially formed in the crucible of American racial turmoil, such global influences infused the leadership style with transnational ideals.

## "Say It Loud!"

After proclaiming, "Say it loud!," James Brown's 1968 Black Power anthem unapologetically declared, "I'm Black and I'm proud!" Such songs, among others, like Nina Simone's "Young, Gifted, and Black," trumpeted the kind of race consciousness that made the Black Power era unique.[60] In the essay "'Black' Is a Country," Amiri Baraka wrote that "Black" constituted a nation within a nation, united by complexion, customs, and culture. He exhorted African Americans to use their peripheral positions as sources of fortitude and encouragement. According to Baraka, African Americans needed to fight for independence over and above separation or assimilation.[61] Of course, most African Americans did not relocate to Africa, nor did they establish an independent North American state, but many did embark on a "resilient" quest for self-determination and identity reinforcement.[62] Black identity, racial and ethnic consciousness, pride, and self-determination stood out as proponents' main concerns.[63] According to The East's Mtamanika Beatty, "Those are the kinds of things that begin to ignite you to look at yourself a little bit differently."[64]

The dynamism of the era and a growing emphasis on racial and ethnic pride shaped Pan-African cultural nationalist women's activist choices. As Azizi Powell pointed out, her affinity for "cultural nationalism, as opposed to other forms," was rooted in the idea that it prompted Black people to better understand and to celebrate their heritage and customs as an African people.[65] Pan-African cultural nationalists were not the first to propose that African American culture was fundamentally African.[66] This essential focus on African heritage deeply influenced Pan-African cultural nationalist women's approaches to leadership. African-centeredness was an important element setting *kazi* leadership apart from servant leadership.

2

# "Agitate. Educate. Organize"

*Women in Kawaida-Influenced Neighborhood Organizations,*
*the Press, and Protest Politics*

One late summer afternoon in 1975, young people in bright T-shirts clapped to the music of drums, filling the sidewalk with rhythmic movement and sound. Dressed in vivid, African-inspired outfits, women kept an eye on the children while men congregated in front of a bookstore with their reading materials. Situated on Claver Place just off the main commercial thoroughfare, Franklin Avenue, shops offered goods ranging from clothes to fresh food and herbs. A newly renovated, two-story cultural and education center overlooked the activity on the street.

Such was the description of everyday life on the north-central Brooklyn block that The East organization occupied, according to a contemporary account in the *New York Times*. In the piece, the author declared that the people of Bedford-Stuyvesant (Bed-Stuy) could be proud of The East's neighborhood enterprises.[1] The organization modeled perspectives of *ujamaa*, from "familyhood" to "cooperative economics," in the middle of a neighborhood that outsiders viewed as a ghetto. When so many educated, hardworking African Americans left rough areas like Bed-Stuy for better neighborhoods, East women stayed, performing *kazi* via essential community work, program administration, and institutional leadership.[2]

Afflicted by the most serious problems of urban America, the environment in much of Bed-Stuy during the 1960s and 1970s belied the East's vibrance. Post–World War II White flight altered the area's ethnic and racial composition, which stood in stark contrast to its population during the first half of the century. Of the more than 250,000 residents who populated postwar Bed-Stuy, 84 percent were Black, 12 percent were Brown, and 4 percent were White or "other." Over time, grim iron grills covered windows and doors that had once been bright and open. Deteriorating, burned-out, and scarred buildings were boarded up. The empty, crumbling shells were left to frame the area's vacant lots and crime-ravaged streets. Incarceration rates were increasing, juvenile delinquency was high, and drug addiction plagued the community. Heroin dependency grew over the course of the 1970s, and crack cocaine had devastated Bed-Stuy families by the 1980s. In the early 1970s, 85 percent of neighborhood residents worked irregularly or part-time. Most toiled as unskilled laborers or in low-level service jobs. More than 50 percent of families made under $5,000, less than half the acceptable standard of living for New York City.[3]

Confronting the rampant problems in neighborhoods such as Bed-Stuy was a driving force behind women's involvement in Kawaida-inspired organizations. Tamisha Peterson, Mtamanika Beatty, and other women in The East sought to address these problems by promoting strong family life. In the process, they were forced to negotiate thorny issues like polygamy, which tested the organization's commitment to "unity without uniformity." Meanwhile, in Pittsburgh, community concerns motivated Tamanika Howze to get involved with the Congress of African People (CAP), where she came to embrace womanist views on gender relations in the process of merging her family life and political activism. Considering the work they performed, the causes they supported, and their involvement with projects like the *Black News* independent circular reveals that a confluence of forces, including the concept of *kazi*, drove the way these women navigated restrictive gender ideologies. Some women began movement work because of the desire to take responsibility for their communities as they faced urban crises, but others eventually challenged gender-based restrictions and integrated women's rights issues into their activism. In the process, the women became leaders in their own right.

Mary Manoni, author of a 1973 study about Bedford-Stuyvesant, defined community as "a group of people who come together to live in a particular area because they have something in common."[4] Perhaps because the author included no local Pan-Africanists and few Black nationalists in her study, Manoni's definition of community overlooked cultural nationalist conceptions of communities bound by commonalities of race, history, interests, goals, and fate but not necessarily by physical proximity. Women in groups such as Pittsburgh CAP and The East tended to define community in both local geographical terms and the broader ideological sense.

## Bed-Stuy: "Why Would Anyone Want to Live There?"

With a rising population of politically underrepresented and systemically marginalized residents, Bed-Stuy became one of the country's largest and most severely crime-ridden and poverty-stricken neighborhoods in the aftermath of World War II.[5] Yet the area had bright facets, and according to many accounts The East was one of them. During an era when upwardly mobile African American professionals composed a minority of the neighborhood's population and most educated residents pulled up stakes to move elsewhere, East advocates lived and worked there, agitating, educating, and organizing to make Bed-Stuy a better place.[6]

At a time when feelings of frustration and powerlessness gripped the neighborhood, The East existed as a nexus that nurtured a sense of pride in the community and facilitated local control over more than a dozen institutions. The East was truly a community project, and local women were irreplaceable strategists, administrators, and participants in this endeavor.[7] According to a *Black News* article, women in The East organization, particularly those in The East Sisterhood, played "a vital role in the organization's day to day operations," including the Uhuru Sasa School, a bookstore, a clothing store, a health food store, a cooperative food buying service, and *Black News*, a community newspaper.[8]

Advocates like Tamisha Peterson remembered the work that she and fellow East sisters performed in the Bed-Stuy community as one of the most satisfying aspects of her time in the organization.[9] Peterson was born and reared in Brooklyn, spending time on her Garveyite grandparents' West Indian street and her parents' African American block. Her story offers a slice of life in what observers called a "bright" part of the borough.[10] Peterson recalled, "My grandparents lived in a house that was in a neighborhood that had brownstones in it." As her narrative unfolded, her words sketched pictures of a childhood spent on sidewalks populated by faces much like her own. Rows of multilevel, ornately embellished brownstone homes lined the streets where she lived, sheltering an ethnically diverse but racially homogeneous community. "On this block there was nothing but islanders. Not even just Black [people], but Black [people] from the islands, all Black and several neighborhoods, and then in my neighborhood were just plain, regular Black folks from . . . the North, born and raised there." Describing a White flight similar to the kind that Newark and Pittsburgh experienced, Peterson explained, "It had been a Jewish community, but once Blacks started moving in, [Jewish people] started moving out."[11]

Considered as a whole, the women's narratives did not reflect the typical tale of a triumphant civil rights movement facilitating African Americans' escape from the social and economic margins in racially segregated communities to better-resourced, integrated environs. Instead, Pan-African cultural nationalist women's narratives are part of a larger story of increasingly ghettoized, stigmatized, and impoverished neighborhoods during a period in which the rising tide of civil rights movement gains was supposed to lift all boats. In this context, women included in this study expressed feelings of alienation from mainstream society and a rejection of integration as a panacea for Black liberation. As Peterson recalled, "Integration, I didn't too much relate to." She saw no appeal in institutions that sought to bring the races together: "I didn't feel that their organizations were any better than ours. . . . We can do just fine, thank you very much."[12] Peterson's recollections confirm the do-for-self tendencies of the *kazi* ethos. Rather than continuing to wait for the painfully slow-moving promise of equality to reach their communities or fleeing their familiar neighborhoods as part of a Black middle-class exodus, the women worked toward gaining control of their embattled communities, redefining spaces and creating institutions within them. They also refashioned their own identities—no longer were they "Negro women," or even "Black." Rather they were "African women," who actively worked to replace the American dream with Pan-Africanist visions of freedom.[13]

Peterson lived in Brooklyn her entire life, except for about two years, which she spent in Puerto Rico with her mother, Iona Anderson, who was there as part of a teachers' exchange program. After Peterson returned to her hometown, she took college courses until she married Fred Richardson, with whom she had one child. It was during this period that Peterson got involved in the movement. She was initially drawn to the Black Panthers, but she ultimately joined The East after selling the Richardson family's Brooklyn bookstore. She put the store on the market after her husband went underground, disappearing amid the Panther 21 episode, in which a group of Black Panthers was arrested and charged for conspiracy to bomb a number of public spaces, carrying dangerous weapons, and plotting to attack several police precincts. Fred Richardson was the twenty-second defendant in the trial.[14]

Peterson's donation of her bookstore's inventory and furnishings assisted The East in founding its Akiba Mkuu shop in 1970. Attracted to the group's familial character, Peterson defined The East as an organization with deep roots in the community. "If things affected [the neighbors]," she said, "that would affect us."[15] East leader Jitu Weusi's "Around Our Way" articles in *Black News* provide a window into community issues that impacted The East. They ranged from police brutality and children's literacy to concerns over local politics and neighborhood crime.[16] For example, East members agitated about unjustly accused and imprisoned African Americans. Peterson recounted that, if community residents were arrested, East family members would raise awareness of their plights and help bail them out.[17] Peterson's sense of The East's solidarity is consistent with the organization's guiding concept of *uhuru sasa*, "freedom now," which helped foster a sense of collective identity for constituents.[18]

Peterson's memories indicate that community work was commonly organized around gender. The East's labor patterns often reinforced women's "proper" roles, which were thought to begin "at home amongst the family" and focused on "inspiring the man to build" and helping "the children to grow."[19] Women's "appropriate" roles were circumscribed within Kawaida-influenced organizations during the pre-1975 years. Many of the female family members' work revolved around domesticity and engaged such public concerns as education and social development. Gender roles were also complex in The East, however. According to Konadu, most women in his study said that they were never entirely subservient, nor were they patently silenced. He reported that some found that they were suppressed in individual relationships, however, a reality they often faced both inside and outside the organization. Some women additionally desired relative sanctuary from the vagaries of the public sphere and sought out forms of reverence and honor typically associated with femininity. The protections assigned to "ladies" within such gender norms were often denied to Black women in the broader society because of their race.[20]

While some might have embraced these roles due to "the promise of protection," others viewed adherence to strictly defined roles for women as a form of *kazi*, or work and sacrifice in service of struggle.[21] Konadu has argued that East advocates never sufficiently theorized gender in the contexts of the organization and the larger freedom struggle to ensure that roles for both women and men were equitable, clear, and consistent with the group's mission.[22] That is to say, women in The East were not completely oppressed; however, gender inequity was not adequately addressed in either the organization or the broader Pan-African cultural nationalist movement, which was directed at bringing about freedom for the entire community. Women navigated these realities, and they actively sought to express themselves and shape the direction of Kawaida-influenced organizations such as The East.

## "It Was a Family Kind of Organization"

Many women advocates were drawn to *ujamaa*—a familial, cooperative principle at the heart of The East's ideology—because it meant that The East operated partially as an "extended family" with several biological kinship groups at its core.[23] The East was a popular, cultural-educational institution consisting of about a hundred people affiliated with multiple organizations. The idea that the organization was more like a family than a group of affiliated institutions recurred in several activists' recollections.[24] Safiya Bandele, a self-described "peripheral" East advocate, liked that the camaraderie she experienced within the group resembled her large, southern family.[25] Shukuru Sanders thought that such a structure was "something even higher or better than an organization." She observed, "We transformed from The East organization to The East family, and to me that changed how we related to each other."[26]

Some activists expounded on the ways East family members related to each other. Mtamanika Beatty stated that adult East advocates referred to each other by the endearing terms "sister and brother." Martha Bright testified, "A lot of us formed our families . . . in The East."[27] Segun Shabaka of The East Brotherhood echoed Bright's sentiments, saying that The East comprised "men and women mainly coming together as families." Shabaka explained, "All the children would first know [adults] as mama, baba, mother, father, and commune together in each other's houses. . . . So it wasn't like most other organizations, I think, who were maybe adult individuals."[28] Shabaka's description suggests that The East embodied the proverb, "It takes a whole village to raise a child." This ideas was confirmed in the testimony of another male member, Adeyemi Bandele, who said that the organization "helped to create a village for the raising of my children."[29] The East family created a space for affirming that "Black lives matter," as they nurtured youth who faced the harsh realities of social marginalization, poverty, crime, and neglect in a White supremacist society.[30] Beyond The East's core family groups, the organization was open to all interested Bed-Stuy community members. Their communal approach to parenting in a neighborhood with such a high incidence of juvenile delinquency was itself an act of resistance.[31]

East family members ate communally on Sundays to foster a sense of togetherness. Providing details about activities that The East family would regularly host, Mtamanika Beatty commented, "It was a good time. . . . We would have the *karamus* [feasts], . . . and everybody brought dishes, and we would eat, . . . and the children would be together."[32] Tamisha Peterson also remembered that "Sundays [were] a time they wanted for us to come together and be family. . . . We'd have different family things, and we'd just eat together and enjoy each other," Peterson recalled. Such acts translated ideas about *ujamaa* into action, Peterson explained. "Since we talked about family," she said, East members had to "promote family."[33] A strength of the concept of family as enacted in The East was that members participated in an act of creating space for marginalized African-descended people to be part of loving, supportive, and affirming relationships in a community that was suffering from the worst effects of urban blight and decay. Yet this concept of family was not without its problems, especially regarding its implications for gender equity. One especially troublesome dimension, which generated diverse responses and significant conflict, was the practice of polygamous relationships.

### "A Bit Controversial": Polygamy, Gender Relations, and *Kazi* Leadership

Family was an important area in women's struggle for agency, as cultural nationalists considered family the cornerstone of organizations, of communities, and, ultimately, of what advocates viewed as a nascent nation. East members saw the family as key for sustaining a cultural and political foundation. They also viewed family as important for maintaining a consistent worldview within the home and in institutional life. Although monogamous couples and their children were the norm, the organization also consisted of "extended families."[34]

Within The East, "extended family" found an expression in polygamy, or marital and marriage-like relationships in which one person had multiple committed mates. The overwhelming majority of extended families took a form similar to polygyny, a plural marriage in which one man maintained spousal relationships with more than one woman.[35] The involved women engaged in a nuptial relationship with only the man and shared familial responsibilities such as parenting with the man and sometimes the other women in the family. While extended families were an option, they were neither necessary nor officially required to develop a sense of belonging to a large family or to be part of The East. The practice provided children of The East and Uhuru Sasa with a community of people who parented them in many ways as extended family mothers and fathers (mamas and babas).[36] Advocates tended to affirm the idea that extended family practices benefited East children. However, their opinions about the nature and outcomes of polygamous practices for women were hotly contested.[37]

Ostensibly, The East's extended family arrangement was not compulsory—although some women did feel pressure to engage in it—and monogamy was more common than plural relationships. Only a small number of East adults actually entered polygamous relationships, and this same pattern was the norm in many non-US cultures. Advocates viewed the practice of extended family through multiple lenses. They saw it as part of a long tradition connecting them with African history and culture, as a countercultural form of resistance undertaken in opposition to Western hegemony, or as a necessity to alleviate some of the problems that African Americans faced, such as shortages of marriageable men and the lack of fathers in households. Opponents viewed plural marriage as inherently problematic and resisted the practice, particularly as it appeared to be a guise for indulging men's promiscuous behaviors, a reflection of broader gender role imbalances, and a burden for women.[38]

Mtamanika Beatty's reminiscences reveal that, besides being based on a particular perception of certain African practices as well as traditions from the broader Muslim world, polygyny was an extension of Kawaida ideologies about gender roles as complementary. She believed that complementary gender roles seemingly represented equality but, realistically, meant that women's places in society were limited. Beatty said, "There was still this way of looking at women from an Afrocentric point of view that . . . women were still . . . on some levels, not equal in that . . . women are intelligent, and they are capable, and they can do things, but women still have their place." Beatty believed that some East advocates "looked at . . . polygamy as a means of being able to have more than one wife so you can grow your family, [the] organization, and for it to be big and for the women to supplement each other with the rearing of the children." She added the following caveat to her explanation: "Ultimately it was the man that was supposed to benefit from that. . . . That's questionable, but that was part of their thing."[39] Beatty's statements reflect the complexity of the debate over polygamy. Proponents believed that extended families were beneficial for fostering the large families that were cornerstones of a nation, especially in the face of sex ratio imbalances. On the other hand, people who contested the practice asserted that polygamy inherently perpetuated gender inequality, devalued wives, and destroyed families.

Some East members viewed polygamy as beneficial and even necessary. Their language suggested that women's participation in polygynous marriages was a form of *kazi*, a method of working toward establishing "solid," heteronormative relationships. They thought of it as a way to enlarge families, institutions, and ultimately "the nation," especially since desirable women outnumbered marriageable men.[40] According to one participant in a radio interview with East women, "There was some polygamy going on in The East. [It] was a bit controversial to take on that kind of lifestyle." Explaining the logic of such practices from her perspective, she said, "I think that there were a whole lot more sisters

than there were brothers, and we, at the time, considered ourselves nation builders, and the way to build a nation is to . . . proliferate. So, some
of us had to take on the responsibility of making certain that the sisters
were capable of having children and should be fertile and ready to bear
children and, at that point in time, have mates, and sometimes we'd have
to share mates. That was the point of the polygamous situation." The
narrator further suggested that, even though polygyny was an extension
of certain men's preferences for multiple female partners, some women
might have viewed participating in polygynous relationships as a part of
the work and sacrifice needed to build a nation.[41]

On both ends of the spectrum of opinions about extended family,
women spoke as if the sacrifice and sharing required to enter polygyny
by consent could essentially be viewed as a form of *kazi*. "There was
a theory behind why it would be a good idea to do it that way," The
East sister in the radio broadcast contended. "That was the theory that
I subscribed to and some . . . other sisters subscribed to, . . . that we had
some good, strong sisters with good, strong genes who needed a man
to help them bring more children into this nation that we were building."[42] Although she opposed polygyny, Tamisha Peterson also indicated
that some women entered or stayed in plural relationships in ways that
could be seen as *kazi* because of their sense of duty to organization and
cause. "The sisters stuck it out. They still stuck it out. They hung in there
because they believed in the organization [and] where the organization
was going," she said.[43]

Some of the women's narratives also reflected the idea that accepting
polygyny as a viable relationship arrangement was part of the process of
unshackling themselves from Western beliefs. From this perspective, the
nominal practice of monogamy as an exclusive marriage form was seen
as one of many types of Western cultural domination.[44] For some East
advocates, the belief that monogamy was the only acceptable marital
form was proof that African Americans were "victims" of their "education and training." Further, some discourse in advocates' narratives suggests that such standards might have imposed disadvantageous values
given the challenges African Americans faced.[45] One overarching belief
was that polygyny was an enduring and viable non-Western tradition
with roots in Africa and the larger Muslim world. Some saw polygyny as
a method of addressing the issue of sex ratio imbalance in the organiza-

tion and the larger community, giving more women the chance to have a husband and a father in the household for their children than would be possible in a society in which monogamy was the only acceptable marital form.[46]

By contrast, some East members saw polygamy as intolerable and destructive. Sometimes this idea sprang from what people perceived as the results of such arrangements. In other cases, advocates implied that polygamy was unacceptable because it fostered inherently asymmetrical relationships in terms of power and expectations. Wives usually got short shrift in terms of rights and privileges.[47] Still other narrators stressed how problematic extended family relationships could be, as they sometimes fomented dissension and in-fighting within The East. A minority of advocates even attributed the organization's demise to the issue of polygyny.[48] Some of the women felt that they were obligated to participate in extended families. Tamisha Peterson explained that someone "had this guy come and lecture, because we used to always have lecturers coming in. . . . He got on the subject of polygamy and, of course, the guys, the brothers, were really, really interested in polygamy, and that actually became something that was forced on the sisters." Polygamous relationships were the most difficult aspect of gender relations in The East for Peterson. She flatly stated that she found she could navigate other issues within the organization, but "the only ugly thing was the polygamy."[49] Mtamanika Beatty expressed similar sentiments in a separate interview. She preferred not to be in a polygynous relationship, but nevertheless felt pressured to do so. Beatty said that coercive attitudes existed among members of The East Brotherhood as well as the sisterhood, and "there was a lot of pressure for a lot of people, . . . for everybody."[50]

Some participants also joined East extended family units at the risk of conflict and strained relationships with their biological families. Relatives often viewed the practice as an unacceptable deviation from the Western norm of monogamous marriages. According to Adeyemi Bandele, who was part of an extended family, "There is the issue of acceptance by the biological families of the people who are involved, and so sometimes they're able to get buy-in and there's . . . at least not rejection." Offering more details, he said, "They may not have full acceptance, but people will honor and respect the lifestyle that they have chosen. . . . I find that, often times, if people honor and respect it themselves, then those around them will do the same, or they're just going to leave them alone."[51]

Some East advocates suggested that enduring the dearth of "balance and openness in male-female relationships, unresolved contradictions, and the absence of provisions for healing" within the polygamous relationships was an act of *kazi*.[52] Other members implied that polygamy could be a form of escapism. Beatty underscored the ways The East's polygamous relationships embodied imbalanced gender relationships: "Having another spouse or having multiple spouses . . . was [men's] right but [was] not necessarily [an option] for women."[53] Peterson provided an example of dysfunction in East extended family practices, explaining how husbands often used second wives to avoid the complexities and problems developing in primary relationships: "If you had a couple that [was] not getting along, [a husband] could just bring in a second wife. [He might say], 'Oh, I don't have to deal with this arguing or rough patch in our marriage, I'll just have a second wife come in.'"[54] Healing such a situation would have entailed facing and resolving the damage and conflict resulting from unhealthy relationships.[55] Instead, the narratives indicated that the conflict brewing in and around many polygynous relationships festered and spread in ways that threatened the long-term viability of certain families and the broader organization.

East narrators suggested that what they viewed as traditional African cultural practices encouraged husbands to obtain current wives' consent and solicit their participation in the process of adding new wives to their families.[56] The dynamics at play in The East's extended family relationships, however, meant that the central spouse inherently had more rights, expectations, and control within the family. That is, the multiple spouses had to commit to one central spouse, who would divide economic resources and family services. The central spouse could engage in intimate physical and emotional relationships with more than one person within polygamous families.[57] In The East, the practice of negotiating with existing wives could and often did play out as an optional courtesy, which husbands could choose to offer or withhold. As family heads, husbands could, in reality, decide not to obtain consent from existing wives. Husbands could invoke the power to become involved with other female partners based on their own wishes and without consent or buy-in from existing wives. According to Peterson, some men in The

East brought women into their families without first consulting their primary mates or against the wishes of dissenting wives. Peterson added that such men sometimes had to be compelled to care for children of troubled earlier relationships. Additionally, some women reported deliberately damaging established relationships in order to obtain a particular husband.[58] Such acts of sabotage were patently inconsistent with the ethics of *kazi* leadership.

Whether or not first wives consented, levels of care and intimacy between members of the plural relationship were frequently imbalanced. Beatty explained that the husband in a polygynous relationship had to divide resources and time "between this woman, that woman, and those children." Implying that subsequent mates often displaced cowives rather than cooperating with or operating under the authority of primary wives, she said, "You want two wives, I tell you what, get rid of me. Let's do that, and you can go get number one and number two, because I'm not going to be number two or number three or whatever." One East brother pointed out that husbands needed to be careful not to favor junior or younger wives at the expense of longer-standing partners.[59] Several women recounted stories of polygyny serving males' prerogatives to seek younger women and newer, more exciting, or seemingly less problematic relationships. Subsequent mates tended to be more positive about polygyny in their narratives than first wives, a tendency reflected in Tamisha Peterson's summary of the situations she observed: "The second wife . . . would always be willing, but the first wife was the resistant one in each case, and that's understandable. That's human nature."[60]

While advocates of extended family relationships touted the benefits of the practice for developing sisterhood and cooperation, critics of polygyny argued that it harmed their friendships with each other.[61] Peterson explained how The East's plural marriage practices changed the organization and eroded the bonds between advocates. She said some East sisters stopped speaking to each other. She also indicated that the adoption of polygyny represented a turning point in the organization's collegial atmosphere, as female advocates began to distrust each other. She explained that women began to question others' intentions, wondering, "Are you sleeping with my man? [Are] you going to become his second wife?" The East "definitely had a different atmosphere with that. I was very sorry about that," Peterson lamented. Explaining that the possibility of being pressured to join an extended family prompted her to avoid forming an intimate relationship with any East man, she said, "Of course I knew I wasn't ever going to deal with any brother in The East because I didn't like that."[62] In this atmosphere, one woman even left the organization rather than undergo the discomfort of extended family living arrangements.[63]

Critics also observed that polygyny tore families apart. In particular, Peterson reiterated that polygyny was generally unacceptable within American culture outside the organization. East women faced challenges within polygynous households that, according to her estimation, might not have been very different from the ones women faced in Africa. She opined, however, that many African women were immersed in cultures that accepted, normalized, and even encouraged polygyny. On the other hand, a number of North American community members, friends, and blood relatives disdained The East's open polygynous practices. Facing pressures from inside and outside the organization, some East women left relationships in which husbands took subsequent mates without their consent. Again, the practice had negative effects on membership. Some women not only withdrew from the organization but also repudiated the overall movement.[64]

Returning to the theme of *kazi*, Peterson further remarked that much of the onus for making extended families work fell on women: "Of course, the women really did try to make it work. If there was going to be another sister in the house, the sisters would really try to work. I didn't find the brothers involved in that as much. . . . Once he had his two women, that was it. . . . How these women were going to get along, . . . raise children, and . . . work this household out was up to the women, really." Peterson's narrative highlighted many ways that The East's extended family practices fostered dysfunction and hurt the overall organization.

Peterson's observations also point to a likely reason that The East, although it was open to the community, never developed a mass following. Many mainstream African Americans eschewed the lifestyle changes that accompanied affiliation with Kawaida-influenced groups. Peterson claimed that the level of *kazi* required to sustain The East family and the larger movement never felt like a job to her, but she did find it challenging. "You would like to see . . . your biological family get a little bit more involved," she reflected. "Well, I don't think too many of us had luck with that. They might pop in every now and then, see a jazz show or something, [and] pop back out." Echoing the kind of sentiment that Scot Brown observed within the Us Organization—that the larger community's reluctance or outright refusal to undergo lifestyle changes reflected a lack of awareness—Peterson said, "I don't know how full the understanding was . . . [of] the whole movement."[65] Such dynamics tended to heighten some women's sense of distance from their biological families, which in turn made the familial character of Kawaida-influenced organizations more attractive to some and alienated others.

While the countercultural lifestyles promoted by groups like The East extended to many other matters, polygyny was at once an extreme and a cautionary example. It was acceptable and even necessary in the eyes of some East advocates, yet unacceptable and destructive to others. Segun Shabaka saw similarities between the extended family and conventional models: "Some lasted, some didn't last, just like some [monogamous] marriages . . . last and don't last." Mtamanika Beatty explained that, although extended family spousal arrangements did not appeal to her as an individual, they could possibly work. "Together with . . . two wives, there may be five or six children. . . . One [wife] can take care of all those children, while the other is able to go out and work and be more productive and not worry about the children. That was the concept," she said. With this notion in mind, Beatty never challenged polygyny outright as a viable practice because, she said, some members of large, extended families could ideally benefit from polygyny.[66] Conversely, the same type of arrangement could pose financial challenges when spouses in the relationship did not work as a team to generate income for the entire family or when adult family members were unemployed or underemployed.[67]

Safiya Bandele's personal experiences in the Bandele extended family bear a lengthy discussion because they reflect such a nuanced perspective on the issue of polygamy in The East. Bandele's story stands out because she considered herself a feminist and a cultural nationalist participating in an extended family, seemingly incompatible positions. She met Adeyemi, the family patriarch, while they were both working as National Black United Front (NBUF) officials. A 1979 Black United Front booklet showed that Safiya (then known as Diann Ellis) served as treasurer and chief of fundraising. A 1981 memo listed her as a member of the central committee alongside many others, including Adeyemi. Additionally, according to her own reflections, she was co-chair of the New York City chapter's central committee and chair of the national women's section. Safiya said that she developed a relationship with Adeyemi through their common commitment to community activism. Safiya became part of the Bandele household in 1980, although she maintained that she never considered herself Adeyemi's wife. Members of the Bandele household were active in The East, and the organization's expression of Kawaida-influenced cultural nationalism was integral to family life, a fact that Safiya found positive and fulfilling. Adeyemi Bandele was an official in The East, and Safiya also participated in organizational life during the short time she lived with the Bandeles.[68]

Safiya expounded on the positive aspects of being part of an extended, or "blended," family, as she called it. She had a daughter from a previous relationship and bore a son while living with the Bandeles. In addition to being active in various other community organizations, she was a professor. She also held a leadership role as director of the Center for Women's Development at Medgar Evers College of the City University of New York (CUNY), a predominantly Black, majority-female institution birthed from Brooklyn residents' late 1960s struggles for community control. Located in Bedford-Stuyvesant, the college focused on contributing to educational equity, social justice, and community uplift in central Brooklyn. As a result of the many hats she wore, Safiya worked to balance her life as a single parent. The Bandeles' extended family was a good fit for her, "because [being] a single mother is really difficult. . . . The more adults you have loving a child . . . the better." She also said, "It was a great time, and I can really see the value of having loving adults in a child's life." She enjoyed seeing her daughter's growth and witnessing the other Bandele children's development. She emphasized that they were truly "loved in that environment."[69] For Safiya, The East's extended family configurations were not constricting but instead an essential component of sustaining her performance of *kazi* and her ascension to leadership positions in the community.

Though part of a Kawaida-influenced cultural nationalist community and a polygynous family for some time, Safiya Bandele also considered herself a feminist, not a subservient woman who walked "two steps behind" men.[70] Safiya engaged in feminist work before, during, and after her affiliation with the Bandeles and The East, through such entities as the Center for Women's Development, the Sisterhood of Black Single Mothers, the NBUF women's section, and the Mother's Day March for Action. She has been cited in the literature as a pioneering African American second-wave feminist, and a supporter of other activists whose devotion to achieving women's equality was inextricably linked with their commitment to Black nationalism.[71] Safiya Bandele asserted that her feminism and participation in an extended family were not contradictory, "because my feminism was grounded in Afrocentricity. My feminism was shaped and informed by being a leader over at [Medgar Evers] College, and so it was no contradiction for me. . . . It was a fit."[72]

Safiya Bandele also explained that her leadership at Medgar Evers and her work in Pan-African cultural nationalism and community activism were parallel. Medgar Evers College developed within the same context as the nearby Ocean Hill-Brownsville strikes that catalyzed the formation of The East's Uhuru Sasa School.[73] Radical feminists founded the college's Center for Women's Development, and The East's Kawaida-influenced cultural nationalism "flavored" the women's center. Safiya also enacted her feminist grounding through her work in The East and NBUF, as she advocated the centrality of women's issues to the Black freedom struggle.[74] Her narrative exemplified the fact that East affiliates' family lives, occupations, community activism, and leadership ethics were closely entwined.

Based on experiences in the Bandele household as well as observations of other Black nationalist groups, Safiya came to believe that polygyny could work for some women who desired to parent, develop careers, serve as activists, and become leaders. Her narrative suggested a belief that polygyny and male chauvinism did not have to be linked, as she disavowed any form of the practice that fostered what she saw as imbalanced gender dynamics.

Even though she believed that polygyny could be beneficial for some women, she discovered that she needed more personal freedom than she had in the Pan-African cultural nationalist extended family household. "The cultural nationalists were really [in] that nuclear family . . . father-as-protector mode," she observed, "and that was not my thinking." Instead, she stressed the desire for independence: "I had my own light to shine, so to speak, my own intelligence, my leadership, my own every-thing." Ultimately, she found that this assertion of individuality did not fit within the extended family relationships of The East. "Even though I had freedom in there, still, I needed more freedom, and so I left . . . physically, but have been emotionally tied to them always, and always will be."[75] Safiya's thinking about polygyny without patriarchy as a potentially ben-eficial arrangement and engagement of extended family relationships as support systems on her path to leadership complicate the binary of two opposing views about polygyny among Kawaida advocates.

East advocates had such varied experiences due to several factors. Primarily, it must be remembered that, as a popular social and educa-tional institution, The East was a big-tent organization. According to Martha Bright, "The East was a 'beacon' for people of African descent." The organization was formed of "multi-tiered, concentric circles of peo-ple who came from different backgrounds and experiences," she pointed out. "I can't emphasize this enough. Multi-tiered, concentric circles, with people who came from all different backgrounds and experiences, and you come to an organization that says 'y'all come.' You're going to have a lot of diversity." She further observed that "some . . . [Kawaida-influenced] organizations were more chauvinistic than others. It de-pends on who was in there. It depends on how open and embracing they were."[76] There was room for such diversity because "*umoja* and *ku-jichagulia* made room for unity without uniformity." She explained that "many things were similar because we have an overriding philosophy of Kawaida [as a] structural framework, but the ways they ran their orga-nizations on a day-to-day basis were not necessarily the same. . . . We could have *umoja* and *ujima* without being exactly alike. We could have self-determination," she added. "We don't have to be exactly alike."[77]

Perhaps the expectation of "unity without uniformity" also explains women's varied experiences in exhibiting leadership regarding polygyny in Kawaida-influenced organizations. "Unity without uniformity," or "operational unity," was a manifestation of *umoja* and one that Karenga endorsed during the 1967 Black Power Conference as a means of assist-ing with the development of a Black united front. The idea meant that group leaders in Kawaida-influenced coalitions should dialogue and de-cide how to "work in parallel and mutually supporting ways," but that individual groups could theoretically maintain their own identities.[78]

The literature spotlights Amina Baraka as a leading advocate of women's rights within the Congress of African People in general, and she specifically fought polygyny.[79] As the top-ranking CAP leadership, both Amina and Amiri Baraka condemned plural marriage practices and established CFUN as "the political headquarters and exemplar for the national CAP organization, projecting a monogamous family ideal." Nevertheless, tensions related to polygamy were widespread and entrenched.[80]

The issue of "unity without uniformity" was contested ground. A December 1973 letter from East/Brooklyn CAP chapter director Jitu Weusi to national CAP chairman Amiri Baraka revealed a growing rift between the groups. Weusi raised concerns about a cult of personality around Amiri Baraka, CAP leadership's insistence that The East be made a "carbon copy" of CFUN, the continued survival of "unity without uniformity," and possible perceptions that The East was "not a Kawaida organization" because of how different some of its practices were from those of Newark CAP. Most pointedly, Weusi wanted to "clarify the concept of the 'Extended Family'" as practiced by advocates of the New York-based East group. Weusi's comments shed light on the intensifying conflicts concerning polygamy. Amiri Baraka pointed out that certain polygamists were ousted from CAP.[81] Female advocates organized and led the resistance to polygamy, which originated in 1971 from CFUN's Women's Division. Women activists produced the leadership models for engaging in an interminable fight against polygyny, opposing larger issues of male chauvinism in both CAP and the broader modern convention movement, and launching CAP's 1974 African Women's Conference.[82]

East advocates' discordant viewpoints on extended family practices reflected an aspect of the struggle over polygyny, and Tamisha Peterson's narrative showed that The East was also a battleground in the conflict around polygamy. Women in the organization exhibited *kazi* leadership by speaking up about the issue. Peterson discussed the challenges that East women faced in resisting polygynous practices and said that those wanting to end the practice were "steamrolled." This issue stood out as an exception to the norm. She recalled that women organized and made decisions about many other issues. Peterson remembered that she and another East sister even joined the elders' council. "We were pretty proud," she said. "We were pretty outspoken. . . . We weren't feeling cowered in any kind of way. . . . We didn't feel like we were oppressed in any way except for the polygamous aspect." Polygynous practices were difficult to thwart due to the dynamics of intimate relationships, she explained. A woman "hooked up with somebody, and the guy says, 'Well, you know, this is my [new wife].' What're you going to do? What do you [say]? 'I'm leaving.' That's your only other option, or you could give him a lecture on, 'Well, this is not how it's done.'"[83]

Why did some East advocates uphold such a controversial practice? In their narratives, advocates suggested that polygyny fostered the kinds of large kinship groups that are a cornerstone of nation building. Members of extended families have said that they established intergenerational networks of members dedicated to East ideologies. These human resources have kept East traditions alive and have enlarged the community of activists who continue some of the now-defunct organization's cultural and political work through a myriad of other groups. The organization's history showed, however, that maintaining institutional leadership and culture among generations proved difficult, and some advocates opined that controversial and contested practices also contributed to the organization's downfall. On one hand, advocates of extended family practices viewed them as a beneficial, necessary form of *kazi* that could enlarge the organization, community, and nation and help overcome a sex ratio imbalance. On the other hand, some advocates exhibited *kazi* leadership initiative by articulating their opposition to polygynous relationships, which they viewed as intolerable, deviant, inherently unequal, and destructive to the kinds of community-building and nation-building work that East advocates undertook.[84] Polygamy, therefore, proved to be a conundrum for The East and for other Kawaida-influenced cultural nationalist organizations.

## *Black News*: "Of, by, and for Our Community"

While cultural nationalist women had different perspectives on the crucial and contentious issue of familial structure in The East and similar organizations, they tended to be more aligned in the belief that community-controlled, Black media outlets were essential components of nation building. Scholars of the Black press often trace its formation to the emergence of *Freedom's Journal* (1827–1829), the first African American newspaper. Fifty years after the Revolutionary War, members of America's free Black communities lived in a state of quasi-citizenship, facing hardships ranging from systemic economic marginalization and political disfranchisement to subtle, individual insults and indignities. In the most basic sense, the Black press strove to counter the kinds of negative narratives emanating from such an environment. African American media outlets also sought to convey Black community values and beliefs as well as expose pressing issues. Over the next 150 years, Black newspapers continued this mission, linking individuals by expressing their common struggles and purpose.[85] Developed in the vein of Black radical papers such as *Rebellion News* (Boston), the *Black Panther* (Berkeley), and *Muhammad Speaks* (Chicago), *Black News*, a "community publication" produced by and for the people of Bedford-Stuyvesant, reported on local and global issues facing African and African-descended people. The work of *Black News* staffers was a form of "agitating," "educating," and helping to "organize" for the purpose of community development. Through such work, *Black News* writers endeavored to use their words and ideas to invigorate action in such areas as politics, education, and entrepreneurship.[86]

Selling *Black News* was one of many activities through which East advocates engaged the "African-based community" on the local, national, and international levels.[87] According to former East member Angela (Weusi) Black, the paper was not just an organizational publication but also a community effort.[88] Peterson characterized *Black News* as "the voice for us to let the community know what was going on."[89] Both men and women sold the *Black News* paper, and the activity was viewed as an integral part of the nation-building effort.[90]

Tamisha Peterson pointed out that *Black News* was important because "it just told what was going on in the community from a Black perspective." In her view, it provided an important counterbalance to mainstream news sources: "[People] always heard the one side of the story; this time they could get the other side." Peterson's term "Black perspective" had a complex meaning.[91] As Maisha Fisher has explained, some East family members believed that the mainstream African American press was inadequate because it was filtered through the lens of White Americans' beliefs and concerns. Specifically addressing the use of the word "Black" in relation to the press, Jitu Weusi branded what he deemed deficient media organs as "'Negro' papers." On the other hand, those circulars that defiantly addressed and reflected the perspectives of African-descended people were "'Black' papers."[92] Although East advocates defined *Black News* as a community effort, they also emphasized that the paper circulated across the nation and around the world.[93] *Black News* was published and distributed with the help of women's leadership, which was frequently implemented informally and in the shadows.

Martha Bright initially got involved with The East as a *Black News* volunteer, and her memories of working to ensure that the paper was distributed in various venues across the globe figured prominently in her remembrances. The newspaper reached an estimated maximum circulation of fifty thousand. Bright recalled that it did not only reach readers all over the city and the nation, "it went into prisons, it went into hospitals, and it went all over the world." Expressing the fact that the periodical had a militant, "tell it like it is" style, Bright went on to say, "In fact the paper was so radical that some countries would not even permit it. When you got to customs, if they saw *Black News,* they confiscated all of them . . . particularly in the Caribbean, some of those countries that were undergoing self-determination struggles at that time." According to Bright's narrative, writing the truth of and for Black communities was an important component of East women's leadership and activism.[94]

Organizing paper sales complemented Tamisha Peterson's work as an Uhuru Sasa teacher. "I used to have my class go out, and we would have them spaced up on a block so they wouldn't be too far from my eyesight and try to sell *Black News* to some people that passed," she said. "We would do that for about an hour or so."[95] This experience speaks to nationalist educational styles that encouraged and celebrated a culture of reading, founded on the belief that community survival depended on literacy and learning. The *Black News* originated in the Ocean Hill-Brownsville uprising, and its essential mission was to "correctly" educate African-descended youth and their families with student-centered content emphasizing parental involvement and Black cultural nationalist values.[96] Women were at the center of this process, particularly in the roles of news writers and teachers.

For New York City native Abimbola Wali, selling *Black News* sparked her interest in joining The East, an act that she described in terms similar to a religious conversion. Wali said, "I was riding the A Train in . . . December 1969, and a young lady was walking through the train selling *Black News*. . . . It was ten cents, and I purchased a copy." Wali remembered that the articles immediately sparked a lively conversation between her mother and her about the possibility of their family having African bloodlines. Wali recounted how writers discussed Black Americans' African heritage, stating, "I just had never heard anything about African heritage or . . . being of African descent. . . . I asked my mother about it. . . . She said, 'Well, nobody in our family was from Africa, and I don't know what they're talking about.'"[97]

Wali said that the incident on the train sparked her interest, and she began selling *Black News* at the New York City office where she was a secretary. "I took it to work. . . . I was working for the city at that time, and I showed it. I start making copies and showing it to people, and then it asked at the bottom . . . if you wanted to sell *Black News*," she said. "Since so many of my co-workers were interested in the *Black News*, I called the number, and one of the brothers who was part of the Black Panthers . . . delivered the papers to my job. So I start selling *Black News*."[98]

Delivering the money Wali collected from *Black News* sales took her to The East's cultural center. "I called The East so I could come and bring the money. . . . When I entered The East, I saw all the people, all the sisters and brothers all around, and I had my permed hair and my miniskirt on, and I was fly. I walked in there, and everybody was cultural. . . . So then I wanted to volunteer my services," she said. Wali explained that group members warmly welcomed her, and The East eventually became her second home. She believed that her affiliation with the group transformed her sense of self as well as her outlook. She recalled that The East changed her lifestyle, and she began to dress and eat differently. She said, "My life changed and has been changed since. So I give praises to Brother Jitu and The East because it just opened up my worldview."[99]

South Carolina native Aminisha (Weusi) Black recalled that she became interested in writing amid community activism with The East. Her passion for reporting was fostered at *Black News* and led to publications in other local media outlets. After she migrated to New York in the late 1960s, she met other East advocates through a friend working in the Ocean Hill-Brownsville district. When Uhuru Sasa opened, Aminisha Black enrolled her two sons and became the school's bookkeeper. She also took on the role of typesetter at the *Black News*. Later, she began investigating and writing stories. The fact that Black reported on politics and was not limited to topics related to domesticity and social organization supports the women's claims that they were not systematically limited to restrictive Kawaida gender roles in The East. Black's narrative also indicated that The East functioned as a space for building Black women's leadership and career skills.[100]

Martha Bright also expressed the idea that The East was a place where women could develop wide-ranging expertise through their community work. She initially came to volunteer at *Black News* with other members of a local Republic of New Afrika formation, a group whose slogan, "Free the Land," reflected its aim of forming an independent nation from the five southern states of Georgia, Louisiana, Alabama, Mississippi, and South Carolina. Bright explained that, as "part of our responsibility with *Black News*, we learned how to do mass mailings and [package] stuff up, and we used to get that stuff out all over the world."[101] According to Bright's account, women filled many roles on the *Black News* staff from its earliest days. "Sister Fujii [Clara Breland] and Penda [Aiken] would type the copy under the leadership of Jim Williams, original editor of *Black News*," she remembered.[102]

When asked how much influence women had on the content of *Black News*, Bright responded, "a lot." She elaborated, "I said the original editor was a brother named Jim Williams, but I named all those women who were there."[103] She recalled that approximately equal numbers of women and men comprised the *Black News* staff. The "East Time-Line" indicates that women actually outnumbered men on the original *Black News* staff. Jim Williams was the paper's first editor, and the original staff (1969–1970) at the Fulton Street location included Ante Brown, Addie Rimmer, Martha Bright, Monifa King, and Fujii Breland. Men joined the staff during the same period, after the headquarters moved to 10 Claver Place. During the years 1969–1972, women appeared to outnumber men on staff, but the latter were the operation's official lead editors.[104]

Although Akili Walker remembered Martha Bright as "a sister . . . who was in charge of the newspaper" and who influenced its content, Segun Shabaka, the final editor, confirmed that all the paper's official editors were males.[105] Shabaka further contended, however, that women played integral roles in *Black News*, The East, and Kawaida-influenced organizations in general. Shabaka noted that he instated an editorial board during his tenure as *Black News* editor. For the years 1978–1983, he explained, "Taaliba and Muslimah," both women, would meet with other board members and decide which items to put into *Black News*. "Taaliba was the key person behind the major interviews we did with the convicted and confessed assassin of Malcolm X. She went into the prison and collected those interviews along with brother Adeyemi, who was [also] on the board," Shabaka attested. Reiterating his point about the important roles women played, not only in composing and disseminating the news, but in the broader East organization, he stated, "I know, when I was there, women were playing major roles in all the different components of the organization especially after [19]74 or [19]75, if not before."[106]

Emphasizing the numerous jobs she performed as part of her community work with the *Black News* staff, Bright said, "I reported, I edited. . . . I did a lot of proofreading. I have *Black News* editions [showing] that I wrote articles." She remembered piling into a car with other female staffers to investigate stories: "We would go places and do original reporting. We had a big say and a big part." Explaining that she was not confined to typical, feminized, mundane tasks and routine office work, Bright emphasized, "We weren't just the typing pool. . . . I didn't know how to type really. I didn't even do hunt[ing] and pecking. That was not me. . . . [*Black News*] was a real hands-on operation and the sisters were a big part of that."[107]

It is important to add, however, that women' appointments to formal, top-level leadership roles were limited. Although some served on the governing boards of the circular, men generally outnumbered them as titled leaders, according to available information.[108] Additionally, there was no woman among the four people who officially held the title of editor. Over *Black News'* years of publication (1969–1984), the editors were Jim Williams, Salik Mwando, Basir Mchawi, and Segun Shabaka.[109] Akili Walker's memories of Martha Bright as "in charge" of *Black News* were important, however. Recognition of women's *kazi* and their unofficial leadership roles within Kawaida-influenced organizations was often based on the informal ways constituents respected and recognized their work and commitment to struggle rather than on titled appointments.

Kwasi Konadu has highlighted the most important legacies of the *Black News* for the communities it served. The periodical carried out the primary function of "liberating and developing the African-based psyche" by promulgating Pan-African nationalist thought and practice in terms that laypeople could understand. It also left a historical record of the internal and external matters of The East organization.[110] For East women, it had another important purpose. Through serving the community as *Black News* staffers, they found that their experiences provided essential skills and training that they could use in other areas of their lives.[111]

## "We Stood for the Community": Women and Political Protest in the East

Producing and distributing *Black News* was not the only way that women affiliated with The East expressed their activism and served the community. Women also participated in voter registration drives, fundraisers, political campaigns, boycotts, and pickets that were, according to Jitu Weusi, a staple of Brooklyn's grassroots politics. Members participated in an array of nonviolent forms of direct action and awareness raising in association with fellow community organizations like the Coalition of Concerned Leaders and Citizens. Focused on specific causes impacting the neighborhood, women passed out leaflets, flyers, and posters, and braved the elements as they occupied strategic swaths of the Brooklyn pavement.[112]

In part, the women undertook such grassroots activism in the context of rising tensions between Black community members and White business owners (of all ethnicities and religious orientations) whom they viewed as interlopers. Frustrated African Americans have historically reported experiencing situations in which shopkeepers desired their dollars but refused to respect them as full citizens and human beings. Such attitudes were reflected in store owners' reluctance to staff their businesses with African-descended people, a lack of local philanthropic projects, and overly punitive attitudes during times of disagreement or conflict. Many African Americans observed that certain rapacious businesspeople drained money from their communities while apathetically watching blight grow.[113]

One tragic example was the case of the Triangle Shoe Store. Several advocates remembered the early 1970s boycott of Triangle as an example of East organizational involvement in direct action.[114] Triangle was located in Bed-Stuy in the 1200 block of Fulton Street near Nostrand Avenue, "right smack in the Black community." The store was robbed of fifty-nine dollars on February 12, 1972.[115] A Triangle manager reportedly chased the alleged thief down the street while "shooting like he was in the wild, wild West."[116] The manager fired a gun at the young man who he believed committed the robbery, and three bullets struck the unarmed teen in the back. According to the account of the incident in *Black News*, the Triangle manager would not allow anyone to aid the youth, who consequently died from his wounds on the sidewalk.[117] "The community was outraged," Walker reported.[118]

In response to the slaying, community members organized a picket line in front of Triangle every day for months in a concerted effort to prevent shoppers from patronizing the business. Capturing sentiments similar to the ones Mtamanika Beatty expressed as a Black mother worried about racialized and gendered violence against young African-descended males, Walker pointed out that East women joined the protests and were especially concerned because the victim was a Black boy.[119] In their analysis of the Triangle Shoe Store incident, Akili Walker, Mtamanika Beatty, and Jitu Weusi reported that the group's actions yielded successful results. Walker explained, "The end result was that the store shut its doors and moved out of the neighborhood."[120] Weusi broadly theorized that the kinds of street-level, grassroots community-control actions, "confrontation politics," and political education projects in which East members participated put hundreds of protestors in the streets, brought attention to important community issues such as predatory business practices and unjust policing, helped raise funds to continue the Black freedom struggle, and set the stage for future coalitions and alliances.[121]

Tamisha Peterson's recollections about women's participation in the strike revealed the subtleties of female participation in East protests in relation to their perspectives on *kazi*. She observed that advocates would assign mostly men and childless women to the picket lines while women with children were home performing family-related tasks, although it was not official organizational policy. Such activities were generally associated with domesticity rather than public action. Many East advocates, however, characterized them as forms of activism in their own right. This association stemmed from the fact that The East was a Kawaida-influenced organization in which advocates viewed fostering strong families and healthy children as a cornerstone of institution building. Peterson pointed out, "We had our own children. So, after we taught [school], we couldn't just go dash out on the picket line. It was time to go home, take care of the kids, do homework, feed them, put them to bed, [and] stuff like that."[122] Politically active and eager to join in boycotts and other actions that did not require extensive time away from family, many of the women apparently viewed the domestic sphere as one of many spaces for carrying out Black resistance. As an act of *kazi*, East mothers conscientiously spent time caring for and uplifting Black children because, in the broader society, they faced formidable challenges.

## "We Saw Ourselves as Soldiers": Women and Gender in Pittsburgh CAP

Pittsburgh-born Tamanika Howze developed into a staunch community activist during the mid-1960s and early 1970s. She remembered initially having an affinity for traditional civil rights organizations like the NAACP. Exposure to activists such as Stokely Carmichael, however, shaped her self-image as a youthful and "idealistic" person who was impatient with the slow pace of change. She said, "I'm this young person wanting things to move more swiftly, and I think they were just moving too slow, and my political thought had changed from civil rights to Black nationalism." As a result of her desire to help Black communities in Pittsburgh quickly grow and prosper, she affiliated with several different organizations. Moving from the city's Hill District to what she characterized as the more "politically astute" and culturally active neighborhood of Homewood during her junior year of high school provided a spark for involvement in various organizations and changed her political as well as her cultural consciousness.[123]

A neighborhood of working-class European immigrant families and upper-middle-class African Americans during the earliest decades of the twentieth century, Homewood was experiencing demographic change by the time Howze and her family moved there. With the mid-1950s construction of the Civic Arena in the Lower Hill District, city and county officials displaced thousands of low-income, majority-Black Lower Hill District residents. Pittsburgh's urban redevelopment program relocated the residents to Homewood. As a result, Black residents comprised nearly 70 percent of the total Homewood population by 1960, up from 22 percent in 1950. In the same decade, the overall population decreased from 34,355 to 30,523 amid White middle-class out-migration. The decades following the watershed year of 1968 witnessed a steady decline of Homewood's business district as well as its overall population. The out-migration was related to uprisings occurring in the aftermath of Martin Luther King Jr.'s assassination and a middle-class African American exodus to nearby neighborhoods as a result of the Fair Housing Act.[124]

Howze resided in the Homewood area from 1965 to 1967, when she was an upperclassman at East Avenue High School. In Homewood, she became involved with various community organizations and projects, including East Avenue's Student Council and the school's Human Relations Committee.[125] She recounted the synergy between returning university students and community activists as one element producing some of the Homewood institutions she joined. Local students left for college and returned to Pittsburgh desiring to start the kinds of Black cultural institutions they had seen elsewhere. One result was Together Inc., an organization of young African Americans that was noted in the press for its contributions to the community's economic and cultural development. Together Inc.'s ventures included the Harambee Bookstore and the annual Homewood-Brushton area Harambee Black Arts Festival.[126] A literacy hub similar to those of The East, the bookstore offered donated books and other reading materials for such populations as imprisoned African Americans; classes and lectures; and space for meetings and events such as fundraisers, plays, music, dancing, and poetry readings by Black Arts Movement luminaries like Sonia Sanchez.[127] The Harambee Black Arts Festival began in 1967, and its initial phase lasted through the early 1970s. Hailed as the third largest of its kind in the country, the festival reflected "the growth and . . . expression of black identity."[128] Howze lived in politically and culturally active neighborhoods in the highly charged decade of the 1960s. Her narrative revealed that entering Pittsburgh CAP was an extension of her community work and personal affiliations during a historical moment.

The exact details about how Tamanika Howze initially became a member of Pittsburgh CAP have faded from memory, and she expressed a belief that her association with the group simply "evolved." She also recalled joining on invitation from the group's leader, Sala Udin Saif Salaam (formerly Samuel Howze).[129] Activists established CAP in her hometown in addition to some twenty-five other urban centers with large Black populations. The groups were formed based on a framework developed in Atlanta and honed at later regional meetings held between 1970 and 1972. The Congress of African People attracted local groups to an expansive national network, within which Pittsburgh CAP was a connected cadre organization.[130] Kasisi Sala Udin, or Sala Udin Saif Salaam (henceforth Udin), was the local chairman.

Howze recalls that her initial job in CAP was taking notes. Remembering the group's strictly defined gender roles, she said that female foot soldiers usually did the secretarial work while rank-and-file men performed such duties as passing out leaflets and hanging posters. Howze stated, "I can't remember what committees I was on, but I do remember that there was a division of roles, very distinctive and, of course, the men were in . . . leadership, and we [women] were more in the subservient roles even though we did a lot of the work."[131]

Tamanika Howze eventually married Sala Udin. The two exchanged wedding vows in a Kawaida-styled ceremony, one of several Pan-African cultural nationalist communal rituals that celebrated the creation of patriarchal, heterosexual Black families as the cornerstone of nation building. Amiri Baraka officiated the wedding on July 7, 1973.[132] A *Courier* article published two weeks after the ceremony detailed the event, painting a vivid picture of the strictly defined Kawaida gender roles, which were common during CAP's early years. Gender difference was inscribed in many details, including the couple's clothing, like they were in mainstream American weddings. Instead of a white dress of the European tradition, the bride was attired in a richly embroidered, bright, flowing, African-styled gown. The outfit was topped with a *gele*, a head wrap fashioned from long pieces of cloth, skillfully tucked and tied to form a high crown. In contrast, the groom wore the austere Nyerere nationalist dress suit consisting of a black, button-down, collarless jacket and matching slacks.[133]

In his address to the couple, Baraka urged that the groom should be the head of his household, providing "emotional, economic, and physical security" for his wife and children. The bride was reminded to be "humble and loving, appreciative and resourceful, faithful, respectful, and understanding" toward her husband. She was also encouraged to inspire him. Finally, Baraka reminded the two of the complementarity concept: "Although you, Sala Udin, are to lead and you, Tamanika, are to follow, there is no superior or inferior one. You are both complementary."[134]

One recurring appraisal of complementarity critiqued the contradiction between the ideal and the praxis. On its face, complementarity suggested equality without sameness; nevertheless, in reality, the theory often bolstered rigid gender roles and stoked practices of gender inequity. Pittsburgh CAP stood as an example. The organization was "top-heavy" with male leaders and populated with female "followers." Additionally, in many Kawaida-influenced organizations, the women were expected to commit to *kazi* through hard work but also to physically display submissiveness with a *salimu*, which involved folding their arms across their chests and bowing when greeting men.[135] In short, Kawaida leaders' and advocates' words and deeds in relation to complementarity often meant two different things.

The wedding ceremony's significance extended beyond its affirmation of unequal gender roles, however. It also suggested Howze and Udin's rootedness in the local community. The couple married in the Hill District, forgoing wedding invitations for an article in the *New Pittsburgh Courier*. Udin wrote "Afrikan View," a regular column that was generally meant to reflect the ideas of Pittsburgh CAP members and that often promulgated Baraka's and Karenga's messages. In the article dedicated to his marital ceremony, Udin wrote, "According to Kawaida customs, wedding invitations are not sent because they would serve to exclude all those who did not receive one. We wish to be inclusive, not exclusive and, therefore, the whole Black community of Pittsburgh is invited to attend." Additionally, outlining the purpose of the union according to Kawaida philosophy, Udin wrote, "To Nationalists a stable Afrikan Family is the cornerstone of a stable Afrikan community, nation and race."[136] Considering this perspective, it is no wonder that the couple's family expanded. They welcomed three sons into the world.[137]

Besides being a wife and mother, Tamanika Howze was a stalwart community advocate and service leader. Even before her marriage to Udin, she was an award-winning activist in her own right. The local New Image NAACP recognized her as one of two CAP members providing "outstanding service" to the Black community in 1972.[138] In her oral narrative, Howze characterized herself and her peers as women who "held it down." That is, they navigated the competing demands of partnering and parenting with careers, community work, and service to CAP. They did so with consistency and composure.[139] News articles confirmed Howze's assessment, reporting that she was part of the Hill Mental Health Team of the Western Psychiatric Institute and Clinic. There, she was a social worker based in a Hill District psychiatric institute's satellite office. Along with performing her wifely duties and work in CAP, she and her team members assisted the local population through such activities as program and business development, awareness raising, and navigating the process of accessing social services.[140]

Despite the accolades and activities, Howze described herself as a behind-the-scenes worker and a "soldier" as opposed to a leader.[141] This characterization is no surprise, given the emphasis placed on masculine leadership models in Kawaida-influenced organizations. Women were expected to support and inspire in auxiliary roles but not necessarily to be visible, official, top-level organizational leaders according to Kawaida philosophy as well as some of the more conservative elements of American society.[142] Many Kawaida-influenced organizations additionally upheld the idea that *kazi* was one of the "Blackest" and most important of all Pan-African nationalist values. According to Kawaida philosophy, "Blackness" was not just skin color but was also determined by one's culture and consciousness. Kawaida advocates thus often viewed hard work as fundamental to both Black identity and the nation-building process.[143]

Accordingly, Howze described a feeling of exhaustion during her time in CAP.[144] The ten or so Pittsburgh members convened weekly 10:00 a.m. meetings on Sundays at a Hill District community center. The small group also sponsored local Kwanzaa festivities and worked to educate the community about the principles and practices of the holiday.[145] Howze labored to assist the organization to reach its overall aims, which involved employing Kawaida as a tool to achieve the lofty goal of organizing African Americans into a cohesive and thriving "national community." She and fellow members worked on the nation-building process at the level of developing institutions aimed at serving Black people's basic needs. Members hoped that the African American population could organize and improve the quality of their lives through such groups. Pittsburgh CAP sought to create and develop institutions in three specific areas: politics, economics, and education.[146]

Pittsburgh CAP participated in various political efforts from its inception. Howze stated that the chapter initially emphasized cultural nationalism, and that it became more politically focused over time.[147] Group members had the goal of employing a united front strategy to help form a grassroots, independent, African American political party in an effort to gain control of local, majority-Black areas, as one aspect of the larger nation-building project.[148] In 1972 the group hoped that the newly formed Allegheny County Black Political Assembly (ACBPA), an arm of the National Black Political Convention, would be a good starting point for building a third party. As a result, Pittsburgh CAP members participated in such activities as organizing voter education projects and registration drives. Additionally, they worked with the ACBPA to hold local, county-wide, and regional conferences as well as conventions during the early to mid-1970s.[149] Pittsburgh CAP members also participated in the Western Pennsylvania Black Political Assembly, of which ACBPA was a branch. Members involved themselves in related activities aimed at "build[ing] a political power base" in Pittsburgh while Howze was affiliated with CAP. Along with Sala Udin, Tamanika Howze was part of a delegation elected by the controversial National Black Assembly (NBA) to represent Allegheny County. She was seated at the 1975 NBA meeting in the District of Columbia.[150]

Although CAP's political activities had begun to fade from Howze's memory, she vividly recalled being most engaged in the organization's instructional projects, endeavors that prepared her for future leadership in the field of education. Besides working with Black Student Unions and teachers' organizations, the Pittsburgh group operated a supplementary educational institution, or what Howze called a "liberation school." According to her narrative, the venture began in her home. A news article informed the city's Black community about the educational institution, announcing its grand opening as African Free School (AFS) in November 1973. The school was slated to offer Saturday classes from 10:00 a.m. to 3:00 p.m. to educate community members on topics such as health and provide physical fitness as well as discipline-related activities like "drill." Focusing on developing a culturally relevant curriculum devoid of what advocates viewed as the hegemonic "hidden curriculum," administrators also hoped to inculcate a "healthy Black personality" in students by teaching "Afrikan values."[151] In the decades following CAP's dissolution, Howze remained active in Pittsburgh, particularly focusing on developing and maintaining local Freedom Schools.[152]

Pittsburgh CAP's work might have been rooted in local concerns, but members agitated, educated, and organized around global issues as well. For example, after the assassination of West African nationalist leader Amilcar Cabral in January 1973, a news article reported that Pittsburgh CAP demonstrated against US companies that continued to conduct business as usual with imperialist forces in countries struggling to throw off the yoke of colonialism. In concert with demonstrators in cities like Newark, New York, and Philadelphia, twenty-five to thirty CAP-affiliated men and women protested downtown in front of the Steel City's Gulf Building, a show of "sympathy and solidarity" with freedom fighters involved in African liberation movements.[153]

Pittsburgh CAP members played important roles in helping establish the national African Liberation Support Committee (ALSC) in 1972.[154] They convened a local work group, which sponsored African Liberation Week celebrations in the city. The gatherings, scheduled around African Liberation Day (ALD) demonstrations, included activities like movies, music, and art exhibits, and were meant to build support for continental African independence struggles. Photographs of a press conference held in Pittsburgh during the ALD commemorations of May 19–29, 1973, pictured a group of men, including The East's Jitu Weusi. They were seated behind a table around Udin, who spoke into a microphone. Such images reinforce the idea that CAP's formally recognized leadership was still male-dominated at the time.[155]

By 1974, CAP had begun to openly embrace socialism, and this turn was reflected in the Pittsburgh branch.[156] In recalling events of the Sixth Pan-African Congress in Dar es Salaam, Tanzania, local members recapped conference sessions covering topics from race and class to the current state of liberation in Africa and the diaspora. The Pennsylvania CAP activists reportedly theorized that the main problem facing African-descended populations was "imperialism versus the people." As a result, the chapter proposed the idea that socialism was the only feasible method for overcoming the marginalized and exploited status of "third-world" people in Africa, the Caribbean, and the United States.[157]

CAP's growing socialism was also reflected in reports of the Pittsburgh branch's activism related to the "woman question." The group held a women's seminar, unity dinner, parade, and political rally as part of its Afrikan Liberation Month activities in May 1974. Amina Baraka was the keynote speaker.[158] An earnest and authoritative leader in CAP who contributed to its ideological and material evolution, Amina Baraka served as the only woman on CAP's Executive Council. As such, she stood alone on the governing body as a proponent of improving women's roles within the organization. It was because of her staunch advocacy that the 1974 African Women's Conference took place in Newark.[159]

The thrust for gender equality in CAP did not emanate only from the top of the organization. According to Howze's account, some of the rank-and-file female advocates' demands for more egalitarian gender roles grew with the organization's increasingly socialistic focus. Expressing appreciation for women in the group who refused to remain silent on the issue of women's inequality, Howze said, "I was glad that the sisters would speak up." She explained that, though some remained submissive, many spoke out about the fact that the organizational structure needed to change because of what she deemed a disproportionate number of male leaders, some of whom should have helped with the organization's grunt work.

Howze believed that the group's shift to socialism changed its gender dynamics. She spoke of a female member who stood up for greater assistance with routine tasks and child-rearing responsibilities at home. Howze also gave an example of how women agitated for organizational change in terms of responsibilities for communal, organizational daycare and cooking in Pittsburgh CAP: "Before, it was just the women who were in childcare, and so we started changing that. The brothers . . . had a duty in childcare. They had a duty in the kitchen [and] that sort of thing." Stressing that CAP's turn toward socialism partly drove these changes, she said that the group eventually transformed, so that it was no longer a Kawaida-influenced organization. Adding an anecdote about her use of personal agency, Howze said, "I remember [at] times developing the schedules, so I made sure to schedule the brothers in childcare [and] schedule them in the kitchen."[160]

Aside from exhibiting *kazi* leadership in relation to struggles over issues of gender inequality in their homes and organizations, Congress of African People advocates publicly kicked off the year 1975 with the "woman question" as a guiding theme for broader community initiatives.[161] In his "African View" column that year, Udin stressed that, like racism, women's rights were of major concern to people struggling for Black liberation as well as those who fought for all oppressed people's freedom and equality. He also wrote that women's issues, like racial discrimination, were by-products of "Monopoly Capitalism."[162] To work on combating these interlocking ills, CAP convened the first national Black Women's United Front meeting during the month of January in Detroit. This action brought CAP under the banner of women's rights, anticapitalism, anti-imperialism, and antiracism with such groups as the All African People's Revolutionary Party, the National Welfare Rights Organization, the Black Workers Congress, Pan Afrikan Students of America, the Youth Organization for Black Unity, and the Ethiopian Students Organization. The overall thrust of the broad coalition was improving the conditions of Black and Third World women while also forwarding the liberation struggle.[163] The Black Women's United Front developed from the conference.

As an individual Pittsburgh CAP member, Tamanika Howze demonstrated a sense of *kazi* leadership by engaging her community around similar causes. A reading of *Courier* articles reveals that Howze's public advocacy, particularly for women's issues, grew within the context of CAP's expanded focus on multiple forms of oppression. For instance, a newspaper journalist cited Howze as a "women's liberation activist" in the series "Are Black Women for or against Women's Lib?" Additionally, the writer quoted Howze's views on the nature of the Black women's liberation movement.

Communicating the idea that her women's rights sensibilities evolved within the context of the Kawaida-influenced Congress of African People as the organization's ideology grew more socialistic, Howze stated, "The Black women's liberation movement is inside and runs parallel to the Black liberation struggle. Racism and sexism are born out of capitalism, as both have been used to psychologically and thus 'existentially' maintain and further develop capitalism." The reporter wrote that Howze said that rich and powerful White males occupied the top positions in capitalistic societies and thus exploited poor White men, people of color, and all women, as they were forced into lower positions on the socioeconomic ladder.[164] Howze further revealed the idea in her self-narrative that she came to her position on women's rights through Black freedom struggle activism. She explained, "I don't subscribe to traditional feminism because traditional feminism is White-oriented. It's not designed for us." Howze instead preferred the designation *womanist*.[165]

Another early 1975 article reported Tamanika Howze's emerging views on women's rights. A group of concerned Pittsburgh citizens sponsored a Free Joan Little rally. The event was meant to bring attention to the plight of an imprisoned, poverty-stricken young Black woman accused of murdering a much older White prison guard, Clarence Alligood, in 1974. The petite and soft-spoken Little testified that she stabbed the brawny jailer in self-defense as he sexually assaulted her in a North Carolina cell. In and out of trouble with the law since she was a youth, Little was being detained on charges of breaking and entering when the rape occurred. Having escaped after managing to get hold of the icepick that Alligood wielded as he sexually assaulted her, Little was declared an outlaw by North Carolina authorities, who issued a "shoot on sight" order. Even though another guard had discovered Alligood with his pants down and a trail of semen on his leg, reporters and prosecutors framed the incident as the vicious murder of a dutiful public servant by a promiscuous Black femme fatale. After Little surrendered, a grand jury handed down a first-degree murder indictment. Little faced the death penalty. Many, including advocates in Kawaida-influenced organizations, rallied to her cause.[166] Historian Genna Rae McNeil described the movement supporting Little's case as an example of the "effective mobilization of progressive social organizations, networks of activists, and movements for justice." Moreover, she pointed out that Little's ordeal was also a moment for women to forge a "sisterhood" across racial and class lines.[167]

It was in this environment that Howze spoke at a Pittsburgh community event where she endorsed Little's right to self-defense. Howze emphasized that Little had the right to protect herself, not only as a poor Black person, but specifically as a woman. Going on record as a CAP member, Howze told a *Courier* reporter, "In the state of North Carolina, committing rape is punishable by death." She declared, "Acting out of self-defense, [Joan Little] was left no other alternative but to fight against an aggressor who was bent on forcibly entering her body."[168]

Little's freedom partially depended on the leadership of activists like Howze. They not only agitated in Little's defense, but also educated people about the multiple, overlapping forms of oppression she faced. The courage of individuals like Howze, who worked within organizations like CAP, was key in assisting Little's defense to secure a 1975 acquittal.[169] Moreover, Woodard points out that female CAP cadres' consciousness raising around the topic of Black women's oppression in the realms of race, class, and gender impacted the philosophies of prominent Pan-African cultural nationalists. Leaders such as Amiri Baraka and Maulana Karenga began to philosophically repudiate male chauvinism, framing Little's act of resistance within the same vein as the larger struggle for human dignity and rights.[170]

It is notable that 1975, the year of the "woman question," with its flurry of activism related to the Little case, marked the first time that readers of the *Courier* heard Howze articulate her own position on any cause. That she addressed women's rights causes within the context of the Black liberation struggle spoke volumes about the leadership of female cultural nationalists, who developed the agency to articulate their own positions and emphasize women's rights within masculinist, Kawaida-influenced groups in general and CAP in particular. Though some may view this as further evidence that Black women lagged behind their White counterparts in terms of women's rights advocacy, historian Danielle McGuire emphasized that the female activists involved with the Free Joan Little movement were part of a decades-old tradition of Black women's testimony and protest against the sexual abuse to which White males subjected them.[171] Marginalized in narratives of the women's rights struggle, and often essentialized in the record because of their initially subservient roles in Kawaida-influenced organizations, female advocates in Kawaida-influenced groups have not received enough attention for their support for women's rights causes such as the Free Joan Little movement.

Even when telling her own story, Tamanika Howze declined to characterize herself as a leader in Pittsburgh CAP. She cited the fact that wives of male CAP leaders were charged with leadership responsibilities as a matter of course. Nevertheless, *Courier* journalists reported that Howze headed the local Black Women's United Front (BWUF) and publicly agitated, educated, and organized for women in various ways.[172] The BWUF arranged employment seminars, discussing important issues and offering resources that exposed neighborhood women to training and job opportunities.[173] BWUF members also helped connect the women with social services organizations, hoping to improve conditions in the community. They conducted a survey of women on public assistance to determine the challenges they faced in locating and utilizing services. The BWUF sponsored a forum to educate women about accessing much-needed welfare resources and offered ideas for creating businesses. As the BWUF had in other instances, the group also planned to charter shuttle buses so interested parties could attend national meetings.[174]

In addition to agitating and educating about gender issues, Howze organized activities emphasizing the struggle for women's democratic rights and working-class solidarity across racial lines as leader of Pittsburgh CAP's BWUF. She told the press, "We feel the conditions now call for a multi-national united struggle for the democratic rights of women, oppressed nationalities and the whole of the working class."[175] Additionally, Howze described the aim of the BWUF as resisting "capitalism, imperialism, racism, and sexism." As an expression of such aims, the group organized a February 1976 conference titled "Women Unite to Fight Back." The summit featured the film *Space to Be Me* and a multicultural panel of women. Both events highlighted the challenges of working-class women in capitalist societies. The local "Women Fight Back" summit was a precursor to the national branch's BWUF conference and International Women's Day demonstration in March, which CAP co-sponsored with the October League.[176] The Pittsburgh CAP branch dissolved later in 1976, according to Howze, who said that the "movement pretty much stopped . . . because we had an enormous task in front of us."

Community concerns and neighborhood involvement often shaped the advocacy work and leadership ethics of women in Kawaida-influenced Pan-African cultural nationalist organizations. Women like Tamisha Peterson in The East and Tamanika Howze in Pittsburgh CAP performed and led integral work in such areas as political organizing, consciousness raising, direct action, education, print media, and nation building via collective institution building as well as household development. They also navigated and challenged confining gender constructs.

Under the CAP umbrella, women from various Kawaida-influenced organizations were also involved in such activities as voter registration and leadership training, both internal and external to their organizations. In particular, the concept of *kazi* provided the foundation for developing women's rights activism as well as female advocates' leadership ethics and abilities, whether such activities, standards, and skills were formally acknowledged or not.

3

## "*Taifa Saa* Means Nation Time"

*Women, Institution Building, and Program Development*

The driving, staccato words of Amiri Baraka's poem "It's Nation Time" delivered a militant ode to "pulsating positive magnetism," "black genius," "unity," and self-determination in service of nation building.[1] Similarly vigorous and definitive, The East organization's Martha Bright described nation building in her oral history narrative. To Bright, "nation time," or *taifa saa*, meant institutional and program development in marginalized communities, like the one in which she was active.[2] The majority of Bedford-Stuyvesant's 1,200 businesses were unprofitable. Additionally, enterprises such as A&P Supermarket, one of the largest grocery store chains in the United States at the time, tended to funnel profits away from the community. The conglomerate had a record of operating in majority-minority neighborhoods but rarely hiring African Americans, keeping them in menial positions, or declining to do business with Black vendors.[3] In such contexts, the Pan-African cultural nationalist concepts of *taifa saa* and *ujamaa* encouraged advocates to help build and maintain self-help entrepreneurial ventures, community programs, and mutual aid groups. These entities focused on generating revenue for Pan-African cultural nationalist organizations, creating jobs, and improving the health of advocates and residents of the broader neighborhoods in which they existed.

In cases where businesses operated, advocates' models seemed to be what is now understood as activist entrepreneurship, rather than extractive capitalism. That is, the businesses made community uplift and humanitarianism their primary reason for existence.[4] For instance, advocates in Us, CFUN, The East, and Ahidiana developed and maintained ventures like boutiques, food cooperatives, kitchens and catering businesses, and women's collectives for the purpose of serving the community. In contrast, extractive business owners obtained Black and

Brown consumers' dollars, funneling resources toward themselves and their own communities with little or no reinvestment in the social and economic welfare of their customers. During Operation Breadbasket's boycotts against A&P during the early 1970s, for example, a local newspaper article informed readers that The East's food co-op was available as a low-cost alternative for local patrons seeking to buy fresh foods. The co-op was touted as an example of *ujamaa*, or cooperative economics.[5]

In this environment, many African Americans welcomed Amiri Baraka's call for nation building, though it was expressed in such masculinist terms as "brothers strik[ing]" and "brothers tak[ing] over the school." Oral narratives like Bright's emphasize women's central roles in nation building, from initial planning and development to the daily maintenance of nationalist institutions and programs.[6] In Ahidiana, Tayari kwa Salaam, Vera Warren-Williams, and other advocates practiced *kazi* through sisterhood gatherings such as the Black Woman's Conferences and their offshoot, the Black Women's Group. Their experiences demonstrate that female cultural nationalists' own gender ideas evolved as they enacted servant leadership and challenged patriarchal views about nation building to support work that they viewed as necessary to the well-being of their communities.

## Making Mavazi: Women's Roles in Clothing the Community

Women were key to the functioning of the Committee for a Unified Newark (CFUN) and East ventures, which were aspects of *taifa saa*, the organizations' nation-building efforts. One gendered project that women undertook was constructing the kind of clothing that was so important to cultural nationalist self-expression. Amina Baraka explained that through "the block associations that . . . women in the community [developed], we taught them to make African clothes." She said that women helped produce various African-influenced clothing styles, including nationalist dress suits for men. In addition to viewing Nyerere, or *mwalimu*, nationalist suits as sartorial and political statements, CFUN leaders envisioned the manufacture and sale of the outfits as a business opportunity, not only for members but also for people in the neighborhoods that the various branches served. Amina Baraka recalled, "This one woman, Ms. Slade, she made it into a business. She made clothes for the men in the organization. . . . You can get African clothes practically anywhere now, but back in the day, you couldn't. So she made a business of it, and she made what we called nationalist dress suits."[7]

Amina Baraka recounted how the dress suits came into fashion among Black nationalist men and, with her help, subsequently grew into a business venture for a woman in the neighborhood. She said, "The people in the community, they were smart." Amina explained that Amiri Baraka had visited Tanzania during Nyerere's presidency. The men there were sporting distinctive suits. "When Amiri brought one back home, I took it apart and made patterns and I started making them myself." Then other women, like Ms. Slade, began to earn money by producing the suits themselves.[8]

When they saw Amiri Baraka don the Tanzanian dress suit, Amina said, the brothers in CFUN would often exclaim, "Ooh, that's a bad suit! I want to wear that. How do you get that?" Ms. Slade, who lived across the street from the organization, had learned to make dashikis from Amina and expressed interest in adding the two-piece men's nationalist outfit to the repertoire of clothing she could produce. Amina Baraka recounted, "I just gave her my pattern and she started sewing suits. She was a working-class Black woman, and she had no other means except her husband working. . . . She found a way to earn money and to do something to serve the community in that sense, because the brothers started wearing the national dress suits. . . . She could make them very well. She had a pattern."[9]

Women also played important roles in East businesses related to garment production and sales because many first-generation advocates viewed African-inspired clothing as "a matter of pride and history," not merely a utilitarian or an aesthetic choice.[10] For example, Muslimah Mashariki sewed the Nyerere nationalist dress suits for The East's Mavazi boutique. Mavazi opened in 1971 and boasted African records, carvings, underwear, dashikis, dungarees, and ready-to-wear as well as custom-made clothing at reasonable prices. Although a male East member, Job Mashariki, was the store supervisor, women like Muslimah also devoted their time, skills, and energy to the enterprise.[11] In other ventures, East women "did bookkeeping and clerical work, cleaning, selling and sewing, typesetting and traveling, and lots and lots of teaching."[12]

Tamisha Peterson summed up women's efforts, her words suggesting that *kazi* undergirded their work ethic: "We did a lot of the footwork, a lot of the office work, a lot of the basic stuff that wouldn't get done, the big stuff." Peterson lamented that she was not surprised that women advocates were not given as much credit as men for such work. Illuminating the importance of women's support networks in navigating their lives as female activists in the organization, she continued, "We took care of each other. We had our sisterhood meetings, and we made a lot of decisions ourselves too on what we were going to do, which direction we were going to go. We handled some of our problems." Reiterating a common theme in the narratives—that gender roles internal to the organization often mirrored those in the broader, patriarchal society— Peterson commented that female East members did "pretty much what women do in everyday life out here."[13] While *kazi* animated the leadership and work ethic of women advocates in Kawaida-influenced Pan-African cultural nationalist organizations as they endeavored to clothe their communities, it guided the work they performed in helping feed them as well.

## "Food for Tradition and Life": Women, Culinary Nationalism, and the East Community

Beginning in 1970 in Brooklyn, East members promoted cultural practices, such as preparing and sharing distinctively African and diasporic foods, as an assertion of Black identity.[14] In doing so, they were linked to a broader movement that popularized what Jennifer Jensen Wallach calls "culinary nationalism." Food production, procurement, preparation, and consumption became central components of the Black freedom struggle for advocates. While civil rights leaders like Ella Baker regarded access to the iconic American meal of a hamburger and a Coca Cola as nonessential to the struggle, younger activists saw it as symbolic of American citizenship. With the rise of Black Power, some African Americans additionally came to regard healthier alternatives to popular American diets as a rebuke of the United States' greed and excess, a symbol of Pan-African cultural nationalism, and a significant factor in Black nationality and identity formation. Mid- to late 1960s Black nationalist activism, according to Wallach, marked a turning point in African American culinary discourses and practices.[15]

The contours of cultural nationalist foodways were gendered.[16] Women held primary responsibility for cooking and serving food according to traditional, mainstream American gender roles as reinforced by those of the Us Organization, CFUN, and The East. The "post-1964 culinary turn" reflected cultural nationalists' belief that consuming a vegetarian or a whole-foods diet was an important part of maintaining self-discipline, personal wellness, and community vitality.[17] As such, women occupied a central role in helping promote healthy habits within Pan-African nationalist organizations because of their gendered roles as cooks for family, community, and nation.

The process of asserting a separate Black identity and value system among nationalists often involved making food an important expression of communal activism. Construction of Black nationalist foodways was one way of reframing the relationship between African-descended people and the United States' nation-state. Moreover, new food habits were at the center of Kwanzaa practices, which included fasting, consuming foods with "African" origins, and eating other dishes that represented continuities across the continent of Africa and the diaspora. "The earliest Kwanzaa observers operated under the assumption that food behavior was an important factor of identity construction," Wallach writes.[18]

Because Kwanzaa was constructed as a harvest festival, foodways were central to its existence and iconography. Beginning in the late 1960s, Pan-African nationalists used food in two ways. Primarily, practices of food production and consumption constituted ways of performing what was considered "a Pan-African food identity." Additionally, they promoted ideals about healthy living.[19] The East's Adeyemi Bandele reinforced this idea when he said that advocates grappled with the "worldwide struggles of people of African descent" and "also addressed the issues of diet and nutrition."[20]

East advocates created and perpetuated Pan-African culinary traditions. They encouraged members to eliminate red meat and to purchase and prepare "good Afrikan food" for Kwanzaa feasts, or *karamus*.[21] Personal interviews and *Black News* articles affirm the importance of assisting community members with what advocates deemed healthy eating practices. East member Basir Mchawi wrote that the process of assisting an individual with switching from celebrating Christmas to embracing Kwanzaa was similar to converting them from meat-eating to a diet replete with "all the protein, vitamins, calories and minerals necessary for proper health" as a vegetarian.[22] As displayed on the pages of *Black News*, books on "diet, nutrition, and exercise" could be the "perfect" Kwanzaa gifts.[23] Assisting with developing the vigor and well-being of the nation's members was especially important, and nationalists promoted their beliefs about healthful living within their communities.[24] Kawaida-influenced foodways, nationalist perceptions of healthy eating, community programs, and institution building were recurring themes in self-narratives, and women were integral to these activities.

Mtamanika Beatty emphasized that one of the ways that East members sought to make a difference was by modeling healthy eating habits and providing wholesome food to the community through the organization's food co-op, school, restaurant, jazz club, and catering business. Beatty asserted that many health issues, which she correlated with harmful patterns of food consumption, remained particularly problematic in the community. She recalled that East advocates encouraged cooks to provide what they viewed as better alternatives by limiting fried foods, using fewer canned goods, and putting more fresh ingredients in their recipes. She also emphasized, "We didn't serve pork at all."[25]

Although its manager was a male, Kwesi Mensah Wali, women were crucial to the operation of The East's food co-op, Kununuana. They assisted with bringing fresh foods and other natural products in bulk form from the Bronx to Bed-Stuy, and at The East, they helped repackage these items for people who pooled money in order to receive them at lower prices.[26] In 1975 the co-op comprised about fifty families and group leaders. Advocates hoped to serve more people as The East's infrastructure expanded.[27]

Kununuana was formed in November 1970 to assist East family members and eventually the larger central Brooklyn community where it was located. Residents there dueled with problems of low-quality, highly processed foods sold at inflated prices. In 1972 Kununuana offered what it called "food for life." A 1973 *Black News* advertisement declared co-op members' goals: "With your support and our determination to provide our community with good food, we may yet become a SUPERMARKET HEALTH FOOD COOPERATIVE in OUR COMMUNITY.... Supporting the EAST stores is like putting money in the bank. You not only get the merchandise you paid for, but we [all] reap the dividends of a developing, beautiful and safe community."[28]

By 1975, the circular advertised that The East co-op occupied a physical store location on Fulton Street, a main Bed-Stuy thoroughfare. At the co-op, shoppers could satisfy all their needs, from "nutritional foods," "herbs," "spices," "fresh fruits," and "vegetables" to "sweets," "meat patties," and "canned foods."[29] Later operating under the names East Co-op Food Store and Uhuru Food Cooperative, the program continued until its closure around 1992.[30] Tamisha Peterson surmised that Kununuana outlasted so many East programs because of its service mission, an indication of its managers' *kazi* leadership ethics. It served a specific function in the community. "I think it was probably the only place in the area that had fresh fruits and vegetables," she said. Peterson further observed that the neighborhood lacked supermarkets and amounted to what would later be labeled a "food desert," an area in which residents are not able to easily access retail establishments offering healthy, affordable food.[31]

The cooperative, or "association of persons for common benefit," was not a new concept, nor was it specific to Pan-African cultural nationalism. The Rochdale Pioneers, an organization of impoverished weavers who decided to work together to overcome the conditions they faced as underpaid laborers in mid-nineteenth-century industrial England, was the first modern example of a cooperative business model. Cooperatives emerged in response to various conditions and at several points in time in the United States. For instance, consumers formed Rochdale-styled cooperatives when food prices spiked from 1910 to 1913. Despite state legislation facilitating such Progressive Era collaborative ventures, they did not fare well outside the British context. Consumer co-ops also emerged during the Great Depression and the American cooperative movement gained short-term support from the New Deal Federal Emergency Relief Administration's Division of Self-Help Cooperatives. The movement subsided as the economy recovered and funding sources dried up. The countercultural movements of the late 1960s and early 1970s stimulated another surge of alternative consumer cooperatives.[32] With the goal of resisting the forward march of extractive capitalism in their community and providing wholesome, affordable food to cope with rising prices, The East's Kununuana developed within a similar struggle for "consumer liberation" through the "insurgent" commercial practices of the 1960s countercultural movement.[33]

Kununuana was also an outgrowth of Black cooperative economic ideas and traditions, and *kazi* leaders were central to its functioning. As Barbara Ransby has pointed out, long-standing practices of mutual aid existed within the African American community. Moreover, many Black organizers viewed cooperatives as pathways to economic uplift.[34] As early as 1907, W. E. B. Du Bois asserted that African American people should band together to form producer and consumer cooperatives as methods of progressing toward moderate socialism within Jim Crow and the dominant capitalist economy. He called this practice "economic co-operation." Du Bois viewed mutual aid societies as forms of such economic cooperation.

Other civil and human rights activists helped promote similar programs of Black cooperative economics. During the Great Depression, Ella Baker spearheaded a program aimed at assisting economically ravaged communities and teaching individuals about socialism. She joined author George Schuyler in 1930 to serve as cofounder and national director of the Harlem-headquartered Young Negroes' Cooperative League, a clearinghouse and training center for affiliated Black co-ops and buying clubs in various locales across the country. In 1969 Fannie Lou Hamer began work on Freedom Farm, a cooperative project in northern Sunflower County, Mississippi. Hamer fought against hunger and poverty in her community through Freedom Farm programs such as a "pig bank," a vegetable farm, a housing project, and a scholarship fund. Freedom Farm also had a business development arm that supported garment operations, including an "Afro-Botique" that sold African-styled garments. From Du Bois, Baker, and Hamer to Tanzanian president Julius Nyerere's 1960s prescriptions for *ujamaa*, which drew on ideologies of African socialism from ages-old extended family traditions, people of African descent had a history of thinking and doing cooperative economics. Viewing Kununuana as *ujamaa*, or "cooperative economics," at work, East members were in the stream of the various histories of collective commerce, and women were at the center of this nation-building activity.[35]

### "Black Women—Hope for the Future": Ahidiana-Inspired Gatherings in New Orleans

Ahidiana administered several enterprises in the spirit of *ujamaa*, including a bookstore, printing press, health and nutrition club, school, and community organization, all based in New Orleans.[36] Also aligned with *ujamaa*, the group's relatively more egalitarian gender roles exemplified "collectivity" by challenging the notion of one-dimensional Black Power masculinism.[37] New Afrika Books was a function of larger Kawaida literacy traditions and an outgrowth of an Ahidiana Sunday study group. The bookstore carried publications from various sources and, significantly, showcased those printed by the organization's press, Ahidiana Habari. The press featured pieces by accomplished writers such as Kalamu ya Salaam, as well as the writings of other African-descended authors who preferred to work with a Black publisher. Notably, Ahidiana Habari also printed works by Tayari kwa Salaam, one of the relatively few women involved in a Kawaida-influenced organization who published during the period of the 1960s to the early 1980s. Her reflections provide a glimpse of women's written expressions about gender roles and the evolving values of Kawaida-influenced organizations. Her writing suggested a growing sense of *kazi* leadership, from the earlier children's books that reinforced complementary gender roles to subsequent pamphlets underscoring the importance of women's leadership and gender equity in the Black freedom struggle.

Not all Ahidiana enterprises focused on literature. Group members also engaged in collective food buying, like East advocates, emphasizing holistic nutrition and buying quantity goods to share with other community members. They bought in bulk to cut costs incurred in providing daily, warm, vegetarian meals for students attending the organization's school.[38] "Ujamaa," a children's story penned by Tayari kwa Salaam, not only emphasized the importance of food co-ops but revealed that youth literature was one of the acceptable venues for women's theorizing within the strictest Kawaida contexts.[39] The tale featured the characters Brother Dog and Sister Cat, two hungry friends with limited funds. Brother Dog suggested that Sister Cat accompany him to buy cheese from a food co-op to fill their stomachs while practicing familyhood and cooperative economics. Dog said, "Let's put our money together and we'll have enough money to get cheese." The characters then "went to town and bought the small block of cheese at Duka Ujamaa, the food co-op." Salaam wrote, "The block of cheese they bought was bigger and heavier than it would have been if they had bought it at a regular store."[40]

The two friends' struggles with their hefty chunk of cheese did not simply spotlight the importance of collective food purchasing and consumption as expressions of *ujamaa*; it also provided a backdrop for presenting ideas about gender. When the time came for coordinating how their weighty meal would be transported, Dog said to Cat, "Brothers have a responsibility to lead; so, I'll take the first turn. And sisters are completers; you can take a second turn." Tayari kwa Salaam's words reflected early Pan-African cultural nationalist values, reminding boys to embrace their duties as leaders and girls to support males in such roles.

Other stories in the larger work, *Who Will Speak for Us?*, were more reflective of the mid-1970s challenges to the kinds of sex roles that excluded women from visible, formal leadership positions. In one tale, Sister Ant emerged as an organizer in the struggle because of her knowledge and skills, despite the fact that she did not possess the large body typically associated with warriors. Sister Green Bird was depicted as a leader in other stories. In part because of Ahidiana's various enterprises, Tayari kwa Salaam's publications remain available in the archival record, adding another woman's voice to those whom Scot Brown cited as members of a Kawaida-influenced stratum of cultural nationalist activist-artists and to the body of work that Ashley D. Farmer introduced as examples of women's gendered cultural nationalist theorizing.[41]

In addition to using literature as a vehicle, Ahidiana members articulated concern over the plight of Black women in Pan-African organizations and stressed the need for female leaders in Black women's gatherings. One such example was the Black Woman's Conference, which Ahidiana established in 1978. The assembly was held annually for four years on the campus of Southern University of New Orleans. According to Samori Camara, the Black Woman's Conference was "local and powerful." The purpose of the forum was to assist Black women with developing themselves by theorizing, planning, and organizing in resistance to race, class, and gender oppression.[42] One Ahidiana activist, Vera Warren-Williams, stated that the conferences highlighted such issues as rape, domestic violence, equal pay, reproductive rights, women's health, nutrition, and fitness.[43]

The Black Woman's Conferences reinforced the concept that both teaching and learning were aspects of *kazi*. Highlighting the importance of women's roles as teachers, Warren-Williams expressed the significance of advancing women's education for entire communities and for the overall nation-building endeavor. "When you educate a woman, you educate a nation," she said. There was a "notion that if the women are educated, then they in turn educated the children, which helped to build a better nation."[44] She recognized the importance of formal education, but also suggested the value of meetings like the Black Woman's Conferences as informal Black nationalist educational spaces with relatively few barriers to entry for women and for entire communities.[45]

The Black Woman's Conference generally followed a standard weekend format.[46] The yearly gathering featured panel discussions, workshops, keynote addresses, films, and a concert. The conferences attracted more than a hundred people each day, and attendees came from many walks of life. They included people from other local and regional social and political organizations, elders, parents of children from Ahidiana, local radicals, individuals affiliated with other independent and supplementary Black schools, and college students.[47]

Organizers held the Third Annual Black Woman's Conference on July 5 and 6, 1980. Ahidiana co-hosted the event on the Southern University of New Orleans campus in conjunction with the Department of Social Welfare. The conference's theme was "Working Together, We Can Make a Change." Conference organizers expressed what could be considered a womanist intent in that they sought to galvanize the entire community to address women's issues. Organizers consciously included males as participants and addressed issues involving children. The purpose of the meeting, as reflected in the program, was to supplement and support Black women's personal development, organizing efforts, and self-defense training, both among themselves and alongside men.[48]

The *kazi* leaders convening the 1980 proceedings followed the standard format for other Ahidiana Black Woman's Conferences. Female nurses and physicians led a workshop offering information for women in their daily struggles with health maintenance. Stressing a key tenet in the credo of nationalist mothering, organizers noted that the assembly was partially aimed at supporting women in the work of rearing offspring who were "strong in their identity, purpose and direction."[49] Emphasizing such themes as communal care for children, the sessions on child-rearing also reflected the event's womanist orientation. They featured presentations from Nilima Mwendo, who spoke on collective childcare, Shawishi wa Watu St. Julien, who explored Ahidiana Work/Study Center as a model school, and Tayari kwa Salaam, who discussed techniques for children's academic development.

Conference-goers could also view *Portrait of Teresa*, a Cuban film about a woman struggling to balance the competing demands of family, job, and self-care. The film portrayed Teresa navigating work at a textile factory, mothering three sons, and struggling to maintain a relationship with her husband. Her marriage to Ramón, a television repairman, was plagued with domestic violence.[50] Convention organizers also noted that the film was important because it depicted a woman "making decisions about developing herself" and centered on "the contradictions that must be resolved if women are to develop themselves as whole human beings."[51]

Organizers developed sessions dealing with Black male-female relationships, women's leadership, and the arts, including speakers such as Kalamu ya Salaam and social worker Morris F. X. Jeff Jr. One panel highlighted several experienced Black female community leaders of the previous generation. The group included Dara Abubakari (Virginia Y. Collins), local grassroots activist, enduring Pan-Africanist, and Republic of New Afrika president; Leah Chase, entrepreneur and internationally known chef; and Aline St. Julien, an outspoken advocate of civil rights and Black Power, an author, and the mother of Tayari, Nilima, and Mtumishi.[52] Sonia Sanchez delivered the keynote address. She also gave a concert performance alongside Sweet Honey in the Rock, an a cappella ensemble of women cultural and political activists.[53]

Warren-Williams, who served on the Black Woman's Conference organizing committee, recalled that she did not give gender roles in Ahidiana much attention prior to the gatherings. "I guess at that point in my development, I didn't really do too much differentiating, but being a female, we were primarily tasked with . . . the education of the children, but the men were also involved in that aspect." She admitted, "I didn't really see tremendous differences, and I don't think, at that particular time, I was focused in on female versus male stuff. I didn't give it much thought."[54]

She went on to explain that participating in the conferences raised her gender consciousness: "Primarily, my consciousness around [gender] began with the advent of the Black Woman's Conferences, which . . . pulled women's issues out and highlighted them; therefore, we organized and brought women from other organizations, groups, and just the community as a whole to address . . . issues."[55] Warren-Williams believed that the assemblies harnessed the energy of Ahidiana members' struggles in relation to uplifting women.

A 1981 booklet entitled *Working Together, We Can Make a Change: Towards Sisterhoods of Struggle* echoed Warren-Williams's sentiments. The brochure, written by Tayari kwa Salaam, reflected the influence of the Black Woman's Conferences on other Ahidiana members' thinking and activism related to women's rights. It mirrored the conferences in its messaging and aesthetics. Salaam wrote the title essay in June 1980 as part of the third conference. The booklet's second essay was dated July 7, 1979, and linked to the prior year's conference, "Identity and Assertiveness." It was meant to serve as a practical guide for women's self-development. Illustrations by local activist and artist Douglas Redd suggested themes of women's work, revolutionary action, unity, and Black pride. One picture, which also adorned the Third Black Woman's Conference cover, depicted a stylized image of a circle of women with cornrowed hair, surrounding what appeared to be a quilt.[56]

In her essay, Tayari kwa Salaam expressed that her thinking about Black women's struggles changed over time, echoing the experience that Vera Warren-Williams and Nana Anoa Nantambu recounted in their oral narratives. Emphasizing the idea that her early focus was on racial issues to the exclusion of gender and class, Salaam wrote, "At first, when asked, 'What issues affect Black Women?' I quickly responded, 'The same ones that affect Black people!'" She then wrote, "Are we not Black people, too? When it comes to oppression and exploitation our enemies make no exceptions. Aren't we daily attacked as African-americans [*sic*] in this white supremacist society?"[57]

Reconsidering the multiple forms of oppression Black women faced, Salaam mused, "On second thought, I remembered that, on a broad scale as women in a sexist society, we do have particular needs and issues because of the blatant sexism practiced in American life." She then went on to provide supporting evidence of gender discrimination, including issues of pay inequity and educational disparities. In a passage that recognized the concept of triple oppression, she wrote, "Looking closer at ourselves, not only as women, but as Black women in a society that is not only sexist, but one that is also racist and capitalist, we face additional struggles based on economic exploitation and racial and sexual oppression." She ultimately advocated for greater self-defense training and personal development among women, arguing that marginalized female activists could only serve as "figureheads" and "decorative fringe" when the time came for serious political organizing. She pointedly stated that only fully developed women whom Black men respected as "comrades, friends, and lovers" could battle sexism, transform themselves and society, and work for the progress of the entire race.[58]

Tayari kwa Salaam exhibited group-centered *kazi* leadership ethics by proposing practical methods for assisting Black women in the process of self-development and achieving greater self-determination. Outlining a program sounding much like what would become the Black Women's Group, she proposed a three-step approach for, first, fostering self-awareness in both women and men; second, planning and implementing programs to include informal women's support groups; and finally, forming women's organizations, or "Sisterhoods of Struggle," which she defined as formal, structured political alliances with clearly stated missions and plans that members should be able to state, write, and understand. The small collectives would be "informal and loosely organized with a de-emphasis on group conformity to values and beliefs." Their activities should accent identity, purpose, direction, and the broad "exchange of ideas."[59] The author suggested that the support groups should work with others to co-sponsor women's rights organizing, demonstrations, and programming. The larger, more formal organizations were to focus on specific aspects of women's empowerment related to the areas of self-determination, self-defense, and self-respect. Members were to operate in conjunction with "other formations of Black and Third World people."[60]

Asserting the need for men to support women in the home as they both worked to liberate entire communities, Tayari kwa Salaam used her personal endeavors and Ahidiana's collective struggles as models. The influences of Amina Baraka and CAP were also evident in her writings. She expressed the idea that she came into greater consciousness about women's rights through the process of working with Ahidiana, organizing locally for CAP's 1974 National Afrikan Women's Conference and the Black Woman's Conferences, as well as by working to implement Kalamu ya Salaam's ideology as outlined in *Revolutionary Love*. "In my own political and social life over the past eight years as a member of Ahidiana," Tayari reflected, "we have gone through a gradual transformation in which men and women in our group are both responsible for housecare [sic] and childcare while both are also actively developing career choices and other interests." This transformation, she continued, was difficult and uneven, but it was clear. "The struggle around sexism was a strenuous ordeal for our organization and most of us grew in varying degrees but we grew. Our school has advanced, we have given annual Black Woman's Conferences since 1978, and we women of Ahidiana are continually developing and taking the lead in projects." Tayari kwa Salaam contended that, with its programs for communal housework and childcare, Ahidiana was a model for "Black men and Black women to struggle and work together as equals." Finally, she asserted that female historical figures from Queen Nzinga to Harriet Tubman were integral to Black history in their roles as "women warriors." In other words, contemporary African-descended women were seen as essential soldiers in the collective struggle against the racist, sexist, and capitalist forms of oppression and exploitation their communities faced.[61]

In addition to generating Tayari kwa Salaam's published work, the Black Woman's Conferences also gave rise to the Black Women's Group (BWG). Consisting of twenty to thirty women and functioning as a support system that met monthly during the mid-1980s in various members' homes, the BWG was more intimate than the conferences.[62] As a child, Kina Joshua-Jasmine attempted to listen in on the serious conversations broached in the BWG meetings that her mother hosted at their home. "It was a group of African American women that wanted to continue to make change in their community," Joshua-Jasmine recounted. She explained that the women began by changing themselves. Much of their service in the community was connected "with them dealing with their own personal issues first."[63] Warren-Williams remarked that, when compared to Ahidiana's general body, the BWG resonated more with the needs of the organization's female members, providing a platform for regularly addressing women's issues.[64]

The Black Women's Group's "interactive sessions" focused on "self-discovery" in an atmosphere of camaraderie and shared governance that reflected the group-centered aspects of *kazi* leadership. The BWG consisted of Ahidiana advocates, as well as women from other walks of life, who came together for a myriad of reasons. They met regularly for peer counseling sessions, discussions, and film screenings. They occasionally planned retreats, which included workshops. Members also shared employment information, participated in communal childcare, and bought food cooperatively. Women in the group dealt with various "personal, social, and political" topics such as domestic violence and leadership skills development.[65]

Black Women's Group members found the circle to be helpful in many ways. For instance, Tayari kwa Salaam praised the BWG for providing an opportunity to practically (rather than theoretically) explore the meaning of her oppression as an African American woman.[66] New Orleans native Carol Bebelle, a *kazi* leader whose values reflect the BWG's imprint, became involved in the group during the mid- to late 1980s. She explained that cultural nationalism influenced the BWG's ideology, and that the Nguzo Saba "were our ten commandments." She said, "Going to the Black Women's Group was like a coming of age." The experience enhanced the way she understood "the importance of culture and how present it is in everything, . . . how important it is for us to essentially use it as a footing . . . to learn how . . . to practice the values . . . that we aspire to." Bebelle is known for speaking and writing about culture as a transformative element. She has advocated using cultural expressions like the performing arts as methods of developing unity between disparate communities.[67]

In her narrative, Bebelle also described the BWG as feminist or womanist in orientation. "At that time, people were working between Alice Walker's womanist . . . [writings] and Audre Lorde's [feminist publications]," she recalled. The BWG was a collective of female African Americans "who were asserting the equality and the importance of women." It helped members develop skills like empathy and increased their tolerance in certain ways. For example, Bebelle said, "I worked through my homophobia in the Black Women's Group."[68]

Such skills were helpful in the work Bebelle performed as cofounder and executive director of the Ashé Cultural Center in New Orleans's blighted, predominantly African American Central City neighborhood. Since its founding in 1998, the center has implemented community and human development projects using culture and creativity. Like the BWG, Ashé is grounded in the African-centered Nguzo Saba, and its group-centered programs highlight African-descended people. It provides space and opportunities for artistic presentations, community development, outreach ventures, artist support, and other related projects. Ashé has played a role in revitalizing both the Central City community and greater New Orleans and is counted among the city's most important post-Katrina cultural establishments.[69]

Although Ashé still exists, the Black Women's Group had dissolved by the 1990s due to conflicts over its purpose and direction. The BWG's imprint on several of New Orleans's community-oriented female activists is its greatest legacy, according to Bebelle.[70] The group was an example of Pan-African cultural nationalists' influence beyond the late 1960s and early 1970s. As Bebelle explained, there was "direct contact" with Kawaida ideals, which influenced Ahidiana, whose members in turn influenced the BWG. Her narrative indicated that the women in the group, many of whom were Ahidiana advocates, exhibited *kazi* leadership within the BWG by modeling a simultaneous practice of Pan-African cultural nationalist values and womanist ethics in their efforts to nurture and strengthen Black women leaders and activists and to positively influence their communities. For instance, during Kwanzaa 1984, the BWG hosted a program titled "Black Women: Hope for the Future," with National Black Feminist Organization founder Patricia Coleman-Burns as the featured speaker. Another example of BWG programming can be found in its "Rap On" Kwanzaa presentation, which took place on the night of Ujima, Saturday, December 28, 1985, at the Xavier University Pharmacy Auditorium. The activity included films and discussions meant to reach teens with instructive messages about sexuality, self-image, and peer pressure. The evening culminated with a contest for the best "message rap," or hip-hop song containing positive or politically meaningful lyrics.[71]

The experiences of women in the BWG demonstrate that the story of cultural nationalism is not solely one in which passive women accepted or were merely victims of masculinist edicts. Narratives like Bebelle's reveal that women demonstrated *kazi* leadership by syncretizing Kawaida-influenced cultural nationalism and expanding the ways the ideology was implemented. Some female advocates of 1960s and 1970s cultural nationalism consciously reshaped a previously masculinist ideology in new ways, using some of its basic values for community programs with specific emphasis on women's equality. In doing so, they created different possibilities for its future uses. Female activists would draw on cultural nationalist values and couple them with feminism and womanism in ways that undergirded the *kazi* they performed in their community work and activism.[72]

Cultural nationalist women's work in Kawaida-influenced community enterprises and programs proved integral to nation building through such activities as garment design, production, and sales. Moreover, *kazi* drove women's motivation to participate in movement activities and molded their leadership styles. Women also occupied a central role in promoting and preserving potential citizens' health and vitality through their practice of Black nationalist foodways for family and nation. While hierarchical notions about gender relations and other authoritarian beliefs plagued Kawaida-influenced organizations, women harnessed cultural nationalism to instate practices like communal meals to help ease the burden of certain feminized tasks, from food preparation and service to cleanup. While some found the gendered nature of nationalist food preparation and service practices restrictive, others viewed the kitchens of Black nationalist institutions as places where women could develop and market professional skills. Black women in Ahidiana's assemblies and conclaves exemplified how cultural nationalist ideologies could be aligned with feminist and womanist values in community programming. The individuals' stories were not those of passive women who fully accepted Black Power masculinism; they were reflections of women who were essential to nationalist enterprises and programs, as they contributed to and expanded the larger efforts of Kawaida-influenced organizations to nation build.

A Woman's Place Is in the Kitchen? Women's Gender Roles in Cultural Nationalist Food Preparation and Consumption

In her autobiography, Black Panther Party leader Elaine Brown provided a snapshot of chauvinistic Kawaida gender conventions related to dining. She described attending a 1967 gathering of activists, many of whom were affiliated with the Us Organization's San Diego branch. After contributing five dollars toward a collective meal and waiting in line for her share, a young woman wearing a long, West African-styled dress declared, "You will have to wait until our Brothers are served." The woman reiterated her stance by stating, "Our Brothers are our warriors. Our warriors must be fed first, sisters." Brown recounted that she and another woman at the event protested their unfair treatment, but they were soon confronted by a man looking much like the other males in Us, bald and wearing a dashiki-type shirt. Arms folded across his chest, he told them that they had been "unsisterly" for wanting to be served with the men. His reaction exhibited to the two women that he thought their attitudes represented a level of impertinence "for which blood could be shed."[73]

Brown's recollections were not anomalous. Deborah Jones recounts having similar experiences while touring with Us's Taifa Time dance troupe in the late 1960s. She said in her memoir that meals at rest stops entailed women serving men first and eating the leftover food.[74] The gendered foodways (in which women generally prepared or served the food, and men ate before women) that Elaine Brown and Deborah Jones recounted about the Us Organization, at least in its earliest phase, were expressions of the broader complementarity ethos. Complementarity meant that men and women should occupy fundamentally different, gender-determined places within the struggle for Black freedom, and that men should be leaders while women must play support roles. Complementary gender responsibilities linked to foodways also showed up in East-related writings, which encouraged mothers, aunts, sisters, and other relatives to "prepare and cook good Afrikan food collectively" for the Kwanzaa feast, or *karamu*. Fathers, uncles, brothers, and other males were only encouraged to "share the expenses of the food and drink."[75]

In CFUN, women enacted *kazi* via the typically feminized tasks of communally cooking and serving food. Komozi Woodard discussed his time in CFUN, explaining a hierarchically organized, communal dining arrangement in which women worked late into the evening to support other members' activism. Because the group's leader and council ate first and the lowest-ranking advocates received their meals last, he chuckled, "I would be waiting in the wings. I guess I would eat at . . . 10:00 at night, because I was so lowly ranked."[76] CFUN sisters were responsible for food preparation and cleaning the kitchen from which all advocates ate, a practice called *chakula ujamaa*.[77] Exhibiting a uniquely group-centered, work-centered, and African-centered form of service leadership, CFUN women developed *chakula ujamaa*, among other practices such as communal daycare, to help female advocates stay active in the organization's political life while balancing housework, child-rearing, and the construction and care of clothing.

Despite the fact that such practices as *chakula ujamaa* reflected a sense of *kazi* leadership, Pan-African cultural nationalist women expressed ambivalence about the gendered dimensions of food preparation, consumption, and distribution. On one hand, East advocates' narratives illuminated the fact that the organization's food preparation and service practices could be restrictive for women. Some of the women lamented being on kitchen duty. They were aware that the task of preparing the food, whether on a daily basis or at occasional meetings, tended to keep women on the fringes of decision making and strategizing. East advocate Akilah Mashariki remembered one of the important inaugural East gatherings with ironic laughter. She said, "I wasn't at the meeting. I was cooking for the meeting in the kitchen of an apartment shared by Job and Seitu Dyson and a couple of other brothers. . . . I was cooking and eavesdropping . . . when Jitu outlined his thoughts for The East to . . . all these brothers who were there at the time."[78]

On the other hand, a closer look at how food preparation in several Kawaida-influenced organizations was remembered reveals that participants viewed the kitchen in complex ways that often exhibit *kazi* leadership ethics. Kitchens functioned as spaces where women could broaden and commercialize the kinds of skills they developed in the process of learning to provide nourishment for their own families inside and outside Kawaida-influenced organizations. For instance, in explaining the importance of The East to the local community, Walker recalled a woman, possibly Lottie Hicks, who began cooking at Uhuru Sasa during a period of unemployment. "Jitu took her skills of being a good cook at home and taught her how to cook for large groups of people," Walker wrote. "This skill allowed her later to get a job at Rikers Island prison from which she eventually retired."[79] Mtamanika Beatty shared a similar recollection, describing how she began cooking the weekday meals for about two hundred Uhuru Sasa students, faculty, and staff after taking courses in quantity food preparation. The hands-on experience she received assisted her when she decided to start her own business venture, T.J.'s Chicken Shack, a take-out restaurant serving home-style meals in the Bedford-Stuyvesant/Fort Greene area during the 1990s.[80]

Martha Bright emphasized that men were part of The East's culture of food preparation, sales, and distribution; however, women figured prominently in the important tasks of providing nourishment for the community and raising funds to support educational ventures through cooking and serving food. "We had a restaurant called the Sweet-East," she explained. "A brother . . . by the name of Brother Abdullah [ran that], but sisters certainly worked in there." She highlighted the important leadership roles that women held in East culinary ventures, adding, "We [sisters] ran the kitchen and East catering service." Bright pointed out that women were heavily involved in The East's program of food distribution as well. "There's no aspect of The East that sisters really weren't involved in except for maybe security. That's the only thing that I can think of that sisters were not really front and center in," she recalled.[81]

A *Black News* article, "Afrikan Women Unite," highlighted the importance of The East women's work. The East Sisterhood, it said, "helps fulfill the organization's function as a cultural and educational institution for people of Afrikan descent." The writer added, "As Afrikan Women, they play a vital role in the organization's day to day operations, which include the Uhuru Sasa Schools, a bookstore[,] a clothing store, a cooperative food buying service, and the newspaper 'Black News' which features 'Fundisha' the official voice of the Congress of Afrikan People." The statement was published in a piece announcing CAP's national Afrikan Women's Seminars on "The Role of the Black Woman in the Revolution," which preceded the Newark-based Afrikan Women's Conference in July 1974.[82]

Amina Baraka spoke at the July seminars, and The East Sisterhood also hosted a spring session with Jitu Weusi as the guest speaker. The objective was to raise awareness of issues plaguing African Americans and caucus Black women for the purpose of problem solving. The topics on the agenda seemed to remain within the "acceptable" bounds of African womanhood, as they included "education, social organization, politics, health, communications, and institutional development."[83] Such documents reveal the multidimensional interplay between advocates' thinking about women's leadership in organizational enterprises and the realities of the nation-building work that women performed within their more typically feminine roles on the ground. Although their realities were complex, what is clear is that cultural nationalist women were guided by the rhythms of *taifa saa* just as men were.

4

# "To Build Our Nation . . . Teach Our Children!"

*Women's Gender Roles in Independent and Supplementary Black Educational Programs*


Four young, Scout-like Simba (lions) stood in line, steely-eyed and disciplined. Samuel Carr-Damu, a dashiki-clad adult male Us member, shouted as he stood behind the young recruits. The boys' yellow shirts were emblazoned with a roaring lion whose fangs clenched the Us Organization's logo. These images of Us's earliest youth education and training efforts were plastered across the July 15, 1966, cover of *Life* magazine as a follow-up on the Watts rebellion that had left the Los Angeles neighborhood deeply scarred a year earlier.[1]

No women or girls appeared in the *Life* cover photo. But Brenda Haiba Karenga's class at the Aquarian Center in Los Angeles was later depicted in Scot Brown's book about Us and struck a visual contrast to the magazine picture of the Simba. At the Aquarian, children sat around a table in front of a bulletin board filled with images of Black subjects as a girl raised her hand and looked at her instructor's pleasant expression. The two pictures illustrate Us's gender values and the ways those roles were transferred to young people through the organization's initial educational endeavors.[2]

Independent and supplementary Black educational programs were some of the most important endeavors that Pan-African cultural nationalist organizations undertook in their communities. Independent Black institutions (IBIs) were places where teachers and administrators reoriented, reeducated, and retrained the next generation of nationalist-minded people. The faculty of independent Black educator training institutes, nurseries, kindergarten through twelfth-grade day schools, after-school programs, and weekend classes sought to advance the Black liberation struggle by providing a politicized education to aid nationality formation in their local communities. Pan-African cultural nationalists' IBIs operated in the "counter-oppressive" spirit of programs like SNCC's Freedom Schools, the Organization of Afro-American Unity's Liberation School, Communiversity's public seminars in Chicago, and the BPP's political education classes and Oakland Community School in that knowledge production and liberatory teaching were critical components of organizing. Community members could attend them to access supplemental education programs, citizenship training, culturally relevant courses in preschool through high school contexts and beyond, co-curricular opportunities, and curricula that exposed pupils to revolutionary ideas such as those related to class struggle via the Black experience. IBIs were some of the longest-running programs of Pan-African cultural nationalist institutions.[3] Often organized in the most difficult of situations, IBIs were seen as practical methods of addressing the vast educational challenges that African Americans faced. In the realm of ideals, the schools could be characterized as maroon zones, *kilombos*, or shelters for African Americans to practice "fugitive pedagogy" true to the legacy of Carter G. Woodson. They were places to envision a world free of European domination.[4]

This chapter explores reflections on women's gender roles and *kazi* leadership in the IBIs of Us, Committee for a Unified Newark and the Congress of African People, The East, and Ahidiana. Within such Pan-African cultural nationalist organizations, which initially drew upon a philosophy limiting women's gender roles to home, education, and supporting males' agendas, these schools were particularly important outlets for women's political expression. For Subira Kifano in Los Angeles, Amina Baraka in Newark, Tamisha Peterson in Brooklyn, Kiini Salaam in New Orleans, and for many others, participation in schools and other educational programs influenced their formation as cultural nationalists and provided opportunities for women to shape the movement. Although advocates framed African womanhood as an essentially African diasporic expression, the concept somewhat resembled the early national period concept of republican motherhood, when middle-class White women promoted republican ideology within the home, the sphere where they possessed power. In this way, White women's ostensibly private action generated a public effect. Likewise, the ideal African woman was seen as a mama who represented, protected, and instructed the nascent Black nation. As Pan-African cultural nationalist teachers, women filled an *in loco parentis* role that was critically important for developing good citizens in the budding nation. Additionally, certain cultural nationalist women used access to the greater education, training, and leadership opportunities to move beyond their limited realms. Not only was their own work as mothers and teachers politicized within the context of African womanhood, but tenacious female Pan-African cultural nationalists drew on African-centered ideas like *kazi* and *ujamaa* to leverage their positions as educators for creating and extending women's leadership positions and for developing programs such as communal childcare, which helped mothers (and fathers) perform important political work outside the home.

## "Knowledge Is the Prime Need of the Hour": The School of Afroamerican Culture and the Mary McLeod Bethune Institute

It has been noted that Us members' masculinism, as depicted in the aforementioned *Life* magazine picture, reflected some of the same problems plaguing other movements within the Black freedom struggle, particularly those associated with Black Power formations. Advocates and scholars have indicated that the initial iteration of Us was highly patriarchal, its organizational philosophy and regulations exceeding the typical sexism of contemporary American life as well as gender relations in certain African cultures. The organization developed what amounted to a cult of personality around Maulana Karenga. Amina Thomas, for example, stated that advocates "agreed to let . . . Karenga . . . dictate our lifestyle at the time" and that the Us leader "had too much power." Similarly, Deborah Jones said, "Us was a cult of personality, and the personality was that of Maulana Karenga." Yet, despite the paramount importance placed on Karenga's leadership, other male and female Us members played important roles in the organization's operations from its inception. From the earliest days, women in Us found ways to negotiate and resist the patriarchy so prevalent within the group.[5]

Even within their circumscribed gender roles, women were important participants in the early phases of Us's political existence. Haiba Karenga and Dorothy Jamal, the wives of Us founders Maulana Karenga and Hakim Jamal, organized and administered Us's nascent School of Afroamerican Culture, and Sanamu Nyeusi taught at the school. Scot

Brown asserts that the school was one of the organization's most important institutions, particularly because it served the children of members
as well as boys and girls from "nationalist-minded families" throughout Los Angeles. Despite a doctrine defining women as "'complementary' rather than 'equal' to the supreme status of the Black man," as Scot
Brown points out, Us's School of Afroamerican Culture developed into
a significant outlet for Us women's activism.[6]

Along with Subira Kifano's, the narratives of former Us members
Amina Thomas, Imani Omotayo, and Deborah Jones confirm that Us
institutionalized and propagated male dominance in its early phases.
Their remembrances also show that organizational norms and values
changed over time, due in part to women's activism and leadership.
Thomas emphasized women's central positions as educators, transmit-
ting Pan-African cultural nationalist values to a new generation of activists. "The sisters were the teachers in the schools," she said. "We taught
[the values] to our children more . . . than the brothers [did]."[7]

Omotayo believed that the School of Afroamerican Culture served an
important basic function in collective childcare and education, because
the Us Organization was filled with youthful advocates, many of whom
had children. "We were all young people, and we all had kids," she said,
"so you had to have a school, you really did." Omotayo observed that most
of the students in the school were the children of organization members.[8]

The School of Afroamerican Culture began as a supplementary educational program in 1967. The institution underwent a name change and
transformation of format in 1971, operating for four years as a full-time
school under the name Kawaida Educational and Development Center.[9] Omotayo explained that the school supported independent and
supplementary programs open to children in the lower-income neighborhoods of South Central Los Angeles, where it was located. "Children
of the community could come," she recounted. "It was a regular, accredited school, and then we had after-school [and] Saturday activities for
children [on] weekends." Omotayo, who helped with poetry and dance
classes in the Saturday program, added, "It was just providing a place
for kids to come to . . . in the Black community." Administrators charged
very little, if any, tuition, and staff and faculty provided students with
"fun things to do, . . . fed them, and gave them some history lessons and
classes." She said that neighborhood children "came for the food and . . .

a lot of their parents did identify [with] and did like the organization being there, because that taught their children to be proud of who they were." Omotayo believed that the school enhanced the reputation of its sponsoring organization in South Central Los Angeles: "I think [the] Us Organization had . . . support in terms of the surrounding community because they were a positive force . . . in the late [19]60's."[10]

Reflecting the African-centered ethics of *kazi* leadership, instructors at Us's School of Afroamerican Culture also served the role of propagating Black nationalist ideas.[11] This fulfilled a fundamental purpose, as one of Us's main goals was catalyzing revolution via cultural education. Us women's greatest contributions to the Black freedom struggle included the development of a novel "cultural archive" of songs, teaching techniques, and educational activities, which they rooted in Kawaida principles and imparted to young African American students at the school.[12] While instructors taught Pan-African cultural nationalist values, they also offered programs focusing on academic excellence. Students "learned about Africa, and they learned about history and the regular things you're supposed to learn when you're in elementary school, but they were also taught cultural things," Omotayo recalled. "A major part of their education was Kawaida."[13] She emphasized that educators at the School of Afroamerican Culture provided nourishment for students' bodies and minds in a fun, uplifting environment and offered a nurturing place for children in a neighborhood needing supportive spaces.

At the same time, Omotayo expressed ambivalence about some of the practices she observed. "Because [of] the structure of the organization, there were men that worked with the boys, but the boys were taught certain things the girls weren't taught." One area of differentiation was instruction in certain African cultural traditions, such as the boot dance, a rhythmic movement with clapping, chants, and songs that had been performed by South African workers since the late nineteenth century. "[The boys] were taught [the] boot dance. . . . They were called the Simbas. We had the group called the Simbas that were older, but the young boys were taught to be, . . . in their words, . . . men. . . . So they kind of tried to do it like you would do it in some parts of the African culture. Girls played a different role than boys, so they kind of adopted that."[14] In hindsight, Omotayo understood the Us Organization's restrictive complementary gender roles for boys and girls to be partially based on essentialized perspectives of "African" traditions.

Men operated a youth weekend school for the Simba Wachanga (young lions), which began in 1965 after the Watts uprising. In 1967 Us shifted its program to encompass Wapinduzi-Wadogo, "the young or [little] revolutionaries." A third group of high school and college students formed the core of the Us Organization.[15] Although men in Us served in the coeducational School of Afroamerican Culture once it was launched, Omotayo recalled that they often focused on working with young males. She said, "If you had boys and girls, they took the boys out and did something different with them, and then the younger children, of course, met together. But the older children, I think it was more of a separate kind of teaching." The men encouraged physical stamina, self-confidence, and discipline by teaching boys such practices as military-style drill exercises.[16]

Like other independent Black institutions, advocates inculcated different "essentialist and hierarchical" skills and traits in girls and women than in boys and men.[17] Advocates taught preteen and teen girls art, poetry, and dance. "Girls were taught to be submissive . . . even at that young age," remembered Omotayo. Older teens as well as marriageable and married women were known as Muminina and often instructed the girls, or Malaika, about what group members deemed appropriate interpersonal relationships and behavior.[18] Patriarchal formulations of Kawaida "social organization" often determined Mumininas' positions within Us's organizational hierarchy. The philosophy limited women's roles to inspiring their men, educating children, and participating in social development.[19]

Some strictly gendered practices became less exclusive over time in the Us Organization, due to changing circumstances and women's resistance. According to the literature and narratives, Us members enacted multiple, complex perspectives about the roles of women over the years. In 1969 the organization began experiencing a period of internal and external conflict, which produced female leaders and ideological changes related to women's roles in the Black freedom struggle. During this period, adult female advocates were called upon to function as "women soldiers," or Matamba, with training activities more like those of the Simba. Women modeled *kazi* leadership ethics by asserting the right to equality during this period, emerging as group members performing vital committee work at all levels in the organization, including the Circle of Administrators.[20]

Several female Us activists' narratives support the idea that many former advocates wanted to move on from the pain of the past. Missteps in developing equitable practices to govern the details of daily organizational life produced negative encounters for Amina Thomas, even though she judged that the overall experience of being a young person in Us and working to improve the African American community was generally positive. Kifano, too, recalled being attracted to the Organization Us during its post-1975 phase because of Maulana Karenga's intelligence and professionalism, and the accessibility of his ideas. Both Deborah Jones and Imani Omotayo, conversely, lamented that their affiliation with the late 1960s Us Organization was a particularly painful time.[21]

Subira Kifano's training as a teacher, as well as the fact that she and other members wanted to engage their own children during Soul Sessions, guided her activism within the Kawaida Groundwork Committee and the reconstituted Organization Us. Kifano's reflections suggested that women exhibited *kazi* leadership through their essential roles in rebuilding and sustaining the group's educational programs. She recalled that, in part, her work with the Kawaida Groundwork Committee grew out of necessity. "I planned the educational activities for the children, because we'd have Soul Sessions. People [from the community] would bring their children, [and] several of the members of the organization had children. I had children. . . . We started as a parent group providing activities. So we'd have child watch, we called it." Although childcare in a separate space from the main Soul Sessions seemed essential to the parents of young children, Kifano explained that a group of advocates had to organize and articulate the benefit of having a different area for teachers to engage the children at their various learning levels.[22]

Kifano added that a group of parents, consisting of both women and men, advocated for and implemented the childcare and education program. "Rather than the children just sitting there, the parents . . . made the hard point . . . that we needed to have child[care] activities. . . . We, the parents, would just take turns watching them." Her experiences as an educator and mother, she said, positioned her to become a leader in developing materials and activities for the collective childcare program. Other women likewise helped develop the program. For instance, Kweli made the art for the materials that were designed to teach the students about such topics as prominent and heroic African Americans. Embodying *kazi* leadership, Kawaida Groundwork Committee members working on the program sought to develop in the children a similar kind of "Afro-centric cultural understanding" as their parents were getting in Soul Sessions.[23]

Kifano recounted that childcare for the Soul Sessions was opened to visitors of the organizational headquarters at the African American Cultural Center, and the program soon overflowed its allotted space and time. The organization's collective childcare during adult-focused programs eventually developed into a Saturday school. Named Mary McLeod Bethune Institute (MMBI), it was subsequently launched as a supplementary Black institution in December 1979. The MMBI was open to the children of Us Organization advocates, while also providing tutoring and literacy support to thousands of students from the Crenshaw community where it was located.[24]

Crenshaw, a district southwest of downtown Los Angeles, had been a White suburb prior to the Second World War. The site of struggles over integration, it became a middle-class African American and Japanese American neighborhood during the postwar era. The area received a tide of Black migrants after the urban uprisings of the 1960s. As a result, multiethnic Crenshaw became known as both an inner-city ghetto and a vibrant hub of African American politics, economics, and culture. In the 1980s, it developed into one of the largest African American communities in the western United States and became known as an iconic Black neighborhood. It was sensationalized in early 1980s and 1990s music, movies, and media as an impoverished, drug-ravaged, and gang-ridden area, although such conditions were not indicative of life in the entire district.[25] Crenshaw's demographics explain why the socioeconomic status of MMBI students varied greatly, with 80 percent residing within a three-mile radius and the balance coming from outlying areas or nearby parochial schools. Their parents, who ranged from highly paid professionals to the unemployed, sought out MMBI to close gaps in their children's education, believing that the area schools put insufficient emphasis on African American history and culture.[26]

The Kawaida-grounded Mary McLeod Bethune Institute was rooted in the Nguzo Saba, and the curriculum focused on the social sciences. MMBI faculty and staff served twenty-five core students and possibly thousands of additional African American learners. MMBI employees also provided outreach via such programs as teacher training for Los Angeles Unified School District (LAUSD) and for other local school districts.[27] Noting that LAUSD rarely acknowledged or celebrated Kwanzaa, Kifano said that part of her outreach work via MMBI involved developing literature and promoting the observance of the celebration. "I wrote a Kwanzaa book—*Kwanzaa: A Special Holiday*—that outlined all the principles [and] talked about different activities that you could do with your children and family," she said. In addition, she "collected . . . Black nationalist songs and shared those with the teachers."[28]

Kifano suggested that women's educational activism and leadership supported Us's work as a vanguard organization focused on wielding "programmatic influence," particularly through the use of the Seven Principles as core tenets. Karenga affirmed this view when he stressed that an important element of the organization's impact was made through the independent school movement, identifying classrooms as key sites of "contestation and struggle."[29] Explaining educators' importance in advancing the Us Organization's philosophy and larger Pan-African cultural nationalist values, particularly among youth, Kifano emphasized teachers' principal roles in encouraging and motivating learning as well as imparting knowledge. "Maulana Karenga, the chair of the Us Organization, advanced the big concept," she said. "The MMBI director and staff developed the concept to explain the meaning for the children attending the institute."[30] Kifano's example shows how women led and sustained these important processes.

Kifano described how the institute's curriculum exposed children to the accomplishments of both Black women and men. One of the school's tenets encouraged "respect for human diversity" and "tolerance." The credo highlighted diversity and asserted the right of individuals and groups to "speak their own special truth and make their own unique contribution to the forward flow of human history." Kifano pointed out that the principle recognized and respected that "the human personality manifested in both genders." Using a frame of reference suggestive of Kawaida womanism to support the importance of teaching youth about the ideas and achievements of both African-descended men and women, Kifano drew on the work of Anna Julia Cooper to support assertions about complementarity as a lens for gender-related theorizing and programming.[31]

Kifano reported that the MMBI curriculum stressed exposing children to a balanced treatment of both men's and women's accomplishments. This seemingly more evenhanded approach marked an improvement in Kawaida-based theories about the importance of women in the struggle for Black freedom. Gone were the 1960s decrees of female domesticity and submissiveness, but the more evolved theories could still be viewed as conservative. Updated ideologies continued to dichotomize masculinity and femininity, promulgating the idea that men and women should uphold different but interdependent gender roles. Nevertheless, Kifano penned a declaration stating that "the new world the Institute struggled to bring into being was of necessity non-racist, non-sexist, and non-classist," which represented, at the very least, theoretical progress over the language of the late 1960s and early 1970s.[32]

Kifano's *kazi* leadership was not limited to the field of education. She had gained organizing experience before joining the Kawaida Groundwork Committee and helping reinstate the Organization Us; she had been active in serving the community; and she functioned as a public speaker, a role that she said Maulana Karenga encouraged her to undertake. While attending Hamline University in St. Paul, Minnesota, she was a member of the Promotion of Racial Identity, Dignity, and Equality (PRIDE) Black students' association and served as its president. She was already theorizing about the miseducation of Black students in American schools and proposing independent educational institutions before she joined the Kawaida Groundwork Committee. Kifano was an officer in the Black Agenda, an organization founded to promote institutional development and growth in the Black community. Over the years, she delivered addresses on a broad range of topics from the socially oriented, Jamaa (Family) series of lectures about interpersonal relationships to more political discussions, such as a talk covering the 1983 Grenada coup.[33] Not limited to the role of helpmate, Kifano served as co-vice chair of the reconstituted Organization Us and director of the children's program from the early 1980s until she left in 1997.[34]

## "Education Is the Root of Development [and] Defense": Black Women and the African Free School

The scene was at the African Free School in Newark in 1971. Young African American teachers, the overwhelming majority of whom were women, led groups of Black children, who stood facing the red, black, and green banner of Pan-Africanism or played at recess. Others chanted Pan-African nationalist slogans, arms folded, eyes forward. Some of the young people smiled, clapping their hands to rhythmic poems. "Red is for the blood of our forefathers which has not been shed in vain. Black is for the color of our faces and the job we must do. Green is for youth and new ideas." Colorful posters with portrayals of Africa adorned the walls.[35] Although depictions of Black nationalists commonly feature gun-wielding men or describe writers and performers mired in rhetoric, female educators demonstrated *kazi* leadership by engaging in the difficult work of nation building.[36]

Both institution building and education were important sites of struggle for nationalists who participated in the effort to transform Black communities. According to Amiri Baraka, "The most revolutionary Afrikans as far as the community will be concerned will be those . . . who can actually run and create schools and transform the present educational process."[37] In his reflections on his tenure as a CAP member, Michael Simanga confirmed the attractiveness of such operations as the African Free School (AFS) to new recruits. Simanga stressed how effectively the enterprises were managed. CAP's African Free Schools stood as concrete manifestations of institution building, organizational growth, and mass political mobilization. He pointed out that these institutions demonstrated self-determination and independence. Advocates formed several social divisions under the CFUN umbrella as new recruits swelled the organization's ranks. CFUN was divided into many departments and had a web of affiliated programs and enterprises. Education was an important department, and the African Free School existed as a significant CAP academic institution.

CFUN literature identified Amiri Baraka as the chief policy maker and described Amina Baraka as the AFS director. Amina performed much of the operation's administrative and intellectual work. Through such labor and leadership, she pursued central nationalist objectives, from seemingly mundane tasks like procuring furniture, to the specialized jobs of curriculum development and publicity. CFUN advocates helped develop and run the daily operations of the multiple independent and autonomous African Free School manifestations in Newark.[38]

The title of the African Free School, named after one of the earliest free public schools in the United States, reflected the institution's mission and its grounding in the history of the long Black freedom struggle. The original African Free School was founded as a one-room schoolhouse in New York to educate free and enslaved African Americans' children. Although White philanthropists associated with the New York Manumission Society established the original African Free School in 1787, the institution developed into a tool for helping achieve Black self-determination. A notable group of leaders, from Alexander Crummell to Henry Highland Garnet, attended the school and became abolitionists, educators, and Black nationalists. The twentieth-century AFS had a commitment to producing a similar body of liberatory Black leaders, a mission that aligned with the people-centered values of *kazi* leadership.[39]

Newark's African Free School grew out of several necessities. Primarily, AFS educators sought to serve local communities by helping to address students' learning gaps. Additionally, the schools were cultural and political education centers where advocates attempted to re-envision Blackness and galvanize change agents within communities consisting mostly of African-descended people. Certain aspects of the AFS initiatives also addressed the fundamental necessity of collective childcare for advocates and the larger goal of educating a generation of children born to the organization's activist families, as was the case in other Kawaida-influenced organizations.[40]

The Newark AFS began in the late 1960s. It was first located in the Spirit House, where a group of young people from the neighborhood regularly gathered. The operation functioned as a theater, multipurpose center, office, and residence. Located in a refurbished tenement at 33 Stirling Street within Newark's deteriorating Central Ward, Spirit House was a hub of activity where the Barakas, a growing group of cultural workers, and various community members organized grassroots political action campaigns, held classes, produced plays, and developed literature. Neighborhood youth performed in Spirit House productions, many of which Amiri Baraka penned specifically for children and teens.

They also helped write a newsletter, a task that many found difficult due to weak writing skills. The Barakas began Spirit House to politicize neighborhood residents and promote the Black Power concept. It soon became clear, however, that residents of the area needed more support.[41]

Newark's AFS, founded as the Community Free School, initially operated three days a week as an after-school class serving elementary and middle school students. The institution quickly grew, expanding to include full-time programs for students as young as three years old. The African Free School ultimately consisted of an independent or "inner" school, featuring a semiautonomous experimental classroom for public school children, infant and preschool facilities, and a youth theater workshop.[42]

Explaining the driving forces of AFS's infant and preschool program growth, Amina Baraka reiterated a common theme in the oral history narratives—that the women who came to Spirit House, and later CFUN, were young and unmarried. Many formed families and gave birth during their time with the organizations. Amina stated that, joining the movement at a mere twenty-three years old, she was the eldest of the Spirit House and CFUN women. "I was the only one with kids in the beginning. . . . I was probably the oldest woman in there, and I was in my twenties," she explained. Emphasizing that the female advocates desired to continue serving in the freedom struggle through all phases of motherhood, she said, "We started to have kids, but the women wanted to be active." Amina's development of daycare programs, supplementary educational institutions, and an independent school was, in part, an answer to their calls for equitable opportunities to participate in various capacities within the movement and typified *kazi* leadership.[43]

Amina Baraka led alongside her husband, Amiri, supervising the African Free School's expanding operations during the late 1960s and throughout the early 1970s. The independent branch of AFS moved to CAP's High Street headquarters, then to a separate building on Clinton Avenue. AFS was further enlarged after a grant of federal Title I funds in 1970, which enabled the creation of an experimental classroom at Robert Treat Elementary, the local public school that Amina had attended as a child. Robert Treat School had been named after the leader of Newark's first European-descended settlers, but community activists renamed the institution to honor Black nationalist leader Marcus Garvey in 1971, an expression of the rising Black political power that helped facilitate the historic 1970 election of Kenneth Gibson, the city's first African American mayor.[44]

CFUN advocates supported broadening AFS operations to challenge the public schools, in part because the pace of independent Black school formation could not serve the majority of African American children, who were in public schools.[45] The people-centered idea behind the Robert Treat semiautonomous classroom experiment was to set up a model for reaching the masses of Black children in public schools, where they would potentially remain for quite some time. Besides offering students more traditional subjects like reading, African Free School instructors taught Pan-African nationalist topics such as Swahili, hieroglyphics, and Zulu folklore. Instructors also imparted a political education for self-determination, emphasized global awareness, and stressed discipline and order. Three or four teachers worked with approximately thirty students in grades five through eight. Additionally, many of the pupils in the AFS semiautonomous classroom had been labeled chronic slow learners.[46] "We asked that we take all the kids that [were] failing, all the kids that they were getting ready to expel from school, and we put them in one classroom," Amina Baraka recalled.[47]

The teachers' work in the AFS classroom was integral to the process of "building a community in the midst of chaos" in Newark's public school system and working toward the ultimate goal of leading the development of a new sense of Black peoplehood.[48] Amina recounted being driven to assist with developing supplements and independent alternatives to the public school system because of family concerns in addition to her worries over the low literacy skills of the neighborhood children. "We had Marcus Garvey. . . . At the time, it was Robert Treat. I had [an] incident in there with my two daughters, and I used to have to go to school . . . every day, and the school was a wreck. It was a mess."[49] The building was located at 131 Thirteenth Avenue, on the corner of Norfolk and Thirteenth, and consisted of a core edifice, constructed in 1888, with a series of additions made between 1891 and 1915. The author of a 1973 article about the institution asserted that Garvey had been a positive model of community participation and academic merit since 1969, citing the addition of the African Free School in the same year. The school system, nevertheless, neglected the building's physical structure as it had many others in the district, resulting in the collapse of a classroom ceiling in 1972. This incident caused missed instruction days and the relocation of students to eight different facilities.[50]

Newark's shifting demographics meant that the student body at Robert Treat had changed from mostly native-born Whites and German, Italian, English, and "Hebrew" immigrants in 1906 to 100 percent Black pupils by 1969. During the 1960s, the overall district population increased from 55 to 80 percent African American students. By 1970, 70 percent of the city's 402,000 residents were Black. Most lived in Central Ward, one of the country's most run-down ghettos and one that had been rocked by rebellions just three years earlier. Although fifty of the seventy-five schools in the area were majority-Black, there were no African American principals at the time of the 1967 Newark uprising. The majority of the schools in the district were old and overcrowded, and had been abandoned by the middle class. The high school dropout rate was high, and literacy levels were low. Many of the city's youth had little chance of escaping isolation and poverty in Newark. Activists at Spirit House began to organize within this context, initially leading a charge to oust Robert Treat's White, status-quo principal.[51]

Hundreds of CFUN advocates were also instrumental in helping elect Kenneth Gibson as the first African American mayor of a major northeastern city, campaigning and organizing alongside United Brothers, a committee that supported individuals who were interested in attaining local leadership positions. The African Free School's semiautonomous classroom emerged as activists won such key battles in their struggle to advance Black nationalism in the arena of municipal politics. Alma Flagg, a Newark public school assistant superintendent who had lobbied for the program, said that African Americans living in the city's poorer neighborhoods had developed the belief that Newark could become a national example of Black achievement. Along with other activists, Amiri and Amina Baraka transitioned to open agitation as a method of pressuring administrators to get to the bottom of why children in the neighborhood could not read, as the full extent of miseducation at Robert Treat and other area schools became apparent. According to Amina, advocates organized for making changes in the public educational system. They demonstrated *kazi* leadership by setting up the semiautonomous classroom, which was small but served as a prototype for other schools. They also participated in a citywide African Education Alliance, which lobbied for renaming several Newark public schools after notable Black freedom fighters.[52]

Amina Baraka further explained how she worked alongside other CFUN advocates and community members to achieve more Black representation in educational leadership. CFUN advocates and community activists essentially formed pressure groups whose actions swayed the school board to secure the AFS semiautonomous classroom and elevated movement sympathizer Eugene Campbell to the top position at Robert Treat in 1970. Campbell, who would eventually become superintendent of Newark city schools, was among several founding members of United Brothers.[53] Amina Baraka said, "This one guy, Gene Campbell, . . . they called him 'Mkuu,' that meant 'principal' in Swahili, . . . [we] put him in Marcus Garvey, and we made it possible. . . . He became . . . a principal of that school. So he let us have an experimental classroom."[54] Reflecting aspects of *kazi* leaders' ideological orientation, the AFS classroom incorporated an African-centered curriculum, which was meant to serve the neighborhood's "educationally deprived" Black students.[55]

Amina Baraka remembered the semiautonomous AFS as an act of Black community self-determination: "We never accepted government funds. We were always leery of accepting government funds because we didn't want to be under the aegis of the government because, you know, COINTELPRO [FBI Counterintelligence Program] was operating heavy, and we knew the minute we spent one dime that was not on [the] charts, that they [were] coming for us. So we had our own bookkeepers."[56] To be sure, news articles reported that intense community interest brought AFS into being.[57] Yet, in terms of funding, AFS was one of the better-subsidized Pan-African nationalist institutions of the era, revealing contradictions between AFS officials' strong sentiments about autonomy and their dependence on subsidies, grants, and external private donations. They nevertheless remained steadfast in implementing African-centered school programs and continued to lodge critiques of public education as it existed.[58]

Amina Baraka felt strongly about the African Free School's successes. "We did pretty good," she reflected with satisfaction, noting progress in the institution's physical plant. "We finally got a building [that] we wanted to move into." She added that advocates entered the realm of "public education to see if we could affect what was going on in public schools."[59] With its red, black, and green liberation flag flying high, AFS received commendations and support from the community and from establishment sources. The school won recognition for its inventive curriculum from the Model Cities Project Class Room program, which awarded the semiautonomous African Free School a $1,020 grant in 1971.[60] The AFS additionally received a letter of endorsement from Congressman William L. Clay of Missouri, advising New Jersey state officials to allocate appropriate levels of Title I funds for the program.[61] AFS held New Jersey Education Association accreditation as an elementary school, and its graduates progressed to high school.

Extraordinarily, AFS educational activists were able to achieve successes despite the overall political environment. The Newark public schools were in crisis, particularly as they were struck by viciously divisive teacher strikes during the early 1970s. The local conflict involved the majority-White teachers' union, which invoked collective bargaining rights against the board of education and the numerically significant groups of Black parents working with community activists, in a similar situation to New York's Ocean Hill-Brownsville struggle for community control of schools. Amid the battles, CFUN leaders and advocates faced accusations of race-baiting to advance their own political agenda. CFUN activists, however, condemned both the union and the African American and Latine school board members, accusing the committee of behaving like neocolonial compradors, using their intermediary, middle-class status to obstruct Newark's Black working class from gaining power.[62]

Although the African Free School's growth was but one example of Black Newark citizens' ability to effect change in their city, ultimately the class of Black officials who grew more influential and powerful in the aftermath of late 1960s and early 1970s political gains failed to effectively address urban blight and other dire social and economic issues. Mayor Kenneth Gibson, who had once been invested with constituents' hopes for breaking the color and class lines demarcating urban politics in the North, ended up functioning as a bureaucrat who was unable to assist (or disinterested in facilitating) the transfer of power and resources to Newark's Black and Brown working-class citizens.[63]

Within Newark's challenging 1970s political environment, AFS remained a priority for its organizers. The school was open to the offspring of CFUN advocates and served neighborhood youth as well. Most of the students from the community were from economically marginalized families. The activists built relationships with parents and grew invested in helping the children succeed.[64] Amina Baraka explained,

> They [were] kids in the neighborhood. [We] didn't really have to look for them. The parents were cooperative. They were glad to have somewhere that the kids could go . . . to do something positive. . . . Later on, we did have applications, but in the beginning, it was just kids off the block. . . . A lot of them used to travel around, especially the male kids, they used to travel around with Amiri. He would take them different places and have [plays], and it was like an extended family kind of thing.[65]

Amiri Baraka recalled that Amina led advocates in developing relationships with other neighborhood women, particularly through block associations, which forged important bonds and "mutual support" networks between advocates and community residents. Additionally, Amina undertook an important leadership role in reforming the school's curriculum. She organized the AFS parents as part of her administrative duties, requiring their involvement in the school's activities. AFS students' parents would also lobby the board of education, especially when it came to the lack of representation for the overwhelmingly Black student body at Robert Treat School.[66]

Operating the AFS was challenging and, although men played significant roles, the mostly female staff was integral to the school's daily functioning. One challenging aspect of running the institution was that it was always in need of funds. AFS was tuition-free and relied on tens of thousands of dollars generated from grants, private donations, CFUN workers' dues, parental volunteerism, and the staff's fundraising efforts.[67] The pay at AFS was so low that teachers had to find supplemental employment. "You've got to remember, these were young college students in the beginning. . . . We lived . . . and we did everything collectively, but as they got older and started to have children of their own and responsibilities," Amina explained, "they had to seek work outside the organization."[68]

Fundraising added to the AFS staff's long list of duties performed according to the *kazi* imperative. Amina recounted, "We had little ice trucks, with the ice on them [for] snowballs and so, in the summer, we would do that, and the money would all go into African Free School." She also pointed out that CFUN advocates did much to help raise money. "We had all types of programs and things that would supplement the school that was coming from the Congress of African People, not so much from the community. . . . We had a lemonade stand and then some of the kids, I think they were selling *Unity and Struggle*."[69] A paper outlining the African Free School structure supported Amina's memories, indicating that the school's economic organization was aimed at achieving self-reliance, with fundraising efforts in the areas of literature sales and a food vending enterprise.[70]

Movement advocates viewed the African Free School as a practical, institutionalized method of addressing the urban crisis in education.[71] Amina Baraka's memories illuminate the ways foot soldiers like the AFS staff practiced *kazi* alongside the Seven Principles of Blackness in this context. Workers at AFS cared for the basic needs of the economically deprived and socially marginalized children of Newark's Central Ward in addition to teaching them to re-envision themselves as a unified, upstanding, self-determining, hardworking, purpose-filled, creative, and faithful people. For instance, teachers helped students with self-care, assembling kits of basic hygiene products for them while attempting to create an environment in which the students from more impoverished backgrounds were not singled out and all would feel included. Amina explained,

> The children . . . we made sure that they had a little bag they had to carry that we used to just find from the Army-Navy store. In the bag was a toothbrush, toothpaste, a hair comb, Vaseline, a washcloth, [and] soap. . . . When they came into school, the first thing they did after they recited the Nguzo Saba [was] go into the washroom. We didn't care if they had just gotten out the tub, but that was to keep other children who didn't have that from feeling like they were different. So we made them go through that process. . . . Then they'd come back and sit down, and we'd have classes.[72]

Amina revealed that, through their work at the African Free School, the mostly female staff members operationalized *kazi* to emphasize so-

cial equity. Because some of the students faced such formidable economic challenges, AFS staff had to assist them with obtaining essential
pieces of their outfits. "We had uniforms, because . . . we could see the
kids were dressed differently, and some of them had on new clothes,
some of them had on old clothes. Some of them had on mostly no
clothes, and so we had green T-shirts, black pants, and . . . we did buy
them shoes."[73]

AFS teachers' exertion of *kazi* leadership extended beyond teaching, fundraising, and caring for students' basic needs. Ashley D. Farmer
has pointed out that women in the Us Organization developed a new
cultural archive in the process of instructing Black youth. This innovative collection consisted of songs, chants, lesson plans, activities, and
teaching materials based in Kawaida principles, some of which are still
used today.[74] Like the women in Us, AFS teachers contributed to enlarging the cultural archive for young African Americans during the Black
Power movement.[75] When discussing the development of the AFS curriculum, Amina Baraka declared, "Our liberation school was run by all
the women. The men [were] off doing other things, but it was organized
by us. We wrote the curriculum."[76]

Amina Baraka's narrative illustrated how women, in their roles as educators, pioneered teaching materials that imparted Kawaida-influenced
values, as well as larger Black Power ideals, aimed at culturally transforming a new generation of African Americans. "We had stories that
we wrote. I wrote one story called 'Coal Black and the Seven Simbas,'"
Amina remembered. Drawing from such groups as the Grandassa Models, she showed how a simple children's story like "Snow White and the
Seven Dwarfs" could be inverted to teach a basic Black Power tenet like
self-love. She continued, "We went through the regular Grimm's fairy
tales and . . . we realized how we had been brainwashed and how Black
was not quite beautiful in those tales. . . . We rewrote them. . . . We would
laugh at how we had been brainwashed, so we decided to reverse it."[77]

The kinds of stories that AFS staff developed for the students not only
enlarged the Pan-African nationalist and Black Power cultural archives
for children, they also filled a need for more stories that spoke to the
experiences of multigenerational African-descended people. Moreover,
Pan-African nationalist tales counteracted depictions like the animated
film *Coal Black and the Sebben Dwarfs*, which was so rife with racial

stereotypes that it had recently been put on a list of offensive cartoons.[78] Providing more details about the story she wrote for AFS, Amina Baraka recalled, "In place of Snow White, it was Coal Black. . . . When Coal Black looked in the mirror, it spoke back to her in a Black voice saying, . . . 'Mirror, mirror on the wall, who's the most beautiful of them all?' And the mirror responded, 'Coal Black is where it's at.'" Amina explained that the AFS teachers wrote several such books.[79] She said that there was a dearth of literature with positive depictions of central Black characters available to the teachers at the time. Her reflections suggested the desire to place African Americans at the center of their own school's literature while developing their literacy practices and reeducating them about their personal value: "I think we had an effect on the community . . . consciousness in terms of the tradition of Black people. . . . It was all right to be Coal Black. You no longer had to be Snow White. It was all right, and you [were] beautiful."[80]

Some of the AFS educators contributing to the Kawaida cultural archive were among the more progressive CFUN women who stood with Amina Baraka and lobbied for the expansion of women's roles in Pan-African cultural nationalism, including Jaribu Hill, Jalia Woods, Salimu Rogers, and Staarabisha (Lydia) Barrett. Hill and Woods served on the Woman Question Commission for a short time, helping chairperson Amina Baraka research, write, and critique the "Woman Question" essay. Woods and Barrett went on to assume leadership roles in the Women's Division, which eventually assumed a vanguard position within CFUN. Barrett had been a founding member of United Sisters. Besides being a freedom singer, trainer, and community organizer, Hill served as a leader of the women's circle, which developed programs such as the African Women's Conference. Amina Baraka and Jaribu Hill also became members of the CAP Political Council. Other AFS teachers included Mumininas Akiba, Ibura, Jalia, Anasa, and Furaha.[81]

Mumininia Jalia was from Dayton, Ohio, and came to CFUN from Kalamazoo College. While in Newark, she served as AFS's principal. Jalia also penned the "Monthly Kiswahili Lesson" in Black New Ark as an extension of her educational administrator role. She sometimes devoted short paragraphs of the column to her views on the importance of African Americans' adherence to Pan-African cultural nationalist values.[82] For instance, Jalia exhorted readers "to identify with our culture [and] our traditional greatness." She further explained, "Self-determination manifests itself in the language that a person speaks."[83] Muminina Jalia's column indicated that women's roles as educators were often politicized, and that some AFS educators leveraged the *kazi* they performed in their feminized teaching roles to reach audiences beyond the classroom.

Komozi Woodard's recollections about Muminina Anasa indicated that African Free School teachers were politically active and astute. He recalled witnessing diminishing numbers of female activists in the New-ark SNCC chapter with which he was affiliated before joining CFUN. Investigating the situation, Woodard recounted dropping in on a local CFUN Soul Session one Sunday, where he saw Anasa. He said that Anasa had also been in SNCC but challenged him to join CFUN and become a Young Lion [Simba Wachanga] if he was a "real man." Woodard said, "In many ways, the sisters were the ones who were challenging [men] to take on the serious commitment of what they were calling nation build-ing back then. So I would have to say that Anasa . . . really spurred me to make my decision" to join CFUN.[84]

AFS teachers used their positions as training grounds and platforms for political expression in other areas as well as for developing their leadership skills. Muminina Furaha served as an administrator at the African Free Schools at Robert Treat and at the Spirit House. "Furaha was . . . the Swahili teacher," Amina Baraka explained. "She was an ac-tress by profession, and she dropped everything and never went back to it."[85] According to Woodard, Muminina Furaha came to New Jersey to help establish the Spirit House Movers and Players, leaving the San Francisco Black Arts West to do so.[86] Amina recounted, "[Furaha] was also part of [the] Malaika Singers. She actually became . . . part of the directors of the Spirit House, the theater group that we had." Amina's reflections highlighted the ways women who staffed AFS were politically driven and how they sacrificed personal ambitions to join the move-ment: "I guess we all were basically artists. . . . My ambition was to be in theater, and I was a dancer. . . . None of us went back to what we [were] really doing [before joining the movement]."[87]

Even the decision to form an AFS daycare illustrated CFUN women's political theorizing and their group-centered, work-centered leadership capacities. The female activists bore what Woodard characterized as an added burden of family responsibilities. Their determination to take part in the political work of the movement resulted in the formation of a twenty-four-hour AFS nursery for CAP families. The center represented the women's effort to institutionalize collective child-rearing. Amina explained how it worked:

> When we gave conferences and conventions and stuff, that's when the daycare was really good for the women. . . . The people who had to do the daycare center, we rotated so that all the women could be active at any given time. . . . There would be women in the daycare for two or three days or weekends or so forth, and the rest of us would be where the conference was, doing what we had to do.[88]

Amiri Baraka wrote that Amina thought that such a center would provide the best way to lighten the child-rearing burdens of women as well as men to free them for political activities.[89] But Amina was especially concerned with the tendency to exclude women from political work in Kawaida-influenced organizations. She wanted to eradicate Kawaida practices that limited women to the fringes of the movement in the realms of social organization, teaching children, and supporting the agendas of their male associates, lovers, and husbands. She spearheaded institutional modifications to facilitate women's appointment to other organizational departments, which dealt with politics, economics, and the arts.[90]

In addition to the African Free School's independent, semiautonomous classroom and daycare programs, the CFUN Women's Division established the Teacher Training Institute to assist other Black educators. The institute was aimed at making AFS's methods accessible to African American instructors across the country. African Free School institutions also served as models for other nationalists who wanted to develop independent educational institutions. Jamala Rogers explained how WATU (St. Louis CAP) developed a small daycare service. WATU advocates were prepared to broaden it into an independent AFS branch before Newark CAP leadership decided to focus on reforming public schools.[91]

Rogers explained that the WATU daycare originated as a resource for community members attending classes at the St. Louis *hekalu*. She also described the main purpose of the program as empowering women for political action: "We had onsite childcare at our *hekalu* so that it freed up the women to do some . . . political work." She explained how the CAP practice of institutionalized communal daycare for busy activists with children has impacted present-day political organizing efforts. "Even now," Rogers said, "the organizations that I'm a part of, we really try to always have childcare so that women can participate. . . . I always saw it as an important role for [an] organization who said that they were committed to full participation by women. . . . If one of the things is, 'I don't have a babysitter,' then you should be building . . . organizational practices to provide childcare."⁹²

Like the students at other Kawaida-influenced Pan-African nationalist independent Black institutions, students at the AFS affectionately called teachers and older advocates "mama," as an African-centered practice of reinforcing community values and performing *ujamaa* (familyhood). "We never referred to ourselves as teachers. We always referred to ourselves as mother [or] 'mama.' . . . People started calling us 'mama' everywhere we went," Amina Baraka explained. Furaha said to a reporter in 1971, "We are like their parents. . . . We want it to be like their family, . . . not dry and distant like the usual school. So, we stress parental respect, and we insist that their parents show up for a session [at the African Free School] once a week."⁹³

Although admitting that such an emphasis on "parental respect" could be read as enforcement of conformity, the practices that the women described were aimed at connecting CFUN advocates as an extended family to members of their Newark community and reflected similarities of custom among a larger network of Kawaida-influenced Pan-African nationalist organizations.⁹⁴ Amina Baraka said that she still encounters students from the African Free School, who often warmly inquire, "How's Mama Furaha? How's Mama Asali?"⁹⁵ The women's narratives contain a common theme: They place community mamas at the heart of independent school programs and practices, functioning as what Rickford called "embryos of the coming nation," in which Black children's lives mattered.⁹⁶

The practice of calling teachers mamas revealed that schools were an extension of women's roles as the mothers and first teachers of the nation. "Just as the mother must set a certain image so should the teacher because they are inseparable. The teacher's role is the role of the mother," stated an *Amsterdam News* article about the African Free School.[97] According to Rickford, the cultural nationalist focus on instilling values in students enhanced female teachers' status. This elevated rank seemed to partially rest on the level of *kazi* required of the educators. Expected to possess the will to work around the clock, if necessary, AFS nationalist teachers were not only accountable for curriculum design, research, text development, and using "correct and innovative" instructional methods, they were also responsible for developing a "high consciousness and being aware of [their] identity, purpose, and direction."[98] "Women were primary bearers of morality and social ethics in the cultural nationalist world view," Rickford wrote. "Since achieving nationhood was thought to require systematic transmission of such knowledge, women were seen as essential agents of national formation." The enhanced status of female teachers in Black nationalist schools was complicated. In one way, the role was predicated on women's continued "willingness to accept male authority." Additionally, the work of teachers in Kawaida-influenced independent Black schools was often an extension of their domestic roles as African women and remained relatively separate from and more feminized than typically masculine roles in the freedom struggle.[99]

Beyond the teachers themselves, Kawaida-influenced schools were sites of women's politicization. Teacher-administrators were activists and leaders in that their work was part of the larger process of Black nationality formation. At AFS, students were taught the standard subjects of history, geography, visual and language arts, science, mathematics, health, and physical education while their teachers also worked to shape them into the next generation of nation builders.[100] Instructors, whose numbers were overwhelmingly female, found the school a place to perform political work within acceptable gender norms according to Kawaida's earliest expressions and based on certain mores, norms, training, and education that women brought to the organization from mainstream society as well. Moreover, the process of forming the AFS was the initial point of attraction for many women to the organization. Woodard wrote that female activists "gathered around Amina Baraka to discuss Black liberation and African culture as she established the African Free School at the Spirit House in 1967."[101] Schools were also places where women could be politically active as well as training grounds for female

leaders and businesspeople, and for the development and encouragement of high levels of education among women and girls.[102]

## The Decline of the African Free School

The Black Power experiment in Newark was in decline by 1974. The
funding for AFS and other CFUN programs was withdrawn as the overarching urban renewal project for neighborhood development, NJR-32
Project Area Committee (PAC), became mired in the corruption of
Newark's "bureaucratic red tape and legal malaise." NJR-32 PAC programs were dismantled, and the Newark Housing Authority demolished
the buildings where they were headquartered, including the African
Free School. These events coincided with growing ideological divisions within CAP. The Congress of African People shifted to "national
communism," as the Barakas' critiques of Pan-African cultural nationalism grew into outright rejection. Woodard wrote that CAP advocates
believed that the Black Power movement "died at the hands of traitorous
black elected officials." Amiri Baraka charged that internal colonialism
in the United States had transformed into neocolonialism. By 1976, "sectarian conflicts" tore apart the Black Women's United Front. According
to Woodard, Amiri Baraka's embrace of cultural nationalism was a key
factor in the development of Black Power. His rejection of the philosophy can thus be viewed as a turning point in the movement's demise.[103]

Jaribu Hill's reflections indicated that, just as the AFS drew women
advocates to Newark, its dissolution amid the changing tides of the Barakas' ideologies pushed activists away from CFUN/CAP. Although Hill
cited that changes both inside and outside the organization prompted
her to leave, she also said, "One of the most challenging aspects of working with CFUN/CAP was abandoning the independent school work for
that of the public school." Hill believed that the leadership should have
continued its educational struggle on multiple fronts, particularly since
certain AFS offerings assisted women in Newark's Central Ward. "Some
of the parents had come to rely on the preschool that we had and, once
we closed that, we lost some momentum," she lamented. "Not totally, but
I think there was a certain amount of disappointment in the community
when we didn't continue that preschool program, which was dire for a
number of women who needed that childcare so that they could go to

work." Suggesting that her time at AFS and in CFUN/CAP influenced the organizing and activism that would characterize her life's work in other areas, Hill said, "Our thinking, of course, was that we definitely needed to focus on public school, because that's where the majority of our children were and are, and that frames my position to this day."[104]

Looking back, Amiri Baraka cited the African Free School as one of the most important endeavors of CFUN and CAP's social organization. He said that the school represented a high level of accomplishment and was influential not only in Newark, but throughout the country as a model and training resource for independent Black schools. Kevin Mumford's assessment of the work that Newark advocates performed aptly sums up their influence. Mumford wrote that the activists inspired a part of the African American community that civil rights leaders had not been able to galvanize. Though Mumford focused mostly on Amiri Baraka's leadership, it is important to note that the women associated with Spirit House and the AFS educational programs were part of the process of influencing and energizing Newark's Black community as well.[105]

## "Freedom Now": Uhuru Sasa School

Operating from 1970 until 1986, Brooklyn's Uhuru Sasa Shule educated hundreds of children and was the longest-running, most influential independent Black institution of the group of IBIs discussed in this chapter. A renewed sense of cultural awareness emanating from the struggles of the 1960s sparked a resurgence of nationalist sentiment, which was often provisionally expressed as separatist inclinations within African American communities. Such impulses toward independent institution building combined with a series of clashes with New York City public school educators and bureaucrats, leading to the creation of Uhuru Sasa as an independent Black institution in 1970.[106]

A group of educators at New York City's Junior High School 271 began an evening school in September 1968, during the Ocean Hill-Brownsville uprising, to provide classes and instruction for youth and adults in Brooklyn. Teachers and administrators offered courses covering a variety of topics that community members deemed useful, from Black history to sewing. Weusi commented, "This told us that if we could do this, and it could be successful, that we could, in fact, develop our own types of schools!" Two years after the Ocean Hill-Brownsville dispute was over, the group developed several programs, including Uhuru Sasa Shule, an independent Black institution in Brooklyn.[107]

Adeyemi Bandele recalled the conditions that produced Uhuru Sasa and the larger East organization. The African American Students Association (ASA) "initially developed as an . . . evening school program so that the high school students could, in fact, work and then come and take classes that were offered by members of the African American Teachers Association (ATA)," he said. "That grew to the extent where we just saw the need for the establishment of our own, independent school." Bandele discussed some of the supplemental adult programming, explaining that organization members ran an after-school program and developed a program designed to reeducate and train teachers who wanted to work in independent schools. He emphasized that the programs of the ATA and ASA led to the establishment of Uhuru Sasa School as well as The East's cultural and education center.[108]

In his narrative, Bandele discussed various roles that women played in Uhuru Sasa. According to his recollection, a few women served on the leadership council, and a woman (Ante Brown) directed the primary school. Bandele recalled male leadership in the middle and high schools, however, while Martha Bright stated that she was a middle school coordinator. Bright also remembered that she and Ayanna Johnson served in leadership positions at the Uhuru Sasa high school. Despite Bright's recollections of women's service in limited leadership positions, Bandele emphasized that women were primarily teachers within the institution. Sixty to seventy percent of Uhuru Sasa's teachers were women, according to Bandele's estimation.[109]

Akili Walker, a student and instructor at Uhuru Sasa during his teen years, confirmed that women played important roles as educators and mentors who reinforced and extended nationalist values. A precocious teen, Walker was a fifteen-year-old dropout, because he became "bored" and "disillusioned" with the public school system. After an independent academy in Massachusetts denied him admission, Walker gained acceptance at Uhuru Sasa. Following a year of courses in math, science, English, Black culture and history, Swahili, and self-defense at Uhuru Sasa, administrators invited him to teach boys aged three to six.[110]

Women played integral roles in training new generations of nationalist educators. Walker specifically highlighted their significance, saying, "The women and the sisters of The East were very influential in the curriculum and [in] training the teachers in the school." Expounding on how experienced teachers educated new instructors, he said, "At Uhuru Sasa, the school was accredited, but not all of the teachers had teaching degrees. So the teachers that did have degrees would teach the [un] credentialed teachers like myself." Walker explained that the older, more experienced educators covered topics from lesson plans to classroom management. "We used to have teacher training classes on Saturdays, and I learned from the sisters how to go about becoming a teacher.[111]

Adeyemi Bandele speculated that two factors influenced the fact that the majority of Uhuru Sasa's faculty and staff members were women. Both elements related to the central functions that women played in Brooklyn's struggle for community control.[112] First, the public educational system's faculty was likewise composed of a greater number of women than men. Many of those teachers decided to work within the experimental district and, later, at Uhuru Sasa School.[113] These instructors, he stated, were professionals, skilled at building and sustaining independent institutions. The teachers trained other instructors and taught students in the experimental district as well as the independent school. According to Jitu Weusi, such educators were not preoccupied with issues like compensation, as were the United Federation of Teachers (UFT) members, who went on strike during the Ocean Hill-Brownsville conflict. Many Uhuru Sasa teachers were affiliated with the ATA and focused more on improving the quality of education and providing overall better opportunities for Black and Latine children.[114] According to Tamisha Peterson, Uhuru Sasa's employees' dedication to transforming the nature of education for the entire community sustained them, especially since they "weren't getting paid a whole bunch."[115]

In addition to New York City public school teachers' influence, the second factor that Adeyemi Bandele highlighted was that some of the concerned mothers in the experimental district also became employees and volunteers at Uhuru Sasa. Women like Aminisha Black revealed several reasons for joining The East's workforce. Black, who became the organization's bookkeeper after enrolling her sons in Uhuru Sasa following the Ocean Hill-Brownsville confrontation, also cofounded the organization's nursery school, Imani Day Care, with Lady Esther Byrd. The child-care center began in Black's home as a cooperative effort of the women, who took shifts to care for the children, while others worked either in East operations or in their careers outside the organization. The center developed to meet working Black mothers' collective needs.[116] As such, Imani Day Care demonstrated one of the important ways Pan-African cultural nationalist women leveraged gender roles, which emphasized mothering, by using daycare operations to achieve more time and space for women's work beyond birth, child-rearing, and housekeeping.

## Teachers as Pan-African Cultural Nationalist "Mothers"

Uhuru Sasa's instructional approach embodied a Pan-African cultural nationalist ethos similar to those of others within the constellation of independent Black institutions. Teachers were community mamas, performing *kazi* to transmit the values necessary to aid nationality formation. As Bright put it, "We were the teachers and the mamas in the school." Uhuru Sasa's teachers also lived in the areas where they worked and were part of central Brooklyn's societal fabric. The women's narratives indicated that faculty members often worked seven days a week. "We had sisters who went on field trips and took the children to camp," she recalled. For example, "We went one fall up to Queen Mother Moore's estate in upstate New York and spent a weekend there." Bright also indicated that Uhuru Sasa faculty spent their summers educating children in the community. Teachers participated in Central Brooklyn Model Cities, taking hundreds of youths to participate in summer programs at HBCUs like Shaw University in Raleigh, North Carolina.[117]

The Ocean Hill-Brownsville experience exposed the reality that the residents in the poor and working-class Black and Latine communities had been marginalized within the city school system, rendering them "nameless and faceless." To help ameliorate the situation, advocates of community control appealed to educators to "make an extra effort" to reach students and their families in the neighborhood.[118] While the UFT asserted that such requests went beyond the contractual duties of public school teachers, Peterson's narrative revealed that activist approaches to education were common among Uhuru Sasa's independent school instructors, who took up such work to fill the void left after the community control movement collapsed. She stated, "The teachers had to make sure that they went to the parents' house, so by the time that the first month [of the school year] was over, we had visited each parent's house [and] knew what their household situation was." Recalling the level of community acceptance they received as reflected in the ways parents welcomed the visiting teachers, she said, "Although we told them we weren't coming there to eat, each family really . . . wanted to make us comfortable. . . . They were so happy that we came to them, because that was rare. They never had any public school teachers to come visit them at their house."[119]

Like the African Free School, Uhuru Sasa educated students of a broad range of talents and abilities in an effort to counterbalance systemic issues. For example, Uhuru Sasa accepted students with behavioral issues and those who had dropped out of the public system. "Many of our students came from the public school system with discipline and other related problems," wrote Walker. He stated in an interview that administrators accepted students with various challenges at Uhuru Sasa, where they learned in an environment emphasizing identity, pride, and order. Walker noted that many of these students enjoyed learning at Uhuru Sasa and that they eventually demonstrated greater academic proficiency than those in the New York City public school system. "After being at Uhuru Sasa," he wrote in his autobiography, "they became disciplined, self-assured, and at least two years ahead of the public school system students academically." Moreover, "I've talked to many students that attended Uhuru Sasa in their adulthood, and they all [say] they benefitted from the school."[120]

Tamisha Peterson confirmed that Uhuru Sasa teachers served an array of Black students from New York City's five boroughs, including those with special needs such as learning, emotional, and behavioral issues. "We had a lot of children that came from what they used to call 600 schools," she said.[121] "They were kicked out of a 600 school because they were bad. Their next road was up the river [to juvenile] detention unless their parents could find someplace else." She suggested that some families came to Uhuru Sasa because they were seeking a last-resort educational option. Peterson added that students in such situations were challenging to teach, but she maintained that many improved under the care and guidance of Uhuru Sasa educators. "There were a few that had become handfuls or *were* handfuls when they came," she said. "Most of them turned around, though. . . . For the most part, they kind of calmed down." Invoking the language of a "community mama" invested in cultivating children of all backgrounds and abilities as members of a formative Black nation, Peterson said, "I think that we always did show love and respect for the children, and you get that back."[122]

Teachers at Uhuru Sasa also had other commonalities with those working in other independent and supplementary Black nationalist institutions. For instance, Uhuru Sasa faculty led single-sex classes, emphasizing what was deemed appropriate behavior for developing manliness and femininity, as did School of Afroamerican Culture teachers. "We had brothers' classes . . . with men teachers and *dadas'* [sisters'] classes with women teachers," stated Bright.[123] Additionally, work in other East enterprises, *Black News* sales, and hosting the annual African Street Festival were essential fundraising activities for educators. Fundraising was a necessary task for teachers, as Uhuru Sasa operated on a tuition-driven budget, which was supplemented by donations. Fees were set low enough so community members could afford them.[124]

Like faculty and staff in the Us Organization, CFUN/CAP, and Ahidiana schools, Uhuru Sasa's educators found a dearth of culturally relevant classroom literature. Also, like Us and CFUN/CAP educators, their ingenuity in creating course texts and activities meant that they contributed to enlarging the possibilities of Pan-African cultural nationalist literature for Black youth. In her narrative, Peterson described the kind of *kazi* that Uhuru Sasa's dedicated and creative teachers performed: "We did everything. . . . We painted our rooms the way we wanted to. I love the fact that we had freedom to create our own curriculum. We drew books with Black faces." She also remembered creating curricular materials. "We didn't have any books, because we weren't going to use the same crappy books they had in the public school, which showed no Black faces [and] no urban settings at all. . . . We were creating a lot of our own stuff, our own curriculum, [and] our own books."[125]

Like others, Peterson asserted that the school was the most important East institution in the community.[126] Her opinion was partly rooted in the idea that Uhuru Sasa's teachers imparted an education focused on preparing students for freedom and self-determination according to a Black nationalist perspective and was partially based on the fact that one of Uhuru Sasa's main goals was educating the whole family. Peterson posed the rhetorical question, "What's more important than the education of your children?" She followed up with a statement suggesting that providing children with a proper, Pan-African nationalist education was the organization's most important endeavor: "There were a lot of other things going on at The East, but the one big thing was Uhuru Sasa."[127] The school's holistic education process consisted of primary, elementary, and secondary education programs for children as well as the adult-focused Evening School of Knowledge, which offered a slate of classes covering subjects like visual arts, math, English language arts and communication, economics, political ideology, food and nutrition, sewing, self-defense, and Swahili. Moreover, Uhuru Sasa contributed to and influenced other East programs, such as the bookstore, food co-op, *Black News*, and the Tamu Sweet-East restaurant. Likewise, these East community programs influenced the school.[128] Thus, the work of Uhuru Sasa's mostly female faculty was integral to The East organization's process of nation building.

In a manner similar to parents at the African Free School, guardians of Uhuru Sasa students were encouraged to take an active role in their children's educational process. East advocates' overall philosophy was that "educating children while the adults remain in the dark is not going to make for a successful unit." The only requirements for African Americans desiring to affiliate with Uhuru Sasa was commitment to "the Black cause," service in The East, and a ten-dollar weekly tuition fee that could be waived through "'working' scholarships."[129] The school thus attracted East affiliates through its instructional programs. Shukuru Sanders recalled walking in her neighborhood on Bedford Avenue and seeing a poster for a new school. After hearing Jitu Weusi explain the institution's purpose and mission, she enrolled her son in the fall of 1970. She began volunteering in the kitchen as part of the school's parental involvement requirement. Her initial job, which entailed serving warm food and beverages during the students' breakfast meals, eventually grew to include the lunch shift, then increasingly greater involvement as an advocate in The East organization.[130] The fact that Uhuru Sasa School often functioned as a gateway for community members underscores educators' and administrators' importance as political agents in the intended process of nationality formation.

## Uhuru Sasa's Decline

Uhuru Sasa faced many of the same challenges as other IBIs. The changing sociopolitical and economic climate of the mid-1970s and early 1980s brought external factors such as continued state repression, economic recession, decreasing philanthropic donations, a drug epidemic, and crime to the doorsteps of IBIs. The Pan-African nationalist movement also faced internal turmoil from ideological conflict over the appropriate path to freedom (racial nationalism or Marxism) and suffered from flagging incomes, activist burnout, and advocate attrition. Jitu Weusi stepped down as headmaster of Uhuru Sasa in 1978. He was succeeded by a series of administrators whose leadership was short-lived. Uhuru Sasa struggled with various issues, including difficulty maintaining the school's physical spaces and paying utility bills. Although the institution continued to allow parents to work off debts through campus service and offered scholarships to approximately a fifth of its students, administrators were forced to raise yearly tuition from $450 to $500, a hefty price for working-class families. Unable to endure the increasing financial strain, the school had closed its doors by 1986.[131] According to Akili Walker, Uhuru Sasa's "closing was a tremendous loss to New York because it was totally focused on teaching children and helping adults to develop their talents to become all they could be."[132]

## "Our People's Future Is Dependent on Our Children's Vital Education": Ahidiana in New Orleans

The seed of New Orleans' Black independent schools germinated in the earliest months of the 1970s within a group of the city's progressive African American activists.[133] An experience with an independent Black school in New York inspired Kalamu ya Salaam's brother, Kenneth Ferdinand, to develop a similar venture in the Crescent City, the family's hometown. Ferdinand met Cicely St. Julien (later Tayari kwa Salaam) after returning south. St. Julien had a "deep love" for and "interest" in developing schools and curricula for African American youth. She wanted to be part of the larger national phenomenon of creating independent Black institutions, which included the Us Organization's, CAP's, and the East's programs as well as the Institute for Positive Education in Chicago. St. Julien worked alongside Ferdinand to reach parents and activists also wanting to build a school. The first institution growing out of this partnership was Dokpwe Work/Study.[134]

In 1972 Ahidiana evolved from a split among Dokpwe's members over the direction and purpose of their work. Those desiring to continue developing Dokpwe solely as a school remained with Kenneth Ferdinand and his wife, Williettatta. Others, including Tayari and another Ferdinand brother, Keith, desired to expand their activities to encompass a new, "full-fledged Pan-African revolutionary organization." Schooling would be only one of the undertakings in the more diversified institution. Advocates of the holistic approach believed that they should not only help liberate the minds of African-descended children in New Orleans, but also develop their organization as a "lifestyle" guided by the Nguzo Saba and aimed at nurturing future activists to assist in liberating the oppressed peoples of the world.[135]

In the aftermath of the split with Dokpwe, advocates developed Ahidiana as a Kawaida-influenced cadre, an "organization of organizers," which attracted between sixteen and twenty-two adult members. Ahidiana's advocates launched their own Work/Study Center. Operations and programming like the Work/Study Center were open to the masses and grew out of Ahidiana's mission to serve the working-class people of the Lower Ninth Ward. The educational institution was an independent Black school founded in November 1973 to educate children between the ages of three and eight.[136] As one of two Ahidiana members responsible for the school's daily functioning and the Work/Study Center's main educational theorist, Tayari kwa Salaam explained several aspects of the school's philosophy and purpose. The center was Black in its constituents' primary commitment to the defense, development, and self-determination of African-descended people, although its literature stipulated that visitors of all races were welcome, and the rights of other peoples were neither excluded nor denied. Tayari kwa Salaam wrote that the Work/Study was independent because its administrator-teachers strove for the greatest possible level of economic self-sufficiency. The Work/Study Center sustained its program with tuition, donations, and Ahidiana membership dues. Ahidiana's dedication to existing as a small, committed group of influential activists was expressed via the center and can be seen in the statement "Our deepest hope is that we will inspire others to start independent black schools." Tayari also explained that Work/Study staff had written a teachers' manual and planned on producing a film to influence the development of other Black independent and supplementary educational institutions.[137]

Women in Ahidiana managed the daily operations of the Work/Study Center and, by consciously shaping it as an affirming and supportive space for Black children in New Orleans's Lower Ninth Ward, they were key participants in the struggle to build a "new society, within and beyond the classroom, at home and abroad."[138] The center started with five students and was located in a remodeled house at 2303 Deslonde Street.[139] Pictures of notable African Americans adorned the walls, reminders of how important it was to uplift the students and teach them self-determination. The placement of the images represented a centering of Black history and culture in the curriculum as well as in the physical learning space.[140]

As in other Kawaida-influenced cultural nationalist organizations, teachers were not only referred to by the Swahili word *mwalimu*, but youth also affectionately called teachers and other older advocates "mama" and "baba" as a practice of reinforcing community values and *ujamaa* (familyhood).[141] Kiini Salaam pointed out in her narrative that Ahidiana was more than its core cadre organization and related school. The organization was composed of various blood, marital, and friendly relationships constituting an extended family where children like her "socialized" and "lived." Practices such as calling community members "mama" and "baba" connected Ahidiana advocates to one another as well as to other groups with similar beliefs. Although some would criticize members as "elitist" and insular, Kiini remembered feeling that together, they could "create a world where people are supporting each other."[142] As far as Work/Study students and young members of the broader Ahidiana/Dokpwe community were concerned, their community mamas were at the center of the process of dreaming and making a better nation and world. The center's role in the wider movement was reflected in Kiini's observation that it was "always hosting different nationalists . . . or freedom fighters from the international community who were coming through New Orleans."[143]

Past students and community members remembered the administrator-teachers as vital and influential. Kwesi Nantambu fondly recalled the center as the first educational institution that he attended. Women at Ahidiana, he said, "were very significant because a lot of them were facilitators at the school."[144] Kina Joshua-Jasmine observed the Work/Study Center as a member of the broader Ahidiana/Dokpwe family. The ladies who ran Ahidiana's school "were powerful women," she affirmed. "They knew their stuff."[145]

Kwesi Nantambu and Kina Joshua-Jasmine went on to recount the details of the women's work and shared observations about elements contributing to their effectiveness as educators in an independent Black institution and as nation builders. Nantambu suggested that the women contributed to Ahidiana's goals of providing a holistic education by teaching more than basic subject matter. Work/Study teachers carried out these aims by "instilling values of respect for the community [and] respect for your fellow person." He said that the instructors "educat[ed] you about . . . your ancestors, your history . . . how [Africans] were brought here, and more." He further commented on Ahidiana teachers' pragmatic approach, saying that they provided insight into interpreting and navigating the social problems that students faced. Joshua-Jasmine highlighted Tayari kwa Salaam in her recollections: "I thought she was a hugely powerful person in the community. She always spoke up. She was always trying to organize something."[146] Ahidiana's educational program was consistent with what Rickford has described as one of IBIs' key thrusts: nurturing children who were "literate and conscious of the world as it was and as it might be." The women who taught at the Work/Study Center carried out the important goal of raising the consciousness of a new generation of leaders, sustaining this important institutional outgrowth of Black Power a decade after the movement began to wane.[147]

Academic instruction in the areas of math, science, communication, and physical education was part of the Work/Study Center curriculum; however, students also received direction in "culture," which reflected Kawaida principles, including the Nguzo Saba.[148] Culture was defined as "the study of the material and social conditions and practices of our people and the World [sic]."[149] Advocates believed that culture was "the most effective means for teaching our people to take an active role in shaping our lives by creating and determining our future. . . . The value of culture lies in how one understands self in relationship to everything else."[150] Kina Joshua-Jasmine explained that cultural nationalist mamas taught students about identity, critical thinking, and independence in a nurturing and engaging environment. She said that they encouraged "learning about who you were" and "where you came from." Their teaching style "was never belittling. . . . You were always questioned in a way that made you think about why you did [something] rather than just being talked to." She had high praise for their skill as teachers: "The women . . . were well organized, and it seemed to me that they really knew their craft and how to motivate kids to want to learn and become more self-sufficient."[151]

Much like East advocates, Ahidiana members opted to redefine spaces and create institutions within their working-class, majority-Black, urban community rather than waiting for the integrationist promise of equality to reach their neighborhood or out-migrating to more affluent areas.[152] One of Kiini Salaam's strongest memories centered on how the Work/Study Center's unique visual and sonic presence transformed part of the Lower Ninth Ward. "From a visual perspective, just being there doing things differently" was important, she said. "We had different clothes, and then every day we would . . . exercise, so we were running around the block. We had our uniforms, and then we had a unity circle. We'd start every day with a circle." Kiini recalled the unique sounds of the center in addition to its distinct look: "We'd sing songs and chant, and that was done . . . outside."[153]

Kiini Salaam also remembered that nearby residents were attracted to the unique Work/Study Center environment, and some eventually enrolled their children. "Certain families in the community saw that, and they kind of were interested. . . . They'd send their children to the school at a very affordable rate. . . . Through that, they would learn about different health choices, and just different cultural possibilities that they may not have been aware of."[154] Vera Warren-Williams was one of the neighborhood residents to whom the Work/Study Center appealed. Warren-Williams had been educated in New Orleans public schools, where she felt marginalized, not least because of her radical outlook and natural hairstyle. She believed in Ahidiana's approach to implementing an independent Black educational institution in the Lower Ninth. They holistically taught Black children "on the level of discipline, cultural and global awareness, proper diet, [and] exercise." Ahidiana's faculty nurtured mature students who did well academically once they left the Work/Study

Center to attend public schools modeled on Eurocentric, middle-class cultural values. Warren-Williams believed that the instructors were "radical and revolutionary" for undertaking such a task.[155]

In a sense, the students' ideas did not pose any challenge to the ideology of complementary gender norms, because young people have historically perceived women as powerful in their mothering and teaching capacities. Teaching, particularly as an extension of mothering, was feminized work both within Kawaida and in mainstream society. Black nationalist schools, however, were a critically important component of the political work of identity formation and nation building, and teachers occupied an elevated status within cultural nationalist ideologies and organizations. An aphorism printed on a Work/Study Center brochure plainly expressed the interconnected nature of nation building and teaching: "To build our nation, build our people. To build our people, teach our children!"[156] Moreover, Mtumishi St. Julien pointed out that Ahidiana's work, including that of the Work/Study Center, was "done in the spirit of changing the minds and hearts of our people to make a positive change in the lives of African people here and abroad."[157]

Rickford has cited the importance of Pan-African nationalist educational institutions in reconstructing African American identity in the post–Jim Crow era. Women were central to what he described as a "vibrant Black Power submovement." Tayari kwa Salaam quoted Mwalimu Shujaa, who wrote that strategic, differentiated education and schooling played significant roles in bolstering "African-American resistance to political and cultural domination" and shaping the development of the Black "cultural nation."[158] Independent Black institutions' roles as "vital mechanisms of 'black consciousness,' which inculcated a sense of pride and awareness, a bulwark against the self-abnegation of 'Negro' mentality," meant that the women who filled the ranks of the schools' educator corps occupied an important position within the Black Power movement.[159]

Like the other schools highlighted in this chapter, the Work/Study Center functioned as an incubator where new groups of nationalists could be developed. Teachers at the Work/Study Center instilled nationalist values, undertaking the tasks of either reinforcing ideals taught in students' homes or introducing the paradigm to children from the broader Ninth Ward community.[160] Notably, although the instructors reinforced Kawaida values such as the Nguzo Saba, theirs was a syncretic version of the doctrine, which openly advocated women's equality.[161] As Rickford has pointed out, Ahidiana developed a "stronger ethic of self-criticism" than other Pan-African cultural nationalist formations. Put differently, the version of Kawaida values taught at the Work/Study Center was more egalitarian than others in terms of gender role socialization.

Teachers at the Work/Study Center instructed students with a curriculum based in Kawaida-inspired values that extended beyond the Seven Principles. For instance, children were also taught the importance of *kazi*, which was underscored in a myriad of ways. *Kazi* was reflected in the term "work" in the school's name. It was embedded in the Darasa/Kazi teaching method. Darasa/Kazi meant "class/work" and differentiated two instructional approaches. "Darasa" referred to formal, structured class time. "Kazi" was the name given to the children's independent study time. Contradicting stereotypes that cast African Americans as lazy, Work/Study teachers regularly reinforced the idea that "Afrikan people have a lot to do. We are always doing Kazi."[162]

The Work/Study teaching philosophies and methods also revealed how Ahidiana members conceived of leadership as closely tied to the concepts of *kazi* and *ujima* (collective work and responsibility). Service was expressed as a key part of collective work and responsibility as well as leadership. Quoting Sekou Toure, Tayari kwa Salaam wrote, "You either serve the people or you use the people. There is no in between." Pupils, she continued, were taught "the value and responsibility of leading and following." As with other Ahidiana projects, all participants were given the opportunity to lead on a rotating basis, regardless of gender. Teachers explained to the students, "We believe in collective leadership and one person cannot always lead."[163] Tayari kwa Salaam's explanations provided a view of leadership models as conceived and operationalized by the rank-and-file women in an informal network of Kawaida-influenced groups rather than by the philosophy's best-known and most powerful male leaders.

Beyond imparting Kawaida-influenced doctrine, the school's mission was also to affirm Black lives and shape students into revolutionaries. School administrators and teachers focused on African Americans' identity, purpose, and direction in the struggle for power and liberation. They asserted "the worth and dignity of Black life and the Black liberation struggle."[164] Like The East family, the Ahidiana organization claimed space in one of the roughest neighborhoods in the United States to affirm Black lives in the process of nurturing their students at the Work/Study Center.[165] As Vera Warren-Williams claimed, "That was revolutionary thinking, . . . that you would choose to educate your own children in a house that was converted to a school that taught more on the level of discipline, cultural and global awareness, proper diet, exercise, and it didn't follow the norm."[166] According to the school's mission statement, the Work/Study staff was "not trying to raise 'cute' simply Black and beautiful children or 'smart' (high IQs) children who will feed into and become a part of the American system." Instead, "We are trying to raise soldiers and warriors, future leaders in our people's struggle for power and national liberation. Power to our people must start with education for our children. . . . Tomorrow will belong to us, only if we educate our children today. Power to our people, education to our children."[167]

Although women were at the heart of the educational process at the Work/Study Center, it would be a mistake to overstate how much agency women wielded in the struggle to overturn male dominance. Patriarchy was embedded in the ostensibly egalitarian missions of independent and supplementary Black institutions. Women founded and operated schools in which they played critical roles, but the masculinist framing of liberation and leadership meant that, for the most part, the institutions reproduced the male supremacy embedded in the majority culture. It is thus important to explore the ways women and girls navigated such realities in local organizations.[168]

The imprint of women's agency can be seen in Work/Study Center literature. Female advocates left their mark, but masculine privilege inside and outside the organization has never been fully obliterated. Though Kawaida-influenced, it reflects Ahidiana's movement beyond the practice of encouraging marginal roles for women. Both men and women were uplifted in school literature, poems, and songs as Ahidiana evolved.

Early Work/Study Center writings promoted males as formal leaders with women and girls as their complements, while later literature contained more egalitarian language. In the 1974 collection of children's stories titled *Who Will Speak for Us?*, female characters were praised for having such traits as organizational skills, technical expertise, wit, directness, and intelligence. The book, nevertheless, culminated with the election of a male character as the representative who would speak for the others.[169] On the other hand, Work/Study students were taught a chant that evolved from the Kawaida saying "Sifa ote mtu weusi" (All praises to the Black man). Earlier versions were taught to children at the African Free School, helped define The East Brotherhood's codes, and can be heard in the 1969 jazz song "Baraka," by James Mtume. The Work/Study Center adaptation entreated students to recite the following in English and Swahili:

> All praises due to the Creator.
> All praises due to the Afrikan man.
> All praises due to the Afrikan woman.
> All praises due to Afrikan children.
> All praises due to Afrikan life.[170]

The more gender-inclusive wording represented a "modernization" of the Pan-African cultural nationalist literacy archive.[171]

Despite its significance as the site of an evolving form of Kawaida-influenced Pan-African nationalism, the Work/Study Center, like many other IBIs, faced external issues and internal weaknesses, rendering it unsustainable. Establishing and sustaining independent schools was a fiscally demanding endeavor. Ahidiana's modest tuition was insufficient to cover operating expenses, yet fees remained out of reach for most Ninth Ward residents. Few revenue streams existed for the school beyond tuition. Although they accepted supporters' donations, advocates eschewed government funding and regulation as a method of avoiding external control. Even if they had sought those resources, municipal or state funds might have been difficult to procure, as federal support for local governments fell by 60 percent between 1980 and 1988. Moreover, African Americans from all walks of life experienced dramatically declining incomes during the [Ronald] Reagan years, a reality that meant that women who may have otherwise sustained the Work/Study Center sought employment outside Ahidiana's enterprises to help their families make ends meet.[172]

Activist burnout, changing values, and social attrition—a feeling among members that they no longer fit or could continue in the group for various reasons—also contributed to the demise of the Work/Study Center, Ahidiana, and the advocates' broader New Orleans Pan-African cultural nationalist network. Ahidiana's children were left to cope with the culture shock of attending public schools as they progressed beyond the Work/Study Center's course offerings. Moreover, the level of *kazi* demanded from the women running the school took its own toll. It became increasingly hard for advocates to commit to sustaining the Work/Study Center after their own children had moved on.[173] To make matters worse, Tayari kwa Salaam, the school's chief administrator/teacher, was struck with a brain tumor. In her narrative, she expressed the feeling of weariness that weighed on many of the teachers: "We [were] tired. Okay? We [were] tired." Besides exhaustion, a general sense of malaise among activists caused attrition. As the radical 1960s and early 1970s succumbed to conservative backlash, some advocates left the organization, deeming it too radical and anti-establishment for the changing times. Others exited the working-class community to which Ahidiana belonged, seeking middle-class professions and more affluent neighborhoods. Still others left as they exchanged the idealism of the early years for jaded critiques of certain group practices. The philosophies seemed too essentialized, "dogmatic," and "socially isolating" to some former advocates.[174]

Many of Ahidiana's core families dissolved in this context. Divorce was a recurring theme in narratives about Ahidiana, particularly as splintered families left some female advocates unable to maintain the level of vigorous *kazi* that the struggle demanded. The erosion of Ahidiana's *ujamaa*-based practices and the dissolution of two-parent households meant that community mamas found themselves emotionally and economically isolated, struggling to function as single mothers focused on making a living for themselves and their children during the era of Reaganomics. As a result, several women, including Tayari kwa Salaam, went into what one former student called "survival mode." Managing daily existence in such difficult circumstances forced the women, who had once been standard bearers of Kawaida-influenced Pan-African cultural nationalism, to move away from their staunch advocacy of Black nationalist values, particularly as related to diet and education. In 1986 the Work/Study Center closed amid the erosion of the other organizations that formed the bedrock of New Orleans-based cultural nationalism.[175]

In his recollections, Kalamu ya Salaam captured the ambivalent character of a period that brought both empowerment and disappointment. "We had our contradictions. We had our problems and so forth and so on," he said. "It was struggle. Let's not romanticize. People start talking about the good old days and all that bullshit. We had some heavy, heavy struggle that we had to go through." Even so, he contended, "we accomplished a great deal."[176]

Schools were important outlets for women's political work within the Pan-African cultural nationalist organizations rooted in earlier iterations of Kawaida, which limited women's gender roles to home, education, and the support of men's agendas. Advocates in Us, CFUN/CAP, The East, and Ahidiana conceptualized womanhood as a characteristically African identity, but the Black nationalist expression of gender roles also resembled the mainstream American early national period concept of republican motherhood. Like republican mothers, members of the majority-female teaching corps associated with Kawaida-influenced IBIs were central to the process of developing good citizens in the budding nation and leveraged their access to the education, training, and leadership opportunities to move beyond prescribed gender roles. Moreover, Pan-African cultural nationalist women employed values like *kazi* and *ujamaa* in their positions as educators to create and extend programs such as communal childcare. Such programs helped advocates, whatever their gender, perform important political work beyond their domestic duties.

# Epilogue

## "Kazi *Like You Mean It*": Kazi *Leadership Lessons in Contemporary Context*

When I began researching this topic, I hoped to avoid reinforcing narratives of Black Power as a period of decline.[1] Examining shortcomings and ebbs in the development of philosophies, organizations, and movements, however, is integral to any serious study. As a movement veteran pointed out, the most painful legacies of the period are the unresolved issues, misinformation, broken relationships, anger, and competing narratives between activists who were once comrades.[2] Remnants of conflict are quite pronounced in several cultural nationalists' testimonies. Academics such as Komozi Woodard, Scot Brown, Kwasi Konadu, Michael Simanga, and Russell Rickford have also documented this type of discord. Some theorists assert that advocates abandoned their initial radicalism. Others observe that 1960s nationalists fell short of their ultimate goal of attaining self-governing, economically self-sufficient, territorially based nationhood; that activists' emphasis on unity masked serious differences; and that their focus on personal change and self-help was ineffective in bringing about structural change.[3] Others point out that many met the "challenge of continuity" through their ideological definitions of nationhood as an enduring sense of community among African-descended people. Advocates produced knowledge, built institutions, and sustained programs as manifestations of Pan-Africanist cultural nationalist ideology.[4] One could argue that these Black nationalists' shortcomings do not constitute a story of degeneration but one of evolution amid changing times.

It is true, however, that Pan-African cultural nationalist organizations were experiencing institutional decline and faced pressure from multiple sources by the mid-1970s. Conflict, internal and external, was a factor that debilitated the advocates and their organizations. Intergroup conflict plagued the Black freedom struggle of the late 1960s and early 1970s, particularly due to the intervening forces of state repression. Other external pressures also crippled the liberation struggle. For example, the FBI's domestic counterintelligence program and Karenga's incarceration caused a fragmentation and transformation of the Us Organization.

The Congress of African People transformed when the leaders' turn from cultural nationalism to Marxism-Leninism-Maoism led to the organization's weakening and ultimate absorption by the League of Revolutionary Struggle, a group mainly consisting of Asian American and Latine Marxist-Leninists. Additionally, throughout the 1970s and 1980s, the general climate of American political conservatism grew, even as the Black middle class expanded, and greater numbers of centrist and left-leaning African Americans won public office. Both The East organization and Ahidiana struggled with limited funds and declined in the face of these challenges.

The Us Organization and the Black Panther Party became embroiled in an ideological conflict over the leadership of the Black revolt. The dispute resulted in the denunciation of cultural nationalism by many of the Panthers and their advocates, who saw it as diametrically opposed to revolutionary nationalism. Cultural nationalists endured such critics' disparagement and disdain. Meanwhile, state programs such as COINTELPRO exploited the conflict between Us and the BPP. Under the direction of J. Edgar Hoover, the FBI surveilled, incapacitated, and destroyed several organizations in an effort to hamper the liberation movement. Among other tactics, agents used propaganda to provoke and worsen conflicts like those occurring between and within cultural nationalist and revolutionary nationalist organizations. As a result, the conflict reached a fever pitch in a January 17, 1969, shoot-out between Us and Black Panther Party members on the UCLA campus that left two Panthers, John Huggins and Alprentice "Bunchy" Carter, dead.[5]

After the UCLA shooting, advocates report witnessing Karenga's deterioration as a leader. He became fatigued, paranoid, and substance-addicted, and his authoritarianism intensified. Karenga's diminished leadership capacity, coupled with state disruption efforts, created conditions for the installation of a violently oppressive form of Us Organization leadership and transformed the organization at its core. The period beginning with the UCLA shooting in 1969 became known as "the Crisis." Individual members' lives drastically changed during this period, as subgroups within Us began to function like security personnel protecting Karenga against the Panthers and the state. A pervasive sense of "paranoia" and a "siege mentality" began to envelop the organization.[6]

Convicted in June 1971 on charges of assault and false imprisonment, Karenga was sentenced to a one-to-ten-year prison term for torturing two female Us advocates, Deborah Jones and Gail Davis. He believed that Davis was attempting to poison him. Karenga and some advocates, however, viewed his conviction as part of a larger conspiracy to discredit him as a leader of the Black revolt.[7] Other activists maintained that the incident reflected Karenga's long-standing personal shortcomings and overall inadequacies as a leader.[8] Certain women who were former Us members remembered "the Crisis" as a turning point that eroded their faith and drove them away from the organization. Amina Thomas, for example, viewed the abuse of the two female advocates and absence of public atonement as a betrayal of Black women. Some former Kawaida advocates continue to assert that Karenga's lack of remorse and failure to apologize openly nullified his ability to effectively represent the Black freedom struggle, explaining this as one reason that they left the organization.[9] Others, like Karenga's second wife, Tiamoyo Karenga (formerly Luz Maria Tamayo), who was also implicated in the attack, continued serving as Kawaida standard bearers, eventually articulating views on Kawaida and women's gender roles.[10] Faithful members such as Subira Kifano also filled post-1975 Us ranks for several decades.

Varying impulses marked the Us Organization's "Crisis" period. On one hand, it was the era that gave rise to the Matamba women's unit, whose members trained in armed self-defense and martial arts to serve the organization in security capacities. According to Scot Brown, women's service in such security functions stimulated the Us Organization's ideological shift away from male supremacy toward greater recognition of gender equality in the early 1970s. Yet increasing militarization coupled with the group's tarnished public perception after the UCLA shooting may have caused some would-be supporters to view organization members as threatening. In particular, many critics claimed that the Us Organization had victimized the Panthers. Although Us continued to perform some of its community activities, popular support waned as its members were increasingly discredited, and the organization lost its core membership as well as larger support networks. During Karenga's "post-1975 reentry into Black nationalist activism," advocates reconstituted the organization in the forms of the Afro-American Movement, Kawaida Groundwork Committee, and the Organization Us. Though active and dedicated, Us has not, however, regained the level of popularity and influence it enjoyed in the 1960s. Only a few active members from the 1960s returned to Us in the late 1970s.[11]

The dissolution of the Us Organization's leadership and the group's decline as a significant actor within the Black Power movement coincided with the rise of the Congress of African People in the movement, with Amiri Baraka and CFUN at its helm. Formed in 1970, CAP reached its zenith during the 1972 National Black Political Convention. Woodard characterized CAP as "the most formidable black nationalist organization in the country" because of its nationwide branch membership as well as its influence on other important groups and individuals within the Black freedom struggle.[12] Despite CAP's growing authority, the organization's most productive years were not conflict-free. For instance, Baraka's security forces clashed with a group of Us Simba at the seminal 1970 Black Power conference at Atlanta University that was aimed at forming CAP. The incident was particularly notable because part of CFUN's security unit consisted of former Us advocates who had moved away from California. The California advocates also left the Committee for a Unified Newark after several months, disagreeing with the leadership over multiple issues, including CFUN's implementation of Kawaida principles. Amina Baraka's strong condemnation of polygyny is reported to have particularly offended several in the California contingent, who continued to maintain such family units while in New Jersey. Despite points of disagreement with former Us members, CAP affiliates played significant roles in advocating for Karenga's release from prison. Additionally, some former affiliates in Brooklyn, Chicago, and New Orleans helped revitalize and maintain cultural nationalist ideologies and Kawaida-influenced practices and institutions into the 1980s.[13]

CAP's leadership struggled to enlarge its reach amid shifting political sands at the height of its influence in 1972. CAP and CFUN leaders began to waver in their own beliefs about the organization's power and the rightness of its approach. CFUN spearheaded construction projects aimed at assisting Newark's African American communities as the growing populations expanded beyond the established boundaries of the ghettoized Central and South Wards. Despite their good intentions, activists faced resistance ranging from legal wrangling and bureaucratic red tape to mob threats and violent attacks from White vigilantes. Additionally, after taking office, mayor Kenneth Gibson seemed to withdraw support for the very Black convention movement activists who had helped him win election.[14]

Because of what Woodard termed a "profound crisis in faith," the Barakas increasingly considered theories of socialism as leading-edge ideologies for the organization, and they turned to Marxism as a culmination of that process. This philosophical turn signaled the decline of CAP-led Pan-African cultural nationalism. Funding for Kawaida Towers, Kawaida Community Development, the Project Area Committee (PAC), and the African Free School was withdrawn, and those programs were dismantled. The Newark Housing Authority ordered the demolition of the buildings housing the PAC office, CAP's theater, the television studio training program, the National Black Assembly, ALSC headquarters, and the AFS classrooms. The New Jersey Housing Finance Agency buried the $1.5 million foundation of Kawaida Towers. Amiri Baraka was further radicalized by these local developments as his national political authority within the Black freedom struggle weakened.[15]

Ideological divisions surfaced beginning in 1974 within the modern Black convention movement and had intensified by 1976. As African Americans' allegiance shifted from independent politics to the Democratic Party, CAP changed its ideological foundation from nationalism to national communism. Additionally, CAP became embroiled in a struggle over the preferred approach to Pan-Africanism (class-based organizing with the Left or race-focused cultural nationalism) among African Liberation Day committee activists, a split from which the organization would never recover. By 1976, the African Liberation Support Committee and the Black Women's United Front were in disarray due to internal conflict. The Barakas ultimately disowned cultural nationalism. This marked the end of the Newark Black Power experiment.[16]

East organizational leaders, preoccupied with institutional survival, were also beset by changing circumstances on local and national levels. While community and institutional development marked The East's formative years from 1969 to 1977, the following decade was a period of decline and ultimate organizational demise. As with other Kawaida-influenced cadres, which were inherently inwardly focused, small-group formations, The East family grew isolated from the larger community in which it existed. Transient membership and a more eclectic organizing style than other Kawaida-influenced groups left the institution with an unclear guiding vision, opening The East to members with a weak sense of commitment or purpose. This porousness may have even led to infiltration by agents provocateurs. Unresolved challenges in interpersonal relationships, unstable leadership of the educational institutions that advocates viewed as The East's centerpiece, and poor business management also contributed to organizational dissolution. The decline of Ahidiana's Work/Study Center, also a central institutional component, spelled the end of the New Orleans organization as well.[17]

In 1976 The East turned the Sumner Avenue Armory into the Uhuru Cultural Center, where all operations were moved after a period of decentralization. The only exception was The East Catering, which remained at 10 Claver Place until a fire destroyed the building that housed the enterprise. The Uhuru Cultural Center went through a period of expansion during which administrators rented it to other community groups, including a gun club that came under government surveillance. Concert organizers also used the venue, and an event-goer was tragically murdered during one of their shows. These events tarnished The East's image among officials and community members, leading to increased scrutiny from city authorities, seizure of the armory in 1986 for use as a homeless shelter, and ultimately the organization's demise in the same year. The International African Arts Festival, which still takes place each June, is the only remaining East enterprise.[18]

In their oral history narratives, second-generation advocates communicated a sense of sadness and frustration that independent Black institutions were so limited in their sustainability and footprint. Kwasi Konadu called the phenomenon "the challenge of continuity." Konadu stated that Black nationalism had been "dormant" or "fragmented" during certain historical periods. He framed the issue of sustainability as a test of courage and determination, asserting that advancing "a sense of self and community in an environment that is hostile to such advancement is a testimony to the African spirit and its humanity." Konadu framed the lasting efforts of Pan-African cultural nationalists via their IBIs as a challenge to the "power relations within the existing social order" and a form of resistance to cultural hegemony.[19] Rickford also spoke to the importance of these projects, writing that Pan-African nationalists' efforts not only served the practical, material needs of movement advocates but also fueled utopian hopes and dreams that self-help initiatives and institution building would rearrange the power relations of an oppressive state.[20] The narratives collected for this book reflected similar themes, as second-generation Pan-Africanist nationalists reported feeling a sense of shock over transitioning from the nurturing environment of their communities to the broader, mainstream society. Such sentiments may speak to the cadre organizing method's shortcomings, as Rickford has pointed out.[21]

Second-generation advocates' sense of malaise after leaving Kawaida-influenced Pan-African nationalist schools also highlights the roots of administrators' *kazi*-driven mission to design and maintain the institutions as bulwarks against Eurocentricity. Young, second-generation advocates viewed their educators' shielding approach to guiding students as both protective and coddling. Kwesi Ayo Nantambu, who was an Ahidiana Work/Study student, explained, "I had the inner-city life of New Orleans, . . . and I had the cultural side. There were some [classmates] who only saw the Ahidiana side . . . and . . . middle-class living, up until they [went] to college, and . . . it gave a false reality [of what] the world was like." Kwesi said that, when he left the Work/Study Center at the age of ten, he experienced "the reality of coming back to New Orleans in the [1980s]."[22]

Kwesi Nantambu suggested that Ahidiana's advocates may have been naïve in their optimism about changing the world. He contended that some of his male classmates battled mental health issues when they had to make their way in mainstream schools after the Ahidiana Work/Study Center closed. Ahidiana members advanced the idea that a "pro-Black world and progressive world" was imminent, he explained. His classmates saw that African Americans outside the Work/Study Center were suffering from "mental slavery" as well as many other issues and observed that Pan-African nationalists possessed a "progressive mindset." He lamented, "Our mindset was more the minority than the majority. . . . Some people couldn't handle that and still have had issues handling it."[23]

*Kazi* leaders, in their roles as mothers, echoed the sense of disappointment about movement institutions' limitations in shielding children from harsh realities such as racism, internalized self-hatred, economic inequality, drug addiction, misogyny, homophobia, and dysfunctional families. There was no panacea in Black nationalism—or in socialism, for that matter. Amina Baraka confessed, "I'm so sad . . . because I can't protect my children. No individual can protect their children. I can't protect them. I [have] a daughter. My oldest daughter is fifty-one and she's a dope addict. She's out on the street. . . . We can't help her." Expounding on the violence that affected her children's lives, she said, "I have had a son shot in the head with a .357 Magnum. We pulled him through. He's alive."[24]

The story of the Barakas' younger daughter, Shani, viscerally demonstrated the need for the Black freedom struggle to address the multiple forms of oppression that all African Americans face. The husband of Shani's older sister, Wanda Wilson-Pasha, stalked the elder sibling and killed the younger in an act of domestic violence.[25] "I have a daughter who was murdered," Amina Baraka lamented. "My [older daughter, Wanda's] husband killed her, shot her in the fucking head. . . . She was gay, and he killed her partner too. He killed her. He killed both of them."[26] At Shani's memorial service, older brother Ras Baraka posed the following incisive questions: "Why couldn't we save her in all of our Blackness, prayers, our revolution talk, our [healing] conferences? Why couldn't we keep her alive? How can we shape a community and let our little sister die?"[27]

The Barakas' story emphasizes the need for a radically inclusive movement, yet researchers and advocates alike have remarked that Kawaida-influenced cultural nationalism was overly focused on racial and cultural unity, and that it glossed over internal diversity and differences. Observers contend that the philosophy fell short on issues of gender and sexuality.[28] Tayari kwa Salaam discussed the ways the idea of "we" in Ahidiana masked differences within their community of activists. "With no idea of multiple subjectivities, I looked only at my ethnic, cultural, and racial subjectivity," she reflected concerning her early years in the organization. "I was also blind to who I was as an African American woman."[29]

While many women navigated and resisted male dominance in Kawaida-influenced organizations, some would ultimately repudiate cultural nationalism altogether. Theorists like Michael Simanga have documented Amina Baraka's ideological transition and influence on her husband.[30] Amina denounced cultural nationalism when she became a Marxist. Explaining why she decided to distance herself from Pan-African cultural nationalism, she said, "There was a whole group of people who [were] willing to talk about Africa, willing to braid hair, willing to run for office, . . . but they [were] not willing to fight for the working class. I left." Describing interactions that catalyzed her migration toward Marxism-Leninism-Maoism, she said, "When I came upon those students [at] Howard University and Central State, all those young students that followed [Stokely] Carmichael and who followed the SNCC people, [in] SOBU [and] YOBU, . . . they [were] talking the kind of talk I wanted to hear!" She explained further that some of the college graduates involved in Left Pan-African nationalism had come from working-class families and challenged cultural nationalists' ideologies and tactics.[31] The evolution in her approach initially caused friction in her own family. "I had to fight my husband then. I said, 'No, I'm with them, I'm with them,' and of course, I made mistakes. I made a lot of mistakes. . . . We fought like dogs. I was so afraid that I was going to lose my children and my marriage, but I took the chance because I'd rather be free or dead than tell a lie."[32]

The activism of committed individuals like Amina Baraka changed gender mandates in Black Power-era Pan-African nationalist groups, but beliefs and practices related to women's equity varied, falling on a continuum. Some responses can be categorized as Kawaida-womanist assertions of complementarity that pose a moderate challenge to masculinist privilege. Other forms of resistance were overt feminist assertions of complete gender equality, which condemned ideas and practices supporting male dominance.

Additional themes of decline and shortcoming surfaced in the oral history narratives.[33] For instance, the emphasis on a narrow self-conception of Blackness, African culture, and identity was also problematic, and has been well documented in the literature.[34] Amina Baraka forwarded the critique that some advocates expressed Black pride in superficial ways and clung to it at the expense of what she deemed more effective ideologies that analyzed multiple forms of oppression.[35] Tayari kwa Salaam anecdotally discussed a class during which she asked her New Orleans-based Work/Study Center students to indicate where they lived on a world map. She wrote that they responded by pointing to the continent of Africa.[36] In essence, the women recognized that the constructed, idealized traditional "Africa" of cultural nationalist ideology was problematic. They critiqued cultural nationalist practices that propagated utopian images of Africa rather than undertaking meaningful engagement with contemporary African Americans and Africans with their varied and dynamic cultures, economic statuses, political orientations, and perceptions of gender.

* * *

Although themes of decline were evident in the women's narratives, they were also filled with positive memories of time spent in Kawaida-influenced formations. Female advocates described the groups as places where families formed and grew. They also remembered the organizations as spaces that catalyzed and fostered their activism, leadership, and long-lasting collegial relationships. Aminisha Black fondly recalled that handsome young men flocked to The East.[37] Martha Bright pointed out that The East was mainly composed of teens and young adults, many of whom came of age, found partners, and became parents during their time in the organization.[38] Positive memories of budding romantic and familial relationships were reflected in the stories of women in other cultural nationalist organizations as well, which is not surprising given the importance of families within Black nationalist ideology. For instance, Jaribu Hill said that she found her "life partner" in the movement. The couple brought a daughter into the world while they were involved with CFUN and the Congress of African People.[39] As families formed, Pan-African nationalist women exhibited *kazi* leadership by developing methods for parents to remain politically active through such practices as communal daycare.[40]

Female East advocates addressed the importance of an "irreplaceable Sisterhood," forging an awareness of themselves, shaping a larger feeling of community, and sustaining their activism.[41] Shukuru Sanders expressed that a sense of family kept her feeling close to the people and ideas of The East once the organization disbanded. Abimbola Wali emphasized in her narrative that she developed "forty-five-year plus" friendships with East women. According to Bright's accounts, The East Sisterhood continued to plan national and international reunions and cultural trips as well as local functions long after The East ceased to formally exist. They also wrote and distributed an annual newsletter at an East Kwanzaa reunion.[42]

Creating an irreplaceable sisterhood was not a trivial achievement. An array of pervasive popular images—such as the domineering, angry matriarch Sapphire from the mid-twentieth-century *Amos 'n' Andy Show*—depict African American women as rude, mean, treacherous, angry, bossy, and unable to trust or work with others.[43] In the face of these stereotypes, real-world examples of Black women's cooperation are important for fostering female leadership, especially so present-day activists in the fight for liberation, justice, and equality can draw on historical examples to shape their own organizing.

Emphasizing these accomplishments is in no way meant to mask underlying discord and vitriol among various individuals and organizations. In particular, the groups that were largely networks of blood and marital relations fragmented when families dissolved.[44] Rickford and others have examined such issues, including the "two-line" struggle, which took the form of an ideological conflict between advocates of various tendencies ranging from African socialism to Marxism.[45] Effective leadership requires the ability to privilege teamwork, and cultural nationalist women's models of *kazi* leadership exhibited the power of what they believed to be "collective work and responsibility."

Some of Jaribu Hill's fond memories highlighted the demanding aspects of the Black freedom struggle and how they shaped her into a *kazi* leader. "I learned how, as a woman, I could use my voice to provide leadership, to provide guidance, to provide friendship and sisterhood," Hill asserted. Through the organizations, she learned to "challenge some of the stark representations of chauvinism and male domination or patriarchy." She saw her time in CFUN and the related CAP united front organization as a turning point during which she grew to embody a "revolutionary" kind of womanhood. Once women in CFUN agitated to broaden their roles beyond the realm of social organization, Hill observed, they took on various tasks like running for office, working on political campaigns, and leading demonstrations. According to her account, women participated in the "theoretical work" and intellectual life of the organization as well.[46]

Hill specified the types of opportunities impacting her development in CAP. She and many other women in the group organized workshops, moderated political discussions, and engaged in similar leadership activities. She described her exposure to politics through what has been called an ambitious African American attempt to form a third political party. "Through the National Independent Black Political Party," she said, "we were able to work as activists and organizers and were treated with a sense of equality and respect. We sat at tables with Shirley Chisolm[,] Charles Diggs, and Richard Hatcher." Hill emphasized that both Amiri and Amina Baraka fostered such opportunities so women and men in the organization could be part of developing the internal framework for key political organizations and interacting with nationally known African American leaders.[47]

Building on her politicized performances with the Spirit House Movers and Players in Newark, Hill went on to compose and perform "contemporary freedom music" with her husband as part of the folk duo Serious Bizness in 1978.[48] Working as a union organizer and adult educator for a time, she later attended CUNY School of Law. Upon graduating in 1995, Hill received the prestigious Skadden Fellowship to support advocacy work, which took her to Mississippi. The following year, Hill founded the Mississippi Workers' Center for Human Rights, focused on advocating, organizing, and training impoverished workers and their families. The workers' center frames issues, from exploitative pay to racism, in the context of human rights violations.[49] Through her advocacy, Hill embodies the *kazi* leadership legacy.

Aminisha Black and Martha Bright also had life-altering experiences in Kawaida-influenced Pan-African nationalist organizations, but theirs took place through The East. Black emphasized that other women experienced The East as an incubator for valuable skills, which they would use in their future roles as community educators, organizers, and administrators. She wrote that Isoke Nia Kierstedt received teacher training and spent a decade as an Uhuru Sasa educator after reading about the school in *Black News* and enrolling her daughter. Kierstedt eventually became director of research and development for the Columbia University Teachers College Reading and Writing Project and the founder of a literacy consulting organization.[50] Black wrote about several other women who served in various capacities after their time at The East, from public educators and higher education professionals to proprietors of independent institutions, some of which still exist. Fela (formerly

Frances) Barclift opened Little Sun People Early Childhood Development and Little Sun People Too!, both in Brooklyn. Ayanna Johnson is the founder of Weusi Shule in Brooklyn's Crown Heights, now known as Johnson Preparatory School.[51]

The topic of women's leadership in the realm of education is significant. Radio show host Dwight Brewster stressed the importance of cultural nationalist women's guidance of independent and supplementary Black educational pursuits, pointing out that women in The East helped develop institutions that were precursors to charter schools.[52] Rickford also highlighted African Americans' enthusiasm for charter schools, partially as a theoretical and practical outgrowth of the 1960s and 1970s independent education movement.[53] Black Power advocates have nonetheless vehemently disagreed over the nature and meaning of charter schooling and other elements of educational choice.

Many activists viewed the movement as "politically conservative" and ultimately corrupted by hostile interests, including "corporate multiculturalism."[54] Some women who were active in the independent and supplementary school movement to build what have been referred to as "parallel structures" through the more left-leaning Pan-African nationalist organizations argued that reformed public schools were the most pragmatic method of educating the masses of Black students. Given the fact that most students were publicly educated, left-leaning Pan-African nationalists opposed mechanisms that could funnel resources away from public schools.[55]

Former CFUN advocate Jaribu Hill spoke to such educational matters in her narrative. "I have issues with charter schools," Hill said. "I don't think you can compare a Freedom School that was operating because there was very little available for people of color . . . to what we're seeing now with the charter schools literally sucking resources out of the public school system, a system that's broken and has been broken." Hill criticized charters because they "will only service a small amount of kids."[56]

Other female advocates of Pan-African nationalism have demonstrated leadership in the realm of educational choice. Advocates of school choice initiatives maintain that they are aimed at giving a broad range of parents opportunities to access good schools for their children, not merely those who can afford private schools or who live in affluent areas. The financial apportionments attached to charters and other school choice programs have been attractive for cash-strapped IBI operators. For instance, education and social policy professor Carol D. Lee (Safisha Madhubuti) developed an independent Black educational institution along with her husband, poet Haki Madhubuti. The school, called New Concept Center, opened in 1972 in an economically marginalized, crime-ridden, majority-Black South Side neighborhood in Chicago and was a unit of the Kawaida-influenced Institute for Positive Education. New Concept became a charter school in the 1990s, eventually expanding to three campuses, the Betty Shabazz and Barbara Sizemore Academies as well as the DuSable Leadership Academy, which Chicago Public Schools began phasing out in 2003. Faculty and staff faced an uphill battle in serving the needs of the academies' student body in terms of achieving academic benchmarks and maintaining charters. Community members praised school administrators, faculty, and staff for instilling pride and self-esteem in the children, who faced daily racial and class struggles.[57]

Similarly emphasizing African Americans' basic right to culturally relevant, self-determined education, former Pittsburgh CAP member Tamanika Howze discussed her post-1980s work in Children's Defense Fund (CDF) Freedom Schools. Freedom Schools are supplementary institutions aimed at shaping college-aged servant leaders to spark a passion for literacy, learning, and social action in primary and middle school students. Inspired by SNCCs example, Marian Wright Edelman resurrected the Freedom School mission through the CDF's Black Community Crusade for Children in 1995. Howze directed the Kingsley-Lincoln Freedom School in Pittsburgh, one of more than sixty nationwide CDF Freedom Schools. The schools still emphasized culture as an indispensable component of an effective educational process, and the children's days at Freedom Schools began with African dance, drumming, and "*harambee* time."[58] Howze has carried on the legacies of Pan-African cultural nationalism as a community leader. She specifically employed aspects of Kawaida alongside the ideas of figures from Ella Baker to Malcolm X in a syncretic way, delivering important life lessons to Pittsburgh-area students.[59]

Howze undertook administrative work in Freedom Schools to help combat the educational and economic disparities that remained entrenched in her community, and her work reflects the tenets of *kazi* leadership in this way. As an education advocate, "Freedom School ambassador," and antiwar agitator, she has continued the types of activities in which she engaged during her CAP years.[60] For instance, she organized events aimed at raising awareness about the challenges that many low-income residents of Pittsburgh faced and educating and assisting them with the process of accessing social services.[61] As a member of the NAACP education committee, she assisted with monitoring African American students' performance in Pittsburgh schools.[62] She was cited in 2004 as an individual who made a significant impact in the field of education.[63] Howze was at the forefront of reviving Pittsburgh's 1960s Harambee Black Arts Festival as its coordinator in the 1980s and early 1990s. Hailed in 2001 for having been a promoter of Black consciousness for more than a decade, she continued to focus on transnational, Pan-African issues in her advocacy.[64]

Historians have pointed out that Pan-African cultural nationalists' methods and models inspired the development of multiple institutions and events, many of which were woman-led. Women also employed some of the skills they acquired in Pan-African cultural nationalist organizations in their roles as community leaders.[65] For instance, Tayari kwa Salaam and Carol Bebelle formed VITAL in 1988. The New Orleans-based venture was an annual seven-week summer supplementary education program that took an interdisciplinary approach to math, science, history, literacy, the arts, and culture. VITAL lasted for a decade, resurrecting some of the effective methods from Ahidiana Work/Study Center while discarding others.[66] In the Organization Us, Subira Kifano continued to be a leader in her community as assistant director of the African American Cultural Center and in her position as a public speaker lecturing on Black history. After she left the group in 1997, she promoted the observance of Kwanzaa and garnered recognition for her acumen as an educator until her death in 2016.[67]

\* \* \*

The recurring theme of family in the narratives included memories of children as indispensable to the goals of institutional and community development as well as nation building. An article headline and a CFUN birth rite seemed to both illustrate this belief. The words "our youth will build our nation" were written above an East-related news article, and the CFUN ritual proclaimed, "Children are life after death, the only way we can live is through children and great works."[68] It is therefore not surprising that women advocates often described their offspring as living legacies. They suggested that their daughters and sons were among the greatest results of their organizing efforts. That Black Power bore fruit in 1990s Afrocentricity reveals the significance of organizing that protected and supported young people but also allowed them to express their own viewpoints and concerns about the ideologies and methods of the Black liberation struggle.[69] Future studies should investigate youth and childhood in Pan-African cultural nationalist organizations, particularly inquiring about advocates involved in Afrocentric institution building and development a generation after their parents, teachers, and mentors. Although there is a growing body of literature on young people and the Black freedom struggle, more work needs to be done to capture the insight and experiences of youthful students and advocates of cultural nationalism. Researchers should also investigate the role of spirituality in advocates' ideologies, activism, organizing, and personal choices. Several Pan-African cultural nationalist activists critiqued the nature or lack of spirituality in certain nationalist organizations.[70]

Female advocates who navigated and challenged male dominance did much to reform Pan-African cultural nationalism, but they obviously did not dismantle patriarchy. The 2016 and 2024 presidential races involved Hillary Clinton, the first major-party female presidential nominee in the United States, and Kamala Harris, the second woman of any race or ethnicity, the first African-descended woman, and the first individual of South Asian ancestry to be a major party's presidential nominee, contending with an openly racist, xenophobic, and misogynistic White male candidate, who was ultimately elected to office in two nonconsecutive terms. There have been no women elected president of the United States to date, yet Harris's historic election in 2020 as US vice president demonstrates the importance of women's advocacy in making strides toward greater gender equity. Still, the fact that Harris has continued to face an onslaught of sexist stereotypes, microaggressions, and slurs reveals how deeply patriarchy remains embedded in American society.[71]

To make matters more complicated, the past few elections again revealed the limitations, fallacies, and fault lines in feminism. Critiques of Black nationalism continue to indict the movement as stubbornly masculinist. In the dominant culture, not solely in Black nationalist sub-cultures, leadership is still often claimed as the domain of cisgendered heterosexual males by default. Black women activists and organizers additionally continue to encounter White women who privilege racial and class allegiances over loyalty to a putative diverse sisterhood of advocates fighting for gender equity. In the face of continued conflicts over culture, identity, equality, and freedom, women like those in Black Power-era Kawaida-influenced Pan-African cultural nationalist organizations impacted policies, ideologies, and group structures. Their approaches to extant circumstances show that more cooperative models of leadership are necessary and possible. One of the great lessons of *kazi* leadership is that people other than cisgendered heterosexual men can and will find the courage to lead, even in the most difficult of circumstances, whether or not their work is formally recognized and rewarded.

## ACKNOWLEDGMENTS

It took a village to bring this book into being. I thank my ancestors, who paved the way for me to exist and who laid the foundation for my academic achievement. I am grateful to my grandparents, Frank and Leola Blevins, who inspected my grade school report cards, celebrated my successes, urged me to keep improving, and modeled the importance of discipline and consistency. I am especially indebted to Dr. Charlotte "Yeye Ifatoki Fagbenro Sillah" Greer. Modupẹ for your mentorship, knowledge, and comments during an Association for the Study of African American Life and History conference that fundamentally contoured the way I thought about the research for this book. I also dedicate this work to the memory of Pan-African nationalist activists— Queen Nzinga Ratibisha Heru, Amiri Baraka, Subira Kifano, and Abimbola Wali—whose imprint is on this work but who have passed into the realm of the ancestors since its inception. May you all rest well.

My big, nurturing family is the cornerstone of my village. My mother and father, Patricia Blevins McCray and Roy McCray, grew up in notoriously segregated Birmingham, Alabama, during a time when the separate and unequal education system was obviously designed to limit the achievements of people who looked like them. Despite the odds, they both attained university degrees and professional credentials. Their high academic achievement and standards were essential building blocks for this pursuit. Also, the family in my immediate household devoted so much emotional support as well as time and insight to bring this project into the world. A special thanks goes to my husband, Michael A. Foster, for opening a way for me to spend the summer months focused on making this book a reality. You gave me an indispensable gift, and I cannot thank you enough. Our daughters also deserve thanks for listening to my ideas, reading chapters, and providing their ever-growing expertise along the way. Additionally, this book could not exist without my aunts, uncles, siblings, cousins, and in-laws. They have not only been my greatest boosters, but they looked after my young children while I studied and wrote during the early days of my research.

Historically Black colleges and universities (HBCUs) are critically important institutions to my village. I was educated at two HBCUs during the 1990s and early 2000s, where I had encountered several 1960s and 1970s Black Power activists' children and associates during my matriculation. Some of those old acquaintances served as touchstones in our conversations or as gatekeepers, introducing me to family and community members who were movement veterans. Kiini Ibura Salaam, a colleague from Spelman College, introduced me to her creative and accomplished family. As a published author several times over, she also led writing workshops and support groups that I found immensely helpful in completing this project. Many other advocates of Pan-African nationalism gave of themselves in immeasurable ways. Amina Baraka, Amina Thomas, Mtamanika Beatty, Nana Anoa Nantambu, Nilima Mwendo, Kina Joshua-Jasmine, Vera Warren-Williams, and Sababa Akili opened their homes and businesses to my family and me, sharing experiences and meals, their offspring connecting with my daughters over common experiences in unspoken ways. A special shout-out goes to Martha Bright, who has become my respected adviser on the pragmatic applications of sisterhood and *kazi* leadership through this project. Thank you all for your kindness and generosity.

The community of scholars at Georgia State University (GSU) provided the structure and support that were essential for completing this project. This study developed from a literature review essay that Akinyele Umoja assigned at GSU for a graduate African American studies class on social movements. Dr. Umoja helped me hone my topic as I sifted through scholarly works on female movement advocates and considered the activism of women Pan-African cultural nationalists. A longtime scholar-activist with roots in Los Angeles, he pointed out that I might think about exploring the literature on women in Kawaida organizations. He also offered some of his contacts, so I could begin conducting oral histories. John C. McMillian and Mary G. Rolinson in the GSU history department also guided and supported me through the research process. The late Jacqueline A. Rouse was a pioneer in the field of Black women's history and an extraordinary adviser who went above and beyond as a mentor. She was a coeditor, with Vicki L. Crawford, of *Women in the Civil Rights Movement: Trailblazers and Torchbearers*, one of the texts that sparked my initial interest in this work. I could never thank any of you enough for your expertise, patience, and valuable feedback.

Many thanks go to the many scholars I have encountered at Clayton State University, Georgia Institute of Technology, Atlanta Metropolitan State College, and via various professional organizations. I greatly appreciate the flexible and supportive leadership of Adam L. Tate, Grady Culpepper, Vance Gray, and Harry Asana Akoh, as I attempted to research and write while maintaining full-time teaching, advisement, and service schedules in the departments they led. Alison M. Parker, Amrita Chakrabarti Myers, David Gilbert, Johnny Smith, Curtis L. Todd, and Stephanie Y. Evans have my utmost gratitude for generously sharing concrete advice about the idiosyncrasies of scholarly writing and publishing.

A multitude of sister-friends are my rock-solid foundation. Ifetayo Ojeleade functioned as a peer-mentor, informal counselor, and so much more. This book would not have seen the light of day without her pouring courage and resilience into me. Thanks also to my colleagues Antoinette Brown-Waithe, Christy Garrison-Harrison, and Nafeesa Muhammad, who lovingly read drafts, gave advice, shared resources, passed along fellowship opportunities, and so much more. I also appreciate all the formal and informal writing group members and conference colleagues I interacted with at some point, from Arika Easily-Houser, Asantewa Sunni-Ali, and Charmayne Patterson to Corliss Heath, Cynthia Stewart, Dione King, Funmilayo Tyson Devoe, Keisha N. Blain, Lisa Bratton, Natanya Duncan, R. Candy Tate, and Y. Falami Devoe. I am especially grateful to the Sister Scholars virtual community and its founder, the generous and brilliant AnneMarie Mingo. To the members of AST, an African Sisterhood, and the Brotherhood of KMT, thank you for seeing me, encouraging me, giving advice and feedback, and providing platforms for intellectual discussion.

I have so much gratitude for the librarians, archivists, and editors who buttressed my writing processes. I appreciate all the individuals who provided me with research support and editing assistance—Joe Johnson, Deborah Striplin, Penda James, and Kevin Schmiesing as well as students Tony Jamal Lee and Nya Harrison. I am grateful for the tireless effort and support of the librarians and archivists who assisted me with finding sources at the Amistad Research Center at Tulane University, Auburn Avenue Research Library on African American Culture and History, GSU Pullen Library, Emory University's Stuart A. Rose Manuscripts Archives and Rare Books Library, the Charles "Teenie" Harris Archive at Carnegie Museums of Pittsburgh, Hamline University Archives, Swenson Swedish Immigration Research Center, and University of California Los Angeles (UCLA) Center for African American Studies. I am also indebted to Kalamu ya Salaam, Komozi Woodard, Kwasi Konadu, Michael Simanga, and Tayari kwa Salaam for graciously sharing their personal archival materials, connections, and reflections. AMSC vice president Mark Cunningham and the Association of Georgia State University Historians, thank you for research travel funds. To the Association of Black Women's Historians, I greatly appreciate your monetary support and public recognition of my work in progress.

Finally, I would be remiss without thanking the powerhouse team at NYU Press Black Power series. Thank you, Ashley D. Farmer, Clara Platter, and Ibram X. Kendi for believing in the potential of this work, and the bevy of NYU Press editors and assistants for shepherding and refining this manuscript. I cannot thank Ashley enough for her kindness and forbearance as well as her extraordinary collegiality and professionalism in working with me to come to the proverbial table. For that, I will forever be grateful. Thank you to my entire village. "I am, because we are."

# GLOSSARY

AHIDIANA. To make a promise or pledge to other people (Swahili).

CHAKULA. Food (Swahili).

DARASA. Class or subject (Swahili).

HABARI. News (Swahili).

HARAMBEE. (1) Working together (Swahili). (2) Advocates of Kawaida often interpreted *harambee* to mean self-reliance.

HEKALU. (1) Temple (Swahili). (2) Affiliate of the national temple (i.e., the physical location) of the Us Organization, which was "the Hekalu." CFUN was such a *hekalu*, and Amiri Baraka carried the title of imamu. Named Hekalu Umoja, it was at 502 High Street in Newark.

IMAMU. (1) Imam or Muslim leader (Swahili). (2) A high priest or spiritual leader in Kawaida who led the spiritual arm of Us or who headed a local *hekalu*.

IMANI. Faith (Swahili), the seventh Nguzo Saba principle.

KARAMU. (1) Party (Swahili). (2) A family- or community-centered feast, usually held on the sixth day of Kwanzaa, December 31.

KAWAIDA. (1) Usual, normal, "regular thing," ordinary, everyday, habit (Swahili). (2) Standard, rule, or regulation.

KAZI. (1) Work (Swahili). (2) A Kawaida principle calling for sustained, vigorous personal effort in service of nation building.

KUJICHAGULIA. Self-determination. From the Swahili words *kuji* (self) and *chagua* (choose), *kujichagulia* is the second Nguzo Saba principle.

KWANZAA. The Kawaida-derived first fruits celebration lasting from December 26 to January 1. The Us Organization spelled the Kwanzaa celebration with two final *a*'s to differentiate it from the Swahili word *kwanza* (first). The use of seven letters was also meant to accommodate the Seven Principles and the initial seven children of the Us Organization. CFUN and East Kwanzaa advocates sometimes spelled the word "Kwanza."

MALAIKA. (1) Good spirit or angel (Swahili). (2) Adolescent girls or young, unmarried women in Kawaida-influenced organizations.

MATAMBA. Matamba was an empire located in present-day northwestern Angola and known for its female political leaders. Named after the historical African nation-state, the Matamba were a group of women mobilized for defense functions in the Us Organization. The Matamba operated during the early 1970s, the organization's "Crisis" period, in which members faced increasing repression. Nzinga, the Us women's security group leader, was named for Queen Nzinga (also spelled Njinga), who ruled Matamba and neighboring Ndongo in the seventeenth century. Scot Brown asserts that the Matamba's existence reflected fundamental changes in Us gender roles.

MAULANA. (1) Urdu from the Arabic term for scholar or Muslim cleric, especially in Central and South Asia. (2) According to Scot Brown, *maulana* had the quasi-religious meaning of high priest in Kawaida.

MAVAZI. Clothing (Swahili).

MUMININA. (1) True believer (Swahili). (2) A woman who was a committed advocate in a Kawaida-influenced organization, a step above Malaika.

MWALIMU. Teacher (Swahili).

NGUZO SABA. The seven principles, also, the Seven Principles of Blackness or Kwanzaa principles. A Kawaida-derived basic moral value system for African Americans. The Nguzo Saba are *umoja* (unity); *kujichagulia* (self-determination), *ujima* (collective work and responsibility); *ujamaa* (cooperative economics); *nia* (purpose); *kuumba* (creativity); and *imani* (faith).

SALIMU. (1) Greet (Swahili). (2) A Kawaida greeting in which women crossed their arms over their chests and bowed slightly when men went by.

SHULE. School (Swahili).

SIMBA or SIMBA WACHANGA. (1) Lions and young lions, respectively (Swahili). (2) The Simba were often the defense formations of Kawaida-influenced organizations, which were composed of young males.

TAIFA SAA. (1) Swahili words meaning nation and hour. (2) Advocates in Kawaida-influenced organizations interpreted *taifa saa* to mean "nation time," a slogan for Black nationalism.

UHURU SASA. (1) Freedom now (Swahili). (2) Uhuru Sasa was also the name of an East organization school.

UJAMAA. (1) Familyhood or socialism (Swahili). (2) Cooperative economics, the fourth Nguzo Saba principle.

UJIMA. (1) Association (Swahili). (2) Collective work and responsibility, the third Nguzo Saba principle.

UMOJA. Unity (Swahili), the first Nguzo Saba principle.

UMUZI. Named after the collective houses or villages of the Zulu, *umuzis* were Amina Baraka's concept for collectives and semi-collectives in CFUN. They were used to foster communal living among advocates.

WATU. (1) People (Swahili). (2) Acronym for the St. Louis CAP affiliate, Working Always Through Unity.

WEUSI. Black (Swahili).

# NOTES

## PREFACE

1 Afrocentricity is an educational philosophy and a cultural movement promoting awareness of African history and culture as the foundation for African Americans' views of the world. African American studies scholar Molefi Kete Asante asserts in his pioneering book on the topic that African Americans should emphasize the history, values, and perspectives of African and African-descended people as a means of defining themselves and understanding the world; decentering and dismantling hegemonic, European-centered standards and beliefs; and, ultimately, helping create a more equitable society. Asante, *Afrocentricity*.

2 Coates, *Between the World and Me*, 34–35.

3 See Davis, *From Head Shops to Whole Foods*, 74–78, for a discussion of hip-hop, African American bookstores, and Black nationalism's late 1980s and early 1990s revival; Coates, *Between the World and Me*, 34.

4 Heterosexism became a contested issue, as outspoken lesbian, bisexual, and queer sisterhood members challenged the group's ideological boundaries. Heteronormativity was never addressed in organizational creeds. See Constitution of Auset.

## INTRODUCTION

1 Halisi and Mtume, *Quotable Karenga*. The price of the *Quotable Karenga* is from FBI Director to Kansas City Special Agent in Charge, memorandum, September 12, 1968, FBI, COINTELPRO Surveillance Files, Black Extremists and Investigation of the Deacons for Defense and Justice, Part 1.

2 Farmer, "Renegotiating the 'African Woman,'" 76.

3 Maulana Karenga, *Kawaida Theory*, 48.

4 Tayari kwa Salaam, *Working Together*.

5 Cole and Guy-Sheftall, *Gender Talk*, 80.

6 Farmer, "Renegotiating the 'African Woman,'" 76.

7 To avoid evoking stereotypes of servility, I opted to use the lesser-known term "service" rather than the more popular "servant" to highlight the activists' display of a leadership tendency established on the desire to work for the betterment and well-being of others. For more information on servant leadership, see Greenleaf, *Servant Leadership*; and Focht and Ponton, "Identifying Primary Characteristics of Servant Leadership."

8  Second-generation Pan-African nationalist Lumumba Bandele said of the term that "*kazi* is the Blackest of all," defining *kazi* as a measurement of advocates' commitment to the cause of Black liberation. He compared it to the colloquialism, "Don't talk about it, be about it," which is akin to the adage "Actions speak louder than words." Lumumba Akinwole Bandele in *Voices of The EAST*, 32.

9  Blain, *Set the World on Fire*, 5.

10  Scot Brown, *Fighting for US*, 6.

11  Umoja and Jones, "Black Power Rivals," 5.

12  Woodard, *Nation within a Nation*, 72.

13  Konadu, *View from The East*, 39.

14  Rickford, *We Are an African People*, 124; *Mashariki Mfan Ya Kazi Mikono: East Worker's Manual*, with a foreword by Kasisi Yusef Iman, n.d., 3, 4, Martha Bright Papers. CFUN members were also called "advocates." Simanga, *Amiri Baraka*, 55.

15  Maulana Karenga, "Kawaida Philosophy and Practice."

16  I will sometimes discuss Committee for a Unified Newark (CFUN) and the Congress of African People (CAP) together as CFUN/CAP. CFUN was the community organization that was founded in 1967 and that catalyzed the formation of CAP in 1970. CAP functioned as a diverse coalition of groups located in several cities across the United States and had an international branch in Surinam, South America. CFUN was CAP's largest branch and its headquarters. Regarding the capitalization of the letter *s* in the Us Organization's name, I will generally refer to the group as Us for the sake of clarity. However, when quoting, I will maintain the source's formatting.

17  Rickford defined Pan-Africanism and outlined various forms of Pan-African nationalism, citing cultural nationalism as a "[shade] of emphasis" rather than a "fundamental difference" in Black nationalist tendencies. Rickford, *We Are an African People*, 99, 129.

18  Maulana Karenga, *Kwanzaa: Origin, Concepts, Practice*, 21.

19  Ukombozi (Michael McMillan), "Reparation for the Descendants of Enslaved Africans." McMillan's membership in Ahidiana is confirmed in St. Julien, *Upon the Shoulders of Elephants*. For a more complex and inclusive origin story about the founding of Kwanzaa, see Kicheko Davis, interview.

20  Bright, interview.

21  Walker and Felton, *Turn the Horns On*, 21.

22  *Mashariki Mfan Ya Kazi Mikono*, 1–2.

23  Bright, interview.

24  Many (but not all) participants expressed that they felt that feminism was tainted by racism and classism in some ways.

25  Alexander-Floyd and Simien, "Revisiting 'What's in a Name?,'" 69.

26  Like other managers and directors, *kazi* leaders could be appointed or elected. Many, however, were emergent leaders, which is defined as group members who exert influence, having emerged due to peer recognition. Others might have been thrust into leadership positions due to their mate's status. Because this manuscript

focuses on memory, it is important to note that some women were remembered by peers as leaders, although they did not hold specific formal leadership roles or their leadership was circumscribed, much like the "bridge leaders" whom Belinda Robnett identified. Li et al., "Multi-Level Study of Emergent Group Leadership," 352; Robnett, *How Long?*, 6.

27 Kerber, *Toward an Intellectual History*, 58. Ashley D. Farmer identifies the "'African Woman' ideal" in *Remaking Black Power*, 3, 93–126. The word "mama" in Pan-African nationalist organizations was used to refer to adult female advocates, organizational and community members, blood as well as marital relatives, elder women, and those who embodied the ideal of African womanhood in terms of representing, protecting, and instructing members of the inchoate Black nation.

28 Konadu reported that Jitu Weusi discussed this commitment to hard work and several other aspects of what I term *kazi* leadership in his assessment of East organizational legacies. Suggesting *kazi*, Weusi claimed that "hard work and respect for good work" were important because they produced results. Konadu, *View from The East*, 134–35.

29 Konadu, *View from The East*, 136. Amina Baraka emphasized that the difficult work of forging freedom and equality necessitated that everyone should be able to participate and lead according to the level and quality of their work. The chance for equality should not have been limited based on personal identity. Baraka, however, associated such inclusive organizing with socialist ideology. Amina Baraka, interview, July 17, 2012 (all citations of Amina Baraka interviews are with the author unless stated otherwise). Collectivity and cooperation also emphasized *ujamaa*, which stressed familyhood as well as a type of activist entrepreneurship focused on cooperative economics. Joshua Clark Davis defines activist entrepreneurs as people who emerged from 1960s and 1970s social and political movements to operate business enterprises promoting social and political change rather than monetary gain as foremost objectives in *From Head Shops to Whole Foods*, 3.

30 For an example, see Ahidiana members' use of the concept Darasa/Kazi for teaching students. Darasa meant "class" or "lesson." Together, Darasa/Kazi, or study and work, exemplified a philosophical approach to activism. That is, study should inform praxis and praxis should, in turn, inform ideology. "The Work Study Center [Teaching Philosophy, Method, and Technique]" (paper prepared for the 1985 Annual Conference of the National Association for the Education of Young Children, November 16, 1985), 1, Tayari kwa Salaam Papers.

31 In Amina Baraka, interview, July 12, 2012; Scot Brown, *Fighting for US*, 65–67, 127, 156; Simanga, *Amiri Baraka*, 73; and Rickford, *We Are an African People*, 123, cult-of-personality leadership was described as circumstances in which organizational literature, practices, rituals, and the like fostered uncritical and at times worshipful praise and admiration for Maulana Karenga and Amiri Baraka.

32 Rickford, *We Are an African People*, 124; Konadu, *View from The East*, 134; Jitu Weusi, "The EAST Legacy," in *Voices of The EAST*, 17–18.

33 The article appeared in *Forward*, the journal of the League of Revolutionary Struggle (LRS). Simanga, "Congress of African People," 177.

34 Jacquelyn Dowd Hall argues for a "long civil rights movement" periodization that begins in the 1930s and challenges the standard 1955–1965 timeline. Jeanne Theoharis, Sundiata Cha-Jua, Clarence Lang, and others argue for the terminology "Black freedom struggle" to point out that the fight for African American liberation was not an unbroken movement but rather a persistent struggle composed of various movements, institutions, actions, and activists who fought in a myriad of eras and regions. I choose to use the term "long Black freedom struggle," as do Jerry Gershenhorn and others. For more information, see Hall, "Long Civil Rights Movement"; Theoharis, "Black Freedom Studies"; Cha-Jua and Lang, "'Long Movement' as Vampire"; and Gershenhorn, *Louis Austin*, 3.

35 Joseph called for a "full length historical study of Black Panther women" in "Black Liberation without Apology," 9. The research that this book is based on was rooted in my belief in the need for a similar study of women in cultural nationalist organizations.

36 Cole and Guy-Sheftall, *Gender Talk*, 79–80.

## CHAPTER 1. "NOBODY KNOWS OUR NAMES"

1 Amina Baraka, interview, July 12, 2012. The acclaimed African American author James Baldwin published a collection of essays titled *Nobody Knows My Name* in 1961.

2 Although scholars like Komozi Woodard, Scot Brown, Kwasi Konadu, Russell Rickford, Michael Simanga, and Ashley D. Farmer have filled some of the gaps in the literature on Pan-African cultural nationalist women's contributions to the Black Power movement, see Moore, *Defeat of Black Power*, 54–55, 77–79, for a treatment of Black nationalist women's participation in the 1972 NBPC, which supports Amina Baraka's claims of invisibility. Moore characterized female Black Power-era nationalists as exceptionally marginalized with few leadership opportunities. Identifying nameless and faceless CAP women by their white dresses and head wraps, he characterized them as "priceless" elements of the NBPC support staff who brought significant organizational experience to the convention's planning and execution teams.

3 See Posey, "Will Black Nationalism Reemerge?" for an example of such popularly held ideas, which cast Black Power as a movement without provenance.

4 Tony Martin has characterized "race first" as the central tenet of Marcus Garvey's program, stating that "the black man was universally oppressed on racial grounds, and any program of emancipation would have to be built around the question of race first." Tony Martin, *Race First*, 23. Martha Biondi's work underscored the idea that "the ethos and political strategy of the Black Power era was indisputably race first." Biondi, *Black Revolution on Campus*, 257. E. U. Essien-Udom emphasized that the ideology of race men was not primarily focused on racism but on identity consciousness, self-definition, group dignity, and

community redemption. The inclusion of women in this definition was implied. Essien-Udom, *Black Nationalism*, 3. For more information on race vindication, or "the project of defending black people from the charge that they have made little or no contribution to the history of human progress," see Moses, *Afrotopia*, 21; and Asukile, "Joel Augustus Rogers' Race Vindication," 281. For more information on efficient womanhood and community feminism, see Duncan, "Efficient Womanhood," 7; Ula Taylor, *Veiled Garvey*, 235–37; and Blain, "'We Want to Set the World on Fire,'" 199.

5  McDuffie, *Sojourning for Freedom*, 203.

6  Cha-Jua and Lang, "'Long Movement' as Vampire," 271.

7  Carmichael and Thelwell, *Ready for Revolution*, 507; Lewis and D'Orso, *Walking with the Wind*, 387–89.

8  See Kinchen, *Black Power in the Bluff City*, 39–40; Joseph, *Stokely*, 102, 114–15; and Yerkey, *He's Coming to Start Riots*, 107–9.

9  Peniel Joseph has asserted that racialized violence flourished in almost every corner of postwar America. He explained that the brutality was manifested in two ways: "hidden" forms and the more self-explanatory "physical" type. Joseph defined the former as unequal educational, residential, judicial, and economic outcomes between Whites and people of color. I selected author and activist Arun Gandhi's term "passive violence," which refers to the same practices, but Gandhi's discourse extends the concept beyond covert actions while also encompassing unintentional deeds. Students for a Democratic Society cofounder Tom Hayden also opined that racism was a form of violence, which all White people in some way supported. Joseph, *Black Power Movement*, xi; Stern, "Conversation with Arun Gandhi"; Hayden, *Rebellion in Newark*, 3.

10  Perkins, *Autobiography as Activism*, xi.

11  While Peniel Joseph wrote about continuity, African American studies experts Sundiata Cha-Jua and Clarence Lang instructed scholars to heed the differences between civil rights and Black Power. Joseph, *Black Power Movement*, 21.

12  Howze, interview. Joseph positioned Stokely Carmichael as a "revolutionary icon" and Malcolm X's most likely successor at the time. Additionally, Joseph makes a similar claim about Carmichael that the Pan-African cultural nationalist women do in their self-narratives. That is, the public imagines the activists as distant from the civil rights struggle, a movement that was ironically a key factor in shaping them (in both its triumphs and its limitations). Joseph, *Stokely*, 3, 327. Direct quote is from Ture and Hamilton, *Black Power*, xv.

13  Ogbar, *Black Power*, 2, 37.

14  Amina Baraka's reference to notoriety relates to Nathan C. Heard's *Howard Street*; Amina Baraka, interview, July 12, 2012.

15  Ongoza, interview; Nana Anoa Nantambu, interview.

16  Joseph, *Black Power Movement*, 9.

17  Umoja, "From Malcolm X to Omowale Malik Shabazz," 31.

18  Glaude, *Is It Nation Time?*, 3; Van Deburg, *New Day in Babylon*, 2.

19 McDuffie and Woodard have underscored the importance of analyzing women as entities who influenced Malcolm X and carried his legacy. The authors wrote about Louise Little, Vicki Garvin, Queen Mother Moore, and Betty Shabazz. McDuffie and Woodard, "If You're in a Country That's Progressive," 529, 532.

20 Ogbar, *Black Power*, 1.

21 Kifner, "Rights Leaders."

22 Kifner, "Rights Leaders."

23 McDonald, *Urban America*, 49–150; Woodard, *Nation within a Nation*, 94.

24 Jamala Rogers, interview.

25 Robin Gregory, interview by Blackside, Inc., October 12, 1988, *Eyes on the Prize Interview Transcripts*.

26 "Overdue Victory." The term "radicalization of a generation" was taken from an Akinyele Umoja quote describing the spirit of the times that produced the Black Power movement. Umoja, interview.

27 "Queen Crowns Queen."

28 Farah Jasmine Griffin explains the importance of aesthetics and activism in "'Ironies of the Saint,'" 220–21. Colorism is also tied to class privilege and oppression. Studies show that many lighter-skinned African Americans have historically been more advantaged than their dark-skinned counterparts in such areas as education, income, and job status. Underscoring the importance of analyzing such issues, some argue that policies designed solely to dismantle racial hierarchy leave intact or even intensify problems of skin-color discrimination. Hochschild and Weaver, "Skin Color Paradox," 643; Ford, "Soul Generation," 20. Tanisha C. Ford writes about style as tactical and political choices in *Liberated Threads*, 105–8, 110.

29 Kathleen Neal Cleaver, a former SNCC member, the first woman to become part of the Black Panther Party's central committee, and wife of controversial Party leader Eldridge Cleaver, was one of the most prominent women associated with the Black Power movement. Amina Baraka, interview, July 12, 2012.

30 Black Rose's colorful moniker suggested commentary about coded messages in the mainstream discourse at the time. She appeared on the cover of jazz musician Lou Donaldson's 1963 *Good Gracious* album. In terms of the beauty politics of the day, reportedly, artists like Miles Davis demanded that Black women be put on their covers; thus, Nelmes's and other Grandassa Models' very appearances embodied the battle against dominant European-centered beauty standards. An example of her notoriety as a natural hair stylist, Black Rose was featured as one of the expert commenters interviewed for the *Ebony* magazine cover story, Garland, "Is the Afro on Its Way Out?" See also Pellegrinelli, "Women Jacketed by Records"; and Blumenthal, "More Jazz and Sex." For more information on Nelmes and Grandassa, see Tinson, *Radical Intellect*, 85–86. For general information on the Grandassa Models, see Aiello, *Artistic Activism of Elombe Brath*, 28–30, 155; and Brathwaite and Ford, *Kwame Brathwaite*, 72, 95, 137.

31 Peterson, interview.

32 Omotayo, interview.

33  Advertisement for Black Rose at Afrikan Beauty Center, *Black News* 2, no. 10 (October 22, 1973): 14.

34  For additional information on African American beauty politics, see Gill, *Beauty Shop Politics*; and Rooks, *Hair Raising*.

35  Joseph, *Black Power Movement*, 14; Woodard, *Nation within a Nation*, 43, 215; Thomas, interview. Several scholars have cited the Vietnam conflict as a defining element of cultural nationalists' anticolonialist and internationalist outlook as well as the long Black freedom struggle's leftward shift during the Black Power era. Woodard, *Nation within a Nation*, 38, 107–8; Scot Brown, *Fighting for US*, 84–88; Black and Angaza, "East Time-Line," in *EAST Sisterhood*, 1; Fisher, *Black Literate Lives*, 60; Konadu, *View from The East*, 68–69; Bright, interview; Shukuru Sanders, interview; Peterson, interview; *Black News* 1, no. 14 (May 12, 1970), cover; summer film festival advertisement, *Black News* 1, no. 17 (July 6, 1970): 8; Kalamu ya Salaam, interview (all citations of Kalamu ya Salaam interviews are with the author).

36  Bright, interview; Beatty, interview.

37  Killens, "Black Man in the New China," 41.

38  Kelley and Esch, "Black Like Mao," 8. Malcolm X, in particular, used the terms "dark world," "dark man," and "dark-skinned people" to articulate the idea of unity among non-Whites and illustrate the concept that, in the context of global imperialism, Whites were considered a "common enemy." Malcolm X, "Message to the Grass Roots," 6. The "Third-World" framing is from Congress of African People's "Woman Question," 9.

39  Killens, "Black Man in the New China," 41–42. See Kelley and Esch, "Black Like Mao."

40  Kalamu ya Salaam, *Our Women Keep Our Skies from Falling*, 5. A West African *lapa* skirt is made of brightly patterned cloth wrapped and tied around the waist. The *lapa* was used as a symbol of African womanhood recognizable to broader cultural nationalist circles. The Egyptian goddess appeared to be Nut, with hands and feet on the earth and body forming the sky. "How to Tie a Lapa."

41  Tayari kwa Salaam, "So-Journeying," 193. Tayari kwa Salaam is also cited as the organizer of a 1977 tour of the People's Republic of China for twenty African American educators; see the back matter of Tayari kwa Salaam, *Working Together*.

42  See Kiini Ibura's website, https://kiiniibura.com, accessed July 8, 2022.

43  Kalamu ya Salaam, interview; Kiini Ibura Salaam, interview. Use of clothing in communist China to promote national unity and equality between men and women has been explored in the literature. According to historian Xurong Kong, the military-styled uniforms came into vogue during the Chinese Revolution and lasted until the end of the 1980s. This assertion further underscores the idea that prevailing trends from other parts of the globe catalyzed and shaped cultural nationalists' activism, not only in terms of their thinking about race and class but also their thinking about gender. Kong, "Military Uniform as a Fashion," 299–302. For a graphic of Ahidiana Work/Study Center's gender-inclusive children's uni-

form, see the school logo, as depicted on "The Work/Study Center Ninth Annual Graduation Celebration," program, May 12, 1985, Tayari kwa Salaam Papers.

44 Kalamu ya Salaam, interview. For a source highlighting the early Kawaida position that women should be fundamentally "feminine," which inherently required "submissiveness," see Halisi and Mtume, *Quotable Karenga*, 20. For a description of requirements for women's dress in the Us Organization from Amiri Baraka's perspective, see Amiri Baraka, *Autobiography*, 386.

45 Amina Baraka, interview, July 17, 2012. Similar views about factors shaping Black nationalist gender roles can be found in "The Woman Question," which stressed the Nation of Islam's influence on Black Power-era cultural nationalism; in the oral narrative of The East's Mtamanika Beatty, where she said the organization's polygynous practices came from "close association [with] the Muslim philosophy of more than one wife"; and in "Africa on My Mind," where E. Frances White claimed that Black nationalist sex roles mirrored those of conservative, mainstream America. Congress of African People, "Woman Question," 13; White, "Africa on My Mind," 76; Beatty, interview.

46 Congress of African People, "Woman Question," 14.

47 Amina Baraka, interview, July 17, 2012.

48 Amina Baraka, interview, July 17, 2012.

49 Panzer, "Pedagogy of Revolution," 810.

50 Mandela, *Part of My Soul*, 60; Magaziner, "Pieces of a (Wo)man," 45, 49.

51 Akili, interview.

52 Konadu, *View from The East*, 34.

53 Campbell, "Making of an Organic Intellectual," 57.

54 Founded in 1964, ASCRIA was a popular organization aimed at assisting Afro-Guyanese populations with identity formation and esteem building through an embrace of African heritage. The leftist political pressure group also implemented programs in support of economic uplift, encompassing agricultural, livestock, mining, and garment-making collectives. Konadu, *View from The East*, 34–36; Kwayana, "Burnhamism," 41; Westmaas, "Organic Activist," 165–67; Campbell, "Making of an Organic Intellectual," 49.

55 Campbell, "Making of an Organic Intellectual," 57; Shukuru Sanders, interview; Cook, "Guyana as Seen by an African-American"; Quest, "Sister Tchaiko Kwayana." For more information on The East's relationship with Guyana and on Ann F. Cook, see Rickford, "We Can't Grow Food," 956, 970, 972.

56 For more information, see Konadu, *View from The East*, 47, 127; and Rickford, "'Kazi Is the Blackest.'"

57 Bright, interview. The construction program to which Bright referred is likely the Self Help Road Project, which began in 1970 and was undertaken with the help of numerous volunteers from Guyana and abroad; Shukuru Sanders, interview.

58 Mumininas, *Mwanamke Mwananchi*, 8.

59 Bright, interview; Shukuru Sanders, interview. At least twelve female advocates made the 1971 trip to Guyana, according to Black and Angaza, "East Time-Line,"

2. The East Sisterhood's purpose is outlined in Konadu, *View from The East*, 50–51. In statements suggesting the significance of *kazi* in influencing a person's work, "Sis. Shukuru" was hailed in *Black News*, in conjunction with the Harlem Hospital Nursing Corp [*sic*] of June 1974, as one who was committed to "suffering, service, [and] sacrifice" for the people. Kasisi Jitu Weusi, "Around Our Way," *Black News*, July 1974, 14; Eusi Kwayana was also a part of the Working People's Alliance.

60  Freeland, "'We're a Winner,'" 261; Beatty, interview.

61  Joseph, *Waiting 'til the Midnight Hour*, 120.

62  Ogbar, *Black Power*, 208.

63  Ogbar, *Black Power*, 2.

64  Beatty, interview.

65  Powell, interview.

66  The belief that African American culture is essentially an African culture was an established viewpoint propagated by academics as far back as Melville Herskovits and Branislaw Malinowski. Moses, *Afrotopia*, 14.

## CHAPTER 2. "AGITATE. EDUCATE. ORGANIZE"

1  Manoni, *Bedford-Stuyvesant*, 2; Surfaro, "The East."

2  The reference to outsiders' impressions of Bedford-Stuyvesant as "the ghetto" is from Heitner, "Good Side of the Ghetto," 48. Manoni also wrote during the early 1970s that Bed-Stuy was called "the largest black ghetto in the country." Manoni, *Bedford-Stuyvesant*, 2. By 1980, singer Billy Joel, in his song "You May Be Right," would juxtapose "Bedford-Stuy" with a "combat zone," emphasizing both as particularly dangerous places. Trymaine Lee, "Fulton Street Journal." See Manoni, *Bedford-Stuyvesant*, 12–14, for information on African Americans able to leave but choosing to stay in the neighborhood.

3  Manoni, *Bedford-Stuyvesant*, 12, 26–27; Trymaine Lee, "Fulton Street Journal"; Davis, *From Head Shops to Whole Foods*, 71–72.

4  Manoni, *Bedford-Stuyvesant*, 10.

5  Konadu, *View from The East*, 7–8. The phrase quoted in the section title, "Why would anyone want to live there?," is from Manoni, *Bedford-Stuyvesant*, 1.

6  Manoni, *Bedford-Stuyvesant*, 7, 13, 26–28; "Bed-Stuy Is Looking Better"; "Storm over Teen Halfway House"; Fried, "Bedford-Stuyvesant Has Bright Side"; "Parents of Young Offenders Meet."

7  Jeffrey Taylor, "'Live from the East'"; Giwa and Giwa, *Sun Rises in the East*.

8  "Afrikan Women Unite."

9  Peterson, interview.

10  Fried, "Bedford-Stuyvesant Has Bright Side." Peterson was also known as Wendie Anderson Richardson.

11  Peterson, interview. Nearby Brooklyn industries employing workers without much formal training or skill attracted Italian, German, Irish, and Jewish immigrants as well as a "trickle" of African-descended migrants during World War I. During World War II, Black families flooded into the area in search of economic

opportunity. Eventually, after World War II, many young European Americans moved away from the community. Manoni, *Beford-Stuyvesant*, 3. A slice of racially integrated World War II-era Brooklyn can be seen in Peterson's parents' 1940 census data. The paternal Anderson side of the family lived in an area where three of four people were native-born African Americans from either the North or South; however, at least two White families and their boarders made up the balance of the reported population. The majority of residents listed as White hailed from Germany. Peterson's mother, Iona Ashby, lived with her British West Indian parents on a majority-African American block. The census taker noted that one White American family, the Gahans, also lived on the block. "United States Census, 1940," index and images, FamilySearch, https://familysearch. org, accessed April 23, 2015, Aeolus Anderson in household of Katie Anderson, Assembly District 18, Brooklyn, New York City, Kings, New York, United States; citing enumeration district (ED) 24–2052A, sheet 3B, family 47, NARA digital publication T627 (Washington, DC: National Archives and Records Administration, 2012), roll 2599; "United States Census, 1940," index and images, FamilySearch, https://familysearch.org, accessed April 23, 2015, Iona Ashby in household of Oliver Ashby, Assembly District 5, Brooklyn, New York City, Kings, New York, United States; citing enumeration district (ED) 24–682, sheet 10A, family 196, NARA digital publication T627 (Washington, DC: National Archives and Records Administration, 2012), roll 2563.

12  Peterson, interview.

13  See Kinchen, *Black Power in the Bluff City*, 36–43, for information about how young African Americans in Memphis comprised a sector of what Kinchen calls the Black Power generation. Also see Farmer, *Remaking Black Power*, 93–126, for a discussion of how women in Kawaida-influenced organizations rethought and revised the African woman concept according to their own needs and interpretations.

14  Peterson, interview. The history of Akiba Mkuu bookstore as well as the nature of its existence as an East effort to engage the community from a nationalist perspective is discussed in Konadu, *View from The East*, 74–75. Akiba Mkuu was also covered in the *Amsterdam News*. The author of the article explained that the bookstore's manager, Akin (Hakim) Bomani, claimed that women interested in "feminism, poetry, mysticism, and children's literature" comprised the largest group of consumers patronizing the store. Philip, "Is the Black Bookstore an Endangered Species?"; notice, *Black Panther*, April 27, 1969, 5; Asbury, "16 Black Panthers Go on Trial."

15  Peterson, interview; Konadu defined The East as a "family-based community institution," explaining that the organization emanated from and centered on intimate and familial relationships. Konadu, *View from The East*, 56.

16  Kasisi Jitu Weusi, "Around Our Way," *Black News 2, no. 12* (December 26, 1973): 12–13; Konadu outlined the areas that *Black News* covered and analyzed, including local, national, and international news pertaining to the Pan-African world,

important political and educational concerns, information for African-descended individuals detained in prisons, and more.

17 *Black News* ran a regular column titled "P.O.W.'s Forum" dedicated to awareness and fundraising for imprisoned individuals of African descent. Also see "Three Homes Are Saved" for commentary on how readers assisted a couple on the verge of losing houses that they had used as collateral for political prisoners who did not report for imprisonment. *Black News* also ran articles and posted commentary about organizing African Americans to halt attacks on Black and Latine community members. Mchawi, "Victor Rhodes"; and Jitu Weusi, "Why Was Arthur Miller Murdered."

18 Konadu, *View from The East*, 56.

19 The entire quote, which apparently came from a participant in The East Sisterhood seminar titled "Organizing the Black Family," read "Our experience—we repeat—taught us that we must organize ourselves and struggle within a movement, that is, our women's organization must be an arm, an instrument of a political movement . . . and women must understand that her [*sic*] role of mobilisation [*sic*] starts first of all at home amongst the family" (ellipses in the original). Kasisi Jitu Weusi, "Around Our Way," *Black News*, June 1974, 12; "Mwanamke Weusi." As an example of women's roles being limited to the area of "social organization," in 1973 all of the CAP Executive Committee members were men, except Bibi Amina Baraka. Amina Baraka served as social organization minister. *Fundisha* 1, no. 6 in *Black News* 2, no. 11 (December 11, 1973): 10.

20 Konadu, *View from The East*, 53–56.

21 The term "promise of protection" is from Griffin, "'Ironies of the Saint.'" Rickford also mentioned the women's view of labor and personal sacrifice in service of struggle, citing it as borderline "self-abnegation" in *We Are an African People*, 154. Ula Taylor similarly refers to the Nation of Islam's mission to distance Black women and girls from predatory labor practices, hurtful social interactions, and lewd immorality, as well as to safeguard them from "the depravity of the white world," as "the promise of patriarchy." Ula Taylor, *Promise of Patriarchy*, 2.

22 Konadu, *View from The East*, 56–57. Akili Walker recalled a similar reality in his reflections about attending Committee for a Unified Newark's brotherhood meetings. In discussing his observations of extended families, he expressed that such relationships were not standard policy; however, he remembered that a minority of advocates unofficially upheld the practice of one man having multiple female partners based on the fact that polygyny was acceptable in "African culture." Thus, in his recollection, there was no official policy normalizing polygyny in The East, nor were extended families expressly discouraged. Akili Walker, interview.

23 The phrase quoted in the section title, "It was a family kind of organization," is from Beatty, interview.

24 The estimate of a hundred East family members came from Bright, interview. East operations were outlined in Konadu, *View from The East*, 157–60. Shukuru Sanders described the organization as a family and Angela Weusi explained that "there

were quite a few large families" and many children in The East, in Angela Weusi et al., "Memories of The East." Advocate Onaje Jua Muid described The East's extended family as "the spark of a nation becoming," in *Voices of The EAST*, 105.

25  Safiya Bandele, interview. East founding member Adeyemi Bandele also stated that Safiya Bandele was a peripheral East member. Adeyemi Bandele, interview.

26  Shukuru Sanders, interview.

27  Beatty, interview; Weusi et al., "Memories of The East."

28  Shabaka, interview.

29  Adeyemi Bandele, interview.

30  Former Organization Us chairperson Subira Kifano highlighted the idea of a common philosophy permeating independent Black institutions beginning in the 1970s. She asserted that the unifying thread was the introduction of an African-centered curriculum in terms of values, views, and lifestyle as part of a commitment to validating the "personal and collective human worth and potential of African-American people, in general, and children specifically." Kifano's assertion can be seen as synonymous with the slogan "Black lives matter." Alicia Garza originated the latter phrase shortly after George Zimmerman's July 2013 acquittal for the murder of Trayvon Martin in 2012. Fellow organizers Patrisse Cullors and Opal Tometi publicized the slogan, which was turned into a hashtag and used to organize online demonstrations. The protests grew beyond social media, as activists took to the streets, picketing, engaging in acts of civil disobedience, and forming several local Black Lives Matter chapters in the United States, Canada, and Ghana. Kifano, "Promise and Possibilities," 44; Michel Martin, "#BlackLivesMatterMovement"; Black Lives Matter, "All #BlackLivesMatter."

31  Bedford-Stuyvesant's rates of juvenile delinquency among those aged seven to twenty were higher than both Brooklyn and New York City's averages at 116 of every 1,000 residents. Manoni, *Bedford-Stuyvesant*, 22. Jitu Weusi asserted the particular importance of providing a space to "educate and redirect" the community's youth. He wrote anecdotally that he stood outside a local department store observing "a virtual army of poor Black and Hispanic youth (male and female) whose only purpose is to steal whatever they can get their hands on." Further, he wrote that he "watched as a police car made trip after trip carting recently arrested youngsters off to jail." "Is this what we can expect from our future leaders and citizens?" he questioned, emphasizing the humanity of the young people rather than focusing on criminalizing them in his discourse. It is no wonder that East programs demonstrated how the associates, male and female, worked to provide a structured, nurturing environment for interested youth in the Bed-Stuy community. Jitu Weusi, "Re-Emergence of B'klyn Grassroots Politics."

32  Beatty, interview.

33  Peterson, interview.

34  The extended family was defined by Kawaida advocates as a voluntary social unit rather than a biologically determined grouping. Social units were based on shared values and perspectives rather than blood relationships. Constituents looked be-

yond descriptors such as half-, step-, and illegitimate in claiming extended family members. Maulana Karenga, *Kawaida Theory*, 54–55.

35  No narrator involved in this project recalled any East policies explicitly forbidding polyandry. Polygyny-like relationships, however, were the norm in extended families. According to Beatty's account, one woman who was affiliated with The East engaged in polyandry. Beatty observed that the woman had spousal relationships with two men at once for a short time. Adeyemi Bandele recalled no such instances of polyandry. Adeyemi Bandele, interview; Beatty, interview. I use the terms "marriage-like" or "spousal-type" because there is no evidence in the narratives that parties maintained, in contravention of New York law, multiple legal marriages at once.

36  Konadu, *View from The East*, 57. For more information on extended family and the identification of adults as mamas and babas from the perspective of a second-generation East advocate, see Lumumba Akinwole Bandele in *Voices of The EAST*, 31.

37  Women's narratives about the Us Organization also indicated that polygamous-type relationships were contested ground, as in Imani Omotayo's recollection of the contention developing between Us Muminina who advocated polygamy and a group of Malaika who did not accept the practice. Omotayo, interview.

38  Konadu, *View from The East*, 57; Adeyemi Bandele, interview. For a defense of extended family practices in Kawaida-influenced organizations beyond The East, see Maulana Karenga, *Kawaida Theory*, 54–55. Woodard specifically described this kind of behavior as invoking "the traditional African concepts of polygamy for the manipulative and vulgar purposes of American adultery and sexual exploitation." Woodard, *Nation within a Nation*, 180. Amina Baraka also described polygamy as the use of "African traditions" to condone manipulative behaviors and reinscribe social hierarchies. Amina Baraka, interview, July 12, 2012. For an explanation of such ideals in the context of other communities of African Americans practicing polygyny, see Dixon-Spear, *We Want for Our Sisters*, xviii, xxx.

39  Beatty, interview.

40  The word "solid" is Adeyemi Bandele's. Adeyemi Bandele, interview. The term "marriageable" is not the language of East advocates but is from Dixon-Spear. Dixon-Spear theorized that, when the number of women was higher than men, competition intensified among female community members looking to secure mates. Securing the types of stable, monogamous, committed relationships and marriages that could help strengthen Black communities became harder for women in racially oppressive environments. In contexts such as that in which The East existed, community demographics intensified the issue by further narrowing the field of possible mates. Problems stemming from racial oppression such as criminalization, drug addiction, unemployment and underemployment, and lack of educational opportunity further limited the number of marriageable women and especially decimated marriageable men's numbers. Once certain cultural nationalists considered the low populations of marriageable men, some deter-

mined that turning away from Western expectations of monogamy as the only acceptable marriage form and toward non-Western and what they understood as "traditional" African practices would legitimize the polygynous-type intimate behaviors regularly occurring in Western society (but in a closeted manner), accommodate the imbalanced marriageable sex ratio, and provide for the kinds of large, heteronormative, male-headed families that could increase the membership of nationalist organizations and thus form support structures for the kind of Black nation that they envisioned. Dixon-Spear, *We Want for Our Sisters*, xxvi.

41 Angela Weusi et al., "Memories of The East."

42 In one type of discourse in the narratives, polygyny was discussed as a way to foster honesty and accommodate men's sexual desires. Discussants implied that male promiscuity was natural, normal, ubiquitous, or inevitable. For instance, Adeyemi Bandele said that polygyny allowed men the ability "to be honest in a relationship so that you don't have to tip[toe] around." A narrator in the podcast with East women opined that a part of the organization's engagement with polygyny "had to do with just what men like to do." Adeyemi Bandele, interview; Angela Weusi et al., "Memories of The East." Dixon-Spear theorized that the "natural tendency for males to engage in sexual multiplicity" was a matter of social circumstance, which the imbalanced sex ratio influenced. Dixon-Spear, *We Want for Our Sisters*, xxxi.

43 Peterson, interview.

44 Dixon-Spear outlines this perspective in her book, asserting that a "closed" or closeted form of polygamy is actually practiced in the West. She also maintains that polygyny is a global norm, and the insistence on monogamy as the sole acceptable marital form represents a Western perspective. Dixon-Spear, *We Want for Our Sisters*, 1–21.

45 Safiya Bandele, interview.

46 Beatty, interview; Adeyemi Bandele, interview; Shabaka, interview.

47 Beatty, interview. For more information on this concept, also see Strauss, "Is Polygamy Inherently Unequal?"

48 Konadu, *View from The East*, 57–58.

49 Peterson, interview.

50 Beatty, interview.

51 Adeyemi Bandele, interview.

52 Konadu, *View from The East*, 57.

53 Beatty, interview.

54 Peterson, interview.

55 Konadu, *View from The East*, 57.

56 Some narrators highlighted as important, and even beneficial, consent among polygamous relationship members, who all should have been informed adults willing to be open and honest. Others emphasized how gendered power dynamics, often unspoken or unacknowledged, were at play in male-female relationships. Adeyemi Bandele, interview.

57 Strauss, "Is Polygamy Inherently Unequal?," 516–17, 529–30.

58 Peterson, interview; Konadu, *View from The East*, 58. See Dixon-Spear for a discussion of the problematic nature of so-called "back-door" marriages and the essential importance of women's consent in polygynous relationships. Dixon-Spear, *We Want for Our Sisters*, 193, 197, 269. The outlined problems, from pressure to accept polygyny to neglecting initial families, were issues in multiple Kawaida-influenced groups, including the Us Organization and Committee for a Unified Newark.

59 Adeyemi Bandele, interview.

60 The East member who broached the topic of polygynous relationships as disguises for men's pursuit of more nubile and possibly more tractable partners was Tamisha Peterson; however, the issue was not unique to The East. It was also a problem in other organizations. Dixon-Spear pointed out that first wives of polygynous relationships involved in her study of African American Muslims, Ausar Auset Society members, and Hebrew Israelites sometimes reported feeling discarded, taken for granted, or tossed away like objects rather than adults on equal footing with their husbands. Peterson, interview; Amina Baraka (CFUN/CAP), interview; Thomas (Us), interview; Dixon-Spear, *We Want for Our Sisters*, 201; Powell (Black Community Defense and Development /CAP), interview; Safiya Bandele (The East), interview.

61 In some narratives, advocates highlighted the positive aspects of sisterhood, which they thought had developed among women in extended families. Segun Shabaka and Adeyemi Bandele, both males, emphasized the beneficial relationships growing out of extended families as well as sisterhood among women. Bandele also suggested that women might gain the ability to spend more time engaging in self-care and experience joy from co-parenting. Shabaka, interview; Adeyemi Bandele, interview; Safiya Bandele, interview. Mtamanika Beatty, however, offered a different view. She explained that some East affiliates viewed polygamy as a way to enlarge institutions and to share parental duties in large family units. Further, she contended, such practices were questionable, particularly in that they ultimately supported male prerogatives more than women's. Beatty, interview.

62 Peterson, interview.

63 Konadu, *View from The East*, 58.

64 Peterson, interview. Imani Omotayo, Amina Thomas, and Amina Baraka reported similar issues of discord over polygamy in interpersonal and family relationships in other Kawaida organizations. In particular, both Amina Thomas (Us) and Amina Baraka (CFUN/CAP) stressed how such discord caused families to break apart. Thomas, interview; Amina Baraka, interview, July 12, 2012.

65 Peterson, interview; Scot Brown, *Fighting for US*, 21. Also see Walker and Felton, *Turn the Horns On*, 22, for commentary about an advocate and his biological father's assessment of him as a Kawaida "fanatic."

66 Beatty, interview.

67 Adeyemi Bandele, interview.

68  Safiya Bandele, interview. Adeyemi Bandele also mentioned Safiya and her role as a National Black United Front leader in his recollections. Explaining the interconnected nature of the two organizations, he said that East family members helped form the NBUF and many participated in it. New York's Black United Front was a citywide, grassroots organization formed of various entities dedicated to eliminating racism, ensuring justice, promoting "collective Black ethics," and seeking complete liberation as well as political, economic, and social power for oppressed people. Adeyemi Bandele, interview; Peter, "4 Evers Faculty Lose Jobs"; Byron and Weusi, *Black United Front*; Adeyemi Bandele to All NBUF Chapters/Organizing Committees, December 2, 1981, Series XIII: National Black United Front, 1979–1981, Komozi Woodard Amiri Baraka Collection. For more information on Medgar Evers College, see Espinal, Barker, and Simmons, " Legacy of Medgar Evers College"; and Tager and Highsmith-Taylor, *Medgar Evers College*, 2–3, 20–21.

69  Safiya Bandele, interview; Safiya Bandele, "Retirement Ceremony," 31, 39.

70  Baxandall, "Re-Visioning," 230; Omolade, "Sisterhood in Black and White," 395. Loretta J. Ross mentioned Safiya Bandele alongside Jamala Rogers (St. Louis CAP) as particularly supportive of feminists in the Black freedom struggle. Ross encountered Bandele and Rogers while working with the NBUF in the early 1980s. Ross, "Personal Journey," 48.

71  Ross, "Personal Journey," 48.

72  Safiya Bandele, interview.

73  East advocate Cynthia Fatima Kierstedt remembered Medgar Evers College as "an extension of Uhuru Sasa School." She attended both institutions. Cynthia Fatima Kierstedt in *Voices of The EAST*, 59.

74  Quotes are from Safiya Bandele, interview.

75  Safiya Bandele, interview.

76  Bright, interview.

77  Bright, interview.

78  Scot Brown, *Fighting for US*, 102. Amiri Baraka commented on "unity without uniformity," asserting that CAP was never meant to be a united front but was supposed to be "an organization with a unitary ideology." "Comments of the Chairman on Resignations of Haki Madhubuti and Jitu Weusi (IPE and The East)," n.d., Series V: Congress of African People, 1960–1976: Congress of African People, Major Topics: Baraka, "Revolutionary Party: Revolutionary Ideology," 1974, Komozi Woodard Amiri Baraka Collection.

79  Simanga, *Amiri Baraka*, 47.

80  Woodard, *Nation within a Nation*, 180–81.

81  Letter from Jitu Weusi to Amiri Baraka, December 12, 1973 (transcribed from the original letter), in Konadu, *View from The East*, 147. Amiri Baraka's response to the letter stated that CAP cadre organizations were to be "carbon copies of each other." Baraka upheld what he termed antifeudalist, antiatavist, antiprimitive nationalist, antielitist ideological development in the Congress of African People.

"Comments of the Chairman on Resignations." Supporting examples for the assertion about cult-of-personality behaviors included Blessed Baraka, an official celebration of Amiri Baraka's birthday as a "high holy day," and buttons with Baraka's face. Leo Baraka paper, n.d., Series IV: Newark (New Jersey), 1913–1980: Committee for Unified Newark, Kawaida Concepts, 1971, Komozi Woodard Amiri Baraka Collection; Amiri Baraka, *Autobiography*, xx; Simanga, *Amiri Baraka*, 86.

82  Woodard, *Nation within a Nation*, 180–81.

83  Peterson, interview.

84  Konadu, *View from The East*, 58; Peterson, interview.

85  Pride and Wilson, *History of the Black Press*, 3; Fisher, *Black Literate Lives*, 59, 61–62, 82.

86  Big Black, "Around Our Way," *Black News* 1, no. 33 (July 17, 1974): 18.

87  The term "African-based community" is from Konadu, *View from The East*, 68.

88  Angela Weusi et al., "Memories of The East." In its first volume, the paper described itself as aimed at various types of African American people making up the neighborhood (male and female, young and old). "'Black News' of Bedford Stuyvesant." That *Black News* was a community effort is also reflected in the circular's publication of a mix of articles authored by East affiliates and members of other Black nationalist organizations such as the Black Liberation Army. Although the magazine became the "official communications instrument of the *EAST*" in October 1969, not all of the articles "reflected the position of the *EAST* organization." According to Konadu, the circular was considered "a communication link within the African-based community," and the circular's subject matter was often contested ground. "General Statement"; Konadu, *View from The East*, 68–71.

89  Peterson, interview.

90  One author reported telling a *Black News* buyer that the twenty-five-cent fee being charged for the paper at the time "would figure big in the resurrection of our people." Mittie Black, "Dialogue with a 'Coloured' Beauty."

91  Peterson, interview.

92  Fisher, *Black Literate Lives*, 60–61.

93  *Black News* reportedly circulated in five countries; however, most sales occurred on New York City streets. Konadu, *View from The East*, 72.

94  Bright speaking during the Angela Weusi et al., "Memories of The East." Maisha Fisher attributed the quote "Tell it like it is" to Jitu Weusi. Fisher, *Black Literate Lives*, 62. See letters to the editor, *Black News* 1, no. 33 (July 17, 1971): 19, and *Black News* 2, no. 12 (December 26, 1973): 22. For more on *Black News* and incarcerated populations see "P.O.W.'s Forum," which was a regular column for incarcerated people of African descent in American prisons. Letters to the editor revealed that readers received *Black News* in locations such as Philadelphia, Wilmington, NC, and Jamaica, West Indies. Letters to the editor, *Black News* 2, no. 10 (October 22, 1973): 11. Estimated circulation and other details about distribution and staff composition can be found in Konadu, *View from The East*, 69, 72.

95  Peterson, interview.

96  Fisher, *Black Literate Lives*, 64, 73; Joshua Clark Davis also discusses advocates' literacy practices in *From Head Shops to Whole Foods*, 53.

97  Abimbola Wali in Angela Weusi et al., "Memories of The East."

98  Abimbola Wali in Angela Weusi et al., "Memories of The East."

99  Abimbola Wali in Angela Weusi et al., "Memories of The East." Wali's use of "permed" meant chemically straightened. "Fly" in this case meant hip, cool, or trendy in style.

100 For an example of stories written by Aminisha (Weusi) Black, see Aminisha Weusi, "Arthur Eve Speaks"; Aminisha Weusi, "Assemblyman Arthur Eve Speaks,"; and Aminisha Weusi, "Bklyn Tenants Fight." Black has more recently written for *Our Times Press*. Angela Weusi et al., "Memories of The East"; Black and Angaza, *EAST Sisterhood*, 3.

101 Angela Weusi et al., "Memories of The East." The Republic of New Afrika (RNA), or the Provisional Government of the Republic of New Afrika (PG-RNA), founded in 1968, had the following additional purposes: to educate people about the existence of African Americans as an "oppressed, colonized nation"; raise awareness about their right to self-determination; and obtain reparations for members of the Black nation from the United States. Citizenship in the RNA was not limited to people of African descent. The Japanese American female activist Yuri Kochiyama was its first naturalized citizen. Ferguson and Ferguson, *Unlikely Warrior*, 204, 284. See Onaci, *Free the Land* for more information on the RNA.

102 Bright, interview. In "A Yoruban Wedding," the author cited that Sister Fujii had been serving as the *Black News* typesetter for more than a year at the time. Penda Aiken was listed as a *Black News* staffer in Konadu, *View from The East*, 68–69. Other female typesetters included Muslimah, Shukuru Sanders, and Oseye (Mchawi). Black and Angaza, "East Time-Line," 1; EAST Timeline, in *Voices of The EAST*, 138; Angela Weusi et al., "Memories of The East." Clara Breland Sister Fujii's reflections on her time as a *Black News* typesetter can be found in *Voices of The EAST*, 41–43.

103 Bright, interview.

104 Black and Angaza, "East Time-Line," 1; EAST Timeline, in *Voices of The EAST*, 138.

105 Akili Walker, interview.

106 Shabaka, email, March 13, 2015. I took the years 1978–1983 from the literature to demarcate Shabaka's tenure as *Black News* editor. Konadu, *View from The East*, 72.

107 Bright, interview. The fact that editor Jim Williams encouraged each staff member to complete an entire issue under his leadership could have lent to Bright's recollections of work at *Black News* as intensive and comprehensive. Konadu, *View from The East*, 69. Bright might have pointed out typing because the occupation has historically been feminized, with low pay in comparison to more male-dominated professional fields such as law, engineering, and accounting. Women held 95 percent of certain typing jobs in 1969. According to a government survey,

these positions paid \$371–\$430 a month on average, in comparison to the lowest-paid professionals (file clerks), who made \$324, and \$2,452 for the highest-paid professionals in the survey (top-level attorneys). US Department of Labor Statistics, "National Survey," 6–8.

108 In October 1969, the *Black News* board consisted of six males and one female, Sia Berhan, a high schooler and member of the African American Students Association (ASA) who had emerged from the Ocean Hill-Brownsville experience and served as the paper's research director. In 1972 the board consisted of all men: Jim Williams, Donald Blackman, Leroy Bowser, Jitu Weusi, George Dudley, Maurice Fredericks (Msemaji Weusi), Andre Womble (Salik Mwando), and Frank Richards. By August 1983, the editorial board reportedly consisted of three males: Segun Shabaka, Adeyemi Bandele, and Msemaji Weusi. Muslimah Mashariki was the only female in the group. See the mastheads in *Black News* 1, no. 2 (October 1969): cover, and *Black News* 4, no 25 (August 1983): 2; see also Isaac, *Inside Ocean Hill-Brownsville*, 184; and Konadu, *View from The East*, 14, 69.

109 Shabaka, email, March 6, 2015.

110 Konadu, *View from The East*, 72.

111 Black and Angaza, *EAST Sisterhood*, 3.

112 Peterson, interview; Jitu Weusi, "Re-Emergence of B'klyn Grassroots Politics"; Allegheny County Black Political Convention, display ad 24, *New Pittsburgh Courier*, January 29, 1972, 19. The phrase "We stood for the community," quoted in the section's title, is from Howze, interview.

113 Trymaine Lee, "Fulton Street Journal." For more commentary on predatory businesses and the African American community, see quote from Malcolm X in "White Merchants and Black Power"; and Martin Luther King Jr., Press Conference on Operation Breadbasket, Chicago, Illinois, July 11, 1967, Martin Luther King, Jr. Papers, 1950–1968. Also see Davis, *From Head Shops to Whole Foods*, 46.

114 In "Re-Emergence of B'klyn Grassroots Politics," Jitu Weusi reported that the Triangle boycott occurred in 1973, but reports of the boycott appeared in a 1972 *Black News* article. Jitu Weusi, "Re-Emergence of B'klyn Grassroots Politics"; "White Merchants and Black Power," 25–26.

115 Jitu Weusi, "Re-Emergence of B'klyn Grassroots Politics"; Walker and Felton, *Turn the Horns On*, 17–18; Triangle Shoe Store advertisement, *New York Amsterdam News*, November 22, 1969, 45. Quote is from Peterson, interview; "White Merchants and Black Power."

116 Walker's account of the Triangle incident seemed to conflate an incident occurring at a different Fulton Street shoe store and the one at Triangle. Walker and Felton, *Turn the Horns On*, 18; "White Merchants and Black Power."

117 "White Merchants and Black Power."

118 Walker and Felton, *Turn the Horns On*, 18. Akili Walker also recounted this story in *Voices of The EAST*, 131.

119 Walker and Felton, *Turn the Horns On*, 18; Akili Walker, interview; Beatty, interview; Beatty also reflected on the incident in *Voices of The EAST*, 35. Such

concerns about the ways gendered violence specifically impacted Black boys may have partially stemmed from beliefs that racial, gender, and cultural stereotypes about African American males as criminal, thuggish, hyperaggressive, and combative fueled state-initiated and state-sanctioned violence against them. Lindsey, "Post-Ferguson," 235.

120 Jitu Weusi, "Re-Emergence of B'klyn Grassroots Politics"; Walker and Felton, *Turn the Horns On*, 18.

121 Jitu Weusi, "Re-Emergence of B'klyn Grassroots Politics."

122 Peterson, interview.

123 Howze, interview. The phrase quoted in the section title, "We saw ourselves as soldiers," is from this interview.

124 Allegheny Department of Human Services, *Homewood*, 4–5; "Public Auditorium Authority Members"; Davis, *From Head Shops to Whole Foods*, 69.

125 East Avenue High School Yearbook, 1967, 47.

126 "F.A.T. Honors Guardians."

127 Trent, "East Area Chatter." Harambee Bookstore is mentioned in Special Agent in Charge, Pittsburgh to Director, FBI, memorandum, March 24, 1971, in FBI, COINTELPRO Surveillance Files for February–May 1971, FBI Files on Black Extremist Organizations, Part 1: COINTELPRO Files on Black Hate Groups and Investigation of Deacons for Defense and Justice, ProQuest History Vault: Black Freedom Struggle in the 20th Century (Folder: 101094-006-0848); display ad 28, *New Pittsburgh Courier*, February 21, 1970, 15; "Inmate Sets Record Straight"; and Fisher, "Earning Dual Degrees," 83.

128 Edwin, "Harambee Arts Festival Returns"; "Awakening of the Harambee Legacy"; "Black Arts Festival Scheduled"; Trent, "East Area Chatter."

129 Howze, interview.

130 Woodard, *Nation within a Nation*, 168; Simanga, "Congress of African People," 113; Daniels, "Toward a Congress of African People."

131 Howze, interview.

132 Stokes, "Arusi!" Tamanika Howze was also known as Bruwana Mundi, Tamanika Mundi, and Tamanika Salaam. Sala Udin Saif Salaam, Afrikan View (column), July 7, 1973. For a discussion of Amiri Baraka's ideological evolution, including his period of engagement with Karenga-inspired "cultural nation building," see Wallach, *Every Nation Has Its Dish*, 184.

133 Like *lapas*, the *gele* (a Yoruba word for a woman's head wrap) is a symbol of African womanhood with long-standing religious, aesthetic, and utilitarian traditions throughout Africa and the diaspora. It became a popular accessory in Black cultural nationalist circles in the United States during the 1960s and experienced a resurgence in the 1990s. The men's outfit, also known as the *mwalimu* suit, was for "discerning nationalists" of the Black Power era. It was initially designed and worn by Julius Nyerere, first president of Tanzania, a newly independent African nation. In addition to wearing the outfits as a fashion statement, men in CAP viewed the suits as a cultural expression of their attachment to their African

heritage as well as a political statement about self-determination, Black nationalist unity, and transnational solidarity. Dorestal, *Style Politics*, 232–33.

134 Stokes, "Arusi!"

135 Tamanika Howze discussed how female members were expected to be submissive and how they folded their arms across their chests when walking past the organization's leader. She also recalled that Pittsburgh CAP was top-heavy with men holding leadership posts. Howze, interview. Amiri Baraka described a similar practice in which he observed women in the Us Organization crossing their arms on their breasts and bowing slightly when Karenga passed them. Baraka called this act of submission "an Afro-American adaptation of West African feudalism." Amiri Baraka, *Autobiography*, 254. E. Frances White opined that complementarity and extended family forms have continued "to work against the liberation of black women." White, "Africa on My Mind," 75.

136 Sala Udin Saif Salaam, Afrikan View (column), July 7, 1973, January 19, 1974.

137 Howze, interview. The couple eventually divorced and lost one son to gun violence. Dyer, "Udin Talks about Slain Son."

138 "'Spiritual Revolution of the Mind' Launched."

139 Howze, interview.

140 "Mental Health Team"; "Hill Mental Health Team Created."

141 Howze, interview; Howze, personal communication. Amina Baraka also described the women in CFUN as disciplined "soldiers," stating that they usually woke at 6:00 a.m. for meetings, performed secretarial work, worked in the communal kitchen, led, cleaned, and organized *umuzis* (dwellings for communal living), ran independent and supplementary educational institutions and childcare facilities, participated in demonstrations, and performed many other tasks. Their work regularly ended after midnight. Amina Baraka, interview, July 13, 2012.

142 Halisi and Mtume, *Quotable Karenga*, 20–21; Mumininas, *Mwanamke Mwananchi*, 4–8; E. Frances White, "Africa on My Mind," 76–77.

143 According to Rickford, Pan-African nationalists viewed *kazi* as both a "moral commitment" and "sustained physical exertion." Rickford, "'Kazi Is the Blackest,'" 99.

144 Tamanika Howze was not alone in expressing such a sense of fatigue. Tayari kwa Salaam of Ahidiana shared a similar sentiment. Tayari kwa Salaam, interview. The importance of *kazi*, particularly in supporting claims of women's organizational indispensability and wide-ranging work duties, was exemplified in "Kazi Like You Mean It," which was the title of a section of Black and Angaza, *EAST Sisterhood*, 7–8.

145 The estimate of about ten Pittsburgh CAP members came from Howze, interview; Cheo Elimu to Imamu Amiri Baraka, memo, December 30, 1970, Komozi Woodard Amiri Baraka Collection. Johnson, "Black Group Holds Feast"; "Blacks Observe Kwanza [*sic*]"; Sala Udin Saif Salaam, Afrikan View (column), December 29, 1973.

146 Sala Udin Saif Salaam, Afrikan View (column), January 19, 1974.

147 Elimu to Baraka, December 30, 1970; Howze, interview.

148 A united front is a coalition formed to oppose a force posing a problem for all constituents. The united front strategy originated in the 1920s Chinese Communist Party and its collaboration with the Nationalist Party to defeat regional warlords. Yee, "Three World Theory," 240. Simanga outlined the origins of the Congress of African People's united front strategy, tracing it back to Malcolm X's call for "a united front of black people regardless of ideology, geography, religion, or affiliation." Simanga also explained that CAP's united front endeavors from 1970 to 1975 were its most important work because advocates helped unify a fragmented struggle into a potent political force. Simanga, *Amiri Baraka*, 93–95.

149 Sala Udin Saif Salaam, Afrikan View (column), January 6, 1973, January 27, 1973, and June 1, 1974. The author of one article recognized that, though the participation of Black officials was lower than the previous year, CAP was the dominant force in the well-organized 1973 Western Pennsylvania Black Political Convention. The author noted that the theme was "Kazi (work) is the blackest of all." "Game of Politics"; Fonville, "Blacks Need Third Party"; Stokes, "Black Politicos."

150 Howze, interview. "Action of Assembly Widens Gap"; Sala Udin Saif Salaam, Afrikan View (column), March 10, 1973; "New Date Set for Parley."

151 Howze, interview; Sala Udin Saif Salaam, Afrikan View (column), January 19, 1974; "Free School." See Williams, *Concrete Demands*, 140, for a discussion of how Black Power activists prioritized quality education, culturally relevant school curricula, and community control.

152 Like the Black Power-era Communiversity, Freedom Schools were modeled on civil rights movement institutions. "Organizers Schedule Black Political Action Forum"; Edwin, "Harambee Arts Festival Returns"; Haynes, "Hill House Program"; Kendrick, "To Tell the Truth." The types of Freedom Schools Howze worked with were first developed by the Children's Defense Fund in 1988. Like the Freedom Schools of the early 1960s, they had the responsibility of educating whole families; however, the more recently formed institutions served a racially and ethnically diverse student body, including Latine pupils. Charles N. Brown, "Pittsburgh Establishes Freedom Schools."

153 "Blacks Demonstrate against Gulf Policy"; Sala Udin Saif Salaam, Afrikan View (column), February 3, 1973.

154 Simanga, *Amiri Baraka*, 6, 68.

155 Sala Udin Saif Salaam, Afrikan View (column), May 19, 1973; group portrait of Ewari "Ed" Ellis, Roland Hayes, Sala Udin Saif Salaam (Sam Howze), Jitu Weusi, and Reverend Rosamund Kay, seated for press conference, with Tim Stevens and Father August "Gus" Taylor seated in back, during African Liberation Week, May-June 1973, 2001.35.4672, Charles "Teenie" Harris Archive, accessed August 10, 2014.

156 Simanga asserted that the mid-1970s period of CAP's development included a turn to socialism, which was expressed through "African revolutionary intellectuals primarily and other Third World revolutionaries secondarily." Simanga, *Amiri Baraka*, 101.

157  "BAS Sponsors Report."

158  Sala Udin Saif Salaam, Afrikan View (column), June 1, 1974.

159  Simanga, *Amiri Baraka*, 83–84.

160  Howze, interview. Pittsburgh CAP's small size may also have played a role in necessitating female involvement on various levels within the group as well as impacting their ability to wield power.

161  Udin, "Black Women's United Front."

162  Monopoly capitalism is a for-profit economic system in which a few private owners, rather than the state, control trade and industry.

163  Udin, "Black Women's United Front"; Fonville, "Groundwork Laid."

164  Fonville, "Are Black Women for or against Women's Lib?"

165  Howze, interview.

166  Joan Little's first name is alternately spelled and pronounced "JoAnn" and "Joanne." McNeil, "'Joanne Is You,'" 259–60, 263, 274–75; McGuire, *At the Dark End of the Street*, 202–3, 208–12, 214–15, 223–24. The New Jersey Black Women's United Front sponsored a fundraiser in support of Joan Little's defense in April 1975. "B.W.U.F.," *Unity and Struggle*, April 1975, 10. After her subsequent arrest pertaining to the original breaking and entering charges, the statement "Free Joan Little" was emblazoned on the pages of *Unity and Struggle*, June 1978, 11, and July 1978, 12; "Legal Updates." Karenga wrote a plea for Little's acquittal. Maulana Ron Karenga, "In Defense of Sis. Joanne."

167  McNeil, "'Joanne Is You,'" 267.

168  Fonville, "Pittsburghers Rally Support."

169  McNeil, "'Joanne Is You,'" 260.

170  Woodard, *Nation within a Nation*, 183; Maulana Karenga, "In Defense of Sis. Joanne." See Greene, *Free Joan Little*, 53–62, for a critique of various Black Power leaders' observations about the meaning of Little's case.

171  McGuire, *At the Dark End of the Street*, xix.

172  Fonville, "Black Women's UF."

173  "Black Women Slate Forum."

174  Fonville, "Black Women's UF"; "Black Women's United Front Plans Conference."

175  "Black Women's United Front Forms."

176  "Black Women's United Front Forms"; "Black Women's United Front Plans Conference."

CHAPTER 3. "*TAIFA SAA* MEANS NATION TIME"

1  Amiri Baraka, "It's Nation Time," in *It's Nation Time*, 21–22.

2  Bright, interview. The quote "*taifa saa*, nation time" is taken from Martha Bright's longer statement, "It was a nation, *taifa saa*, nation time. . . . Any aspect of a nation that you could think of, we had at The East."

3  Manoni, *Bedford-Stuyvesant*, 25.

4  Joshua Clark Davis defines "activist entrepreneurs" in *From Head Shops to Whole Foods*, 3.

5  Operation Breadbasket, which operated from 1962 until 1972, was aimed at helping African Americans gain greater access to the American economy and was spearheaded by the Southern Christian Leadership Conference. Big Black, "Around Our Way," *Black News* 1, no. 28 (February 7, 1971): 10; "Breadbasket Maps A&P Confrontation"; Stanford, "Reverend Jesse and the Rainbow/PUSH Coalition," 152–57. For more information on the influence of Black Power as one of several transformations inspiring activist entrepreneurship and "participatory economics" during the 1960s and 1970s, see Davis, *From Head Shops to Whole Foods*, 3–4, 43–49.

6  Amiri Baraka, "It's Nation Time," 22; Bright, interview. Simanga also pointed out that women in Newark CAP were key to the organization's businesses, which were an expression of self-reliance and self-determination. Simanga, *Amiri Baraka*, 82.

7  Dorestal, *Style Politics*, 233; Amina Baraka, interview, July 13, 2012.

8  Amina Baraka, interview, July 13, 2012.

9  Amina Baraka, interview, July 13, 2012.

10  Wilson, "Our Generation," in *Voices of The EAST*, 134.

11  Black and Angaza, *EAST Sisterhood*, 7. Although the Mavazi store did not do well, women like Muslimah nevertheless contributed their labor to such ventures, which were part of a larger economic-nationalist effort to develop institutions that would help sustain the organization, the surrounding community, and the Black nation within the United States. For more information about Mavazi's offerings, see Konadu, *View from The East*, 83–84; and Mavazi Clothing Co-op advertisement, *Black News* 2, no. 4 (June 2, 1973): 37, and *Black News* 2, no. 12 (December 26, 1973): 14.

12  *The EAST Sisterhood* booklet included self-narratives from Martha Bright, Muslimah, Inuka, Olabisi, and Nassoma, all women who described their various tasks as East family members. Black and Angaza, *EAST Sisterhood*, 7. Other female advocates recalled performing jobs like clerical and administrative work, typesetting, and teaching, listing such duties among a host of tasks that either reinforced or increased their workforce readiness and their entrepreneurial and leadership skill sets. See Oseye Mchawi, Isoke Nia, Mama Carrie Ansar Roberson, and Shieba Ellerbee Watson in *Voices of The EAST*, 98, 107–8, 111–12, 130.

13  Peterson, interview. Another advocate reflected on her time in The East, stating that *kazi* became a guiding force for her lifelong values, and that it is a "profound work ethic" dictating persistence until the ultimate goal is achieved. Oseye Mchawi in *Voices of The EAST*, 98.

14  The wording for the section title, "Food for Tradition and Life," is from a Kununuana Co-op advertisement, which read, "Food for Life, Shopping in Tradition." *Black News* 1, no. 37 (January 1972): 7.

15  Wallach, "How to Eat to Live"; Wallach, *Every Nation Has Its Dish*, 161, 173, 177. Also see Davis, *From Head Shops to Whole Foods*, 192–93, where the author explains foodways, which Black nationalists theorized as important for reducing dependence on the industrial agriculture complex and the Eurocentric consumerism controlling it.

16 Foodways encompass diet, culinary customs, and eating habits.

17 Wallach, "How to Eat to Live"; Wallach, *Every Nation Has Its Dish*, 185.

18 Wallach, "How to Eat to Live."

19 Wallach, "How to Eat to Live." Advocates did not limit their health-related activism to culinary concerns and foodways. For instance, a 1972 *Black News* article reported a plea for a neighborhood mobile health clinic that would provide such services as vision screening, x-rays, and sickle cell testing. "Mobile Clinic for Our Community."

20 Adeyemi Bandele, interview.

21 Kweli Campbell (Weusi) in *Voices of The EAST*, 41. The quote was printed in an article that was part of the 1975 and 1976 *Black News* Kwanzaa commemorations. The 1975 layout informed the public about the origins and meaning of the holiday celebration, and invited them to East Kwanzaa programs every day from December 1 to December 19. "Kwanza [*sic*], a Tradition," *Black News* 3, no. 5 (December 1975): 17, and *Black News* 3, no. 13 (October 1976): 12.

22 Mchawi, "Which Way Kwanza [*sic*]."

23 East Publication and Distribution advertisement, *Black News* 2, no. 12 (December 26, 1973): 16–17.

24 Wallach, "How to Eat to Live."

25 Beatty, interview. The East Caterers were managed by Brother Mzee Moyo. East Caterers advertisement, *Black News* 4, no. 25 (August 1983): 22. The East Catering service was also mentioned in Angela Weusi et al., "Memories of The East." One narrator suggested that the venture was a good organizational fundraiser. Akili Walker emphasized East women's role in preparing food for the jazz club. Walker, interview.

26 Bright, interview; Angela Weusi et al., "Memories of The East"; Konadu, *View from The East*, 79; Muslimah Mashariki in *Voices of The EAST*, 95.

27 Surfaro, "The East."

28 Kununuana Co-op advertisement, *Black News* 1, no. 39 (April 1972): 15; Kununuana Co-op advertisement, *Black News* 2, no. 11 (December 11, 1972): n.p. Also see Davis, *From Head Shops to Whole Foods*, 192.

29 East Co-Op advertisement, *Black News* 3, no. 4 (October-November 1975): 17.

30 Konadu, *View from The East*, 82.

31 Peterson, interview. The term "food desert" was first used in the 1990s. The literature reflects that low-income neighborhoods and communities with a high African American population had fewer supermarkets and chain stores than economically and racially advantaged areas. There were also correlations between residence in food deserts and issues with diet and diet-related health outcomes, such as obesity, heart disease, and high blood pressure. More than three decades after the work of Black nationalists involved in this study, the Centers for Disease Control suggest such corrective policies as governmental support of local cooperatives and development of community food projects. Cummins and Macintyre, "'Food Deserts,'" 436; Beaulac, Kristjansson, and Cummins, "Systematic Review of Food Deserts," 1, 5.

32 Macleod, "Food Prices," 382; Marc D. Brown, "Building an Alternative," 298–301; Konadu, *View from The East*, 82; Davis, *From Head Shops to Whole Foods*, 1–5.

33 Joshua Davis asserts that, although Black capitalism was never a panacea, Black-owned businesses did benefit African American communities. Davis, "Consumer Liberation," iii, 9, 38; also see Davis, *From Head Shops to Whole Foods*, 43–49.

34 Ransby, *Ella Baker*, 88.

35 The Kawaida Groundwork Committee and the Organization Us participated in the Inner Cities Food Cooperative with the National Council of Negro Women (NCNW). The NCNW's goal was to help counteract the negative effects of rapidly divesting outlets for reasonably priced healthy foods in urban areas by bulk purchasing items and selling them at discounted rates to residents, who paid a small fee to be members of the co-op. Buttressing my claim that such activities resembled what would later be called social-entrepreneurship business models more than the extractive capitalism of critics' accusations, the NCNW co-op's president explained, "Our co-op is people-oriented not profit-oriented." Subira Kifano served as board member of the NCNW's Inner City Food Cooperative in 1983. The Sunflower County section of the NCNW had also contributed to Freedom Farm, particularly providing the first fifty pigs that started the program's initial "pig bank" program. Such connecting threads suggest the importance of women's contributions to a long tradition of Black cooperative economics and underscore the idea that women in Black Power cultural nationalist groups used tactics that were similar to those of their counterparts who participated in earlier phases of the long Black freedom struggle. "NCNW Opens Inner Cities Food Cooperative"; Ransby, *Ella Baker*, 82; Nembhard, *Collective Courage*, 99–100; Chana Kai Lee, *For Freedom's Sake*, 147–52; Blain, *Until I Am Free*, 121–22.

36 Kalamu ya Salaam, interview. The wording of the subsection title is from the title of a 1984 conference; see "Black Woman's Group Presents Black Women: Hope for the Future," flyer, 1984, Tayari kwa Salaam Papers.

37 In reference to egalitarian gender roles, Samori Sekou Camara asserted that women and men were equal partners in Ahidiana. He contrasted the organization's "mutual respect" between members to the "power struggles and masculine posturing" in other Black Power groups. Camara, "'There Are Some Bad Brothers and Sisters,'" 193, 200–201. For more information on Ahidiana's various enterprises, also see St. Julien, *Upon the Shoulders of Elephants*, 14.

38 Camara, "'There are Some Bad Brothers and Sisters,'" 193; Tayari kwa Salaam, "Practice the Values," 46; Tayari kwa Salaam and Kalamu ya Salaam, *Who Will Speak for Us?*, n.p. Another Ahidiana activity related to larger Black Power cultural nationalist foodways included vegetarian cooking workshops for parents of Work/Study Center students. The classes were intended to encourage healthy eating at home. Madzimoyo, "Afrikan-Americans Educate Their Own."

39 Tayari kwa Salaam, "Ujamaa," in Salaam and Salaam, *Who Will Speak for Us?*, n.p. *Who Will Speak for Us?* is a reflection of Kawaida philosophy, as Tayari kwa

Salaam not only explores the Seven Principles in the work, but also reinforces the importance of adhering to the teachings of both Maulana Karenga and Imamu Baraka.

40  Duka Ujamaa was the name of a cooperative grocery story in Newark. Duka Ujamaa advertisement, *Black Newark*, February 1973, 5; Woodard, *Nation within a Nation*, 135.

41  Scot Brown, *Fighting for US*, 153–57; Farmer, "Renegotiating the 'African Woman,'" 76.

42  Camara, "'There Are Some Bad Brothers and Sisters,'" 201, 203. Perhaps, in using the word "powerful," Camara referred to Tayari kwa Salaam's claim that "each year women participants would be moved by the conference proceedings and become inspired to start an organization for Black women." She offered the Black Women's Group as an example. Tayari kwa Salaam, "So-Journeying," 112.

43  Warren-Williams, interview.

44  Warren-Williams, interview.

45  The Black Woman's Conference required registration. The registration fee was twelve dollars in advance to attend and fifteen dollars on-site. Third Annual Black Woman's Conference, "Working Together, We Can Make a Change," program.

46  Camara, "'There Are Some Bad Brothers and Sisters,'" 202; Second Annual Black Woman's Conference, "Understanding Black Women," program, 1979, Tayari kwa Salaam Papers.

47  Warren-Williams, interview.

48  Third Annual Black Woman's Conference, program.

49  Third Annual Black Woman's Conference, program.

50  Maslin, "'Portrait of Teresa.'"

51  Third Annual Black Woman's Conference, program.

52  Third Annual Black Woman's Conference, program; Farmer, *Remaking Black Power*, 141; Pope, "Virginia Evalena Young Collins." For more on Aline St. Julien's reflections on racial and ethnic identity, see Gehman, "Toward an Understanding of the Quadroon Society," 54–55; Tayari kwa Salaam, "So-Journeying," iv; Aline St. Julien, *Colored Creole: Color Conflict and Confusion in New Orleans*, pamphlet, 1987 reprint of 1972 essay, Warren-Williams Papers; Simmons, *Crescent City Girls*, 56, 61–63, 164–65.

53  Third Annual Black Woman's Conference, program.

54  Warren-Williams, interview.

55  Warren-Williams, interview.

56  Tayari kwa Salaam, *Working Together*, 2, 9, 10.

57  Warren-Williams, interview; Nana Anoa Nantambu, interview; Tayari kwa Salaam, *Working Together*, 3.

58  Tayari kwa Salaam, *Working Together*, 3–4. Highlighting the intersectional challenges of racism, sexism, and classism, Black communist women of the Old Left pioneered what would become known by the 1970s as Black feminist theories of triple oppression. McDuffie, *Sojourning for Freedom*, 3–4.

59 Organizational structure and size should be considered as elements giving rise to ideas and policies supporting greater women's equality in Kawaida-influenced groups. Kalamu ya Salaam discussed how Ahidiana was more consensus-based than other Kawaida-influenced groups. Rickford has claimed that Ahidiana possessed a "stronger ethic of self-criticism" than other nationalist formations. Kalamu ya Salaam, interview; Rickford, *We Are an African People*, 146.

60 Tayari kwa Salaam, *Working Together*, 4, 7.

61 Tayari kwa Salaam, *Working Together*, 5–6, 8.

62 Warren-Williams, interview; Joshua-Jasmine, interview, May 28, 2013.

63 Joshua-Jasmine, interview, May 28, 2013.

64 Warren-Williams, interview.

65 Warren-Williams, interview; Tayari kwa Salaam, "So-Journeying," 112–13. Quotes are from Bebelle, interview. Ahidiana was a consensus-based rather than an autocratic and hierarchical organization. Kalamu ya Salaam, interview; Tayari kwa Salaam, "Practice the Values," 42.

66 Tayari kwa Salaam, "So-Journeying," 114.

67 Bebelle, interview; "Carol Bebelle"; Michna, "Performance and Cross-Racial Storytelling," 49.

68 Bebelle, interview.

69 "Ashé" means "life force" in the Yoruba language. Bebelle cofounded Ashé with Douglass Redd. Michna, "Performance and Cross-Racial Storytelling," 49, 50, 56–57; Bebelle and Rowell, "Carol Bebelle with Charles Henry Rowell," 1212; Ashé Cultural Arts Center website, accessed November 26, 2015, www.ashecac.org; "Carol Bebelle."

70 Bebelle mentioned such community advocates as former Ahidiana member Nilima Mwendo (Lower Ninth Ward activist) and Vera Warren-Williams (Community Book Center proprietor) as well as local nurse Teja Carey. Bebelle, interview.

71 "Black Woman's Group Presents Black Women: Hope for the Future," flyer, 1984, Tayari kwa Salaam Papers; "KWANZAA News," brochure, 1985, Tayari kwa Salaam Papers.

72 Joshua-Jasmine described the BWG's work as "feminism." Joshua-Jasmine, interview, May 28, 2013.

73 Elaine Brown, *Taste of Power*, 108–9.

74 Jones and Chimurenga, *What We Stood For*, 52, 58. The protocol of men eating before women is also noted in Wallach, *Every Nation Has Its Dish*, 186.

75 This quote was printed in an article that was part of the 1975 and 1976 *Black News* Kwanzaa commemorations. "Kwanza [*sic*], a Tradition," *Black News* 3, no. 5 (December 1975): 17 and *Black News* 3, no. 13 (October 1976): 12.

76 Woodard, interview.

77 Amina Baraka, interviews, July 12, 2012, July 13, 2012; Woodard, interview; Woodard, *Nation within a Nation*, 135; Simanga, *Amiri Baraka*, 82.

78 Angela Weusi et al., "Memories of The East"; Akilah Mashariki, panel discussion. Amina Baraka told a similar story about Martin Luther King Jr.'s 1968 visit to her home, although she stated that she was cleaning rather than cooking. Amina Baraka, interview by Kim Brown.

79 Walker and Felton, *Turn the Horns On*, 17. Akili Walker also recounted this story in *Voices of The EAST*, 131. Esenga McCrakin told a similar story about how her affiliation with The East helped her develop essential skills. She discussed enrolling her child at Uhuru Sasa and working in the Parent Council office during a period when she was laid off from her job. From the council office, she moved into serving in The East's kitchen with "sisters Lottie and Kadijah" for a decade. McCrakin began to take food service and cake decorating courses as well as cooking class at a local technical during that time. Esenga McCrakin in *Voices of The EAST*, 96.

80 Beatty, interview. See Black and Angaza, *EAST Sisterhood*, 3, for a general statement and example of women using skills they acquired and developed in The East in their future careers and community work.

81 Bright, interview; Angela Weusi et al., "Memories of The East."

82 "Afrikan Women Unite."

83 "Afrikan Women Unite."

CHAPTER 4. "TO BUILD OUR NATION . . . TEACH OUR CHILDREN!"

1 *Life*, July 15, 1966, cover; Scot Brown, *Fighting for US*, 40. The phrase quoted in the chapter title is from "Work/Study Center Ninth Annual Graduation Celebration."

2 *Life*, July 15, 1966, cover; Scot Brown, *Fighting for US*, n.p.; Omotayo, interview. Founded by Alfred and Bernice Ligon in 1941 and operating for over fifty years, Aquarian was one of the longest-lived Black-owned bookstores in the country. It was also a spiritual center for studies of metaphysics and astrology and a meeting place for exploring African American history and culture. "Alfred and Bernice Ligon Aquarian Collection"; Aquarian is also mentioned in Jones and Chimurenga, *What We Stood For*, 43.

3 Emery, Braselmann, and Gold, "Freedom School Curriculum"; Robin J. Hayes, *Love for Liberation*, 16–17; Felber, "'Harlem Is the Black World,'" 210; Abioye, "Vanguards in the Classroom," 560; Brock, "Selected Projects in Labor Education." Benson refers to the Communiversity as a site of "counterhegemonic instruction and curricula" in "Learning Laboratory for Liberation," 193. Jamala Rogers, interview; Nana Anoa Nantambu, interview.

4 Rickford did not consider IBIs to be *kilombos*, free spaces, or safe spaces for African-descended people fleeing hegemonic oppression; instead, he considered IBIs *potential* seedbeds of revolution in the late 1960s and early 1970s. He cast IBIs as superficially and symbolically Afrocentric, mere reflections of the extant conservatism by the late 1970s and early 1980s. Scot Brown suggested, on the contrary, that a variety of nationalists looked toward advocates of cultural nationalism for ideological clarity and support during the post-1960s period of

conservative ascendance. Citing feminist and civil rights advocate Pamela Allen in a discussion of businesses, Joshua Clark Davis pointed out that free spaces were activist-created environments welcoming marginalized and nonconformist people, functioning as movement cultural hubs, and promoting alternative political and business values. He also discussed community control, parallel institutions, and dual power as methods for affording African Americans more intellectual and political self-determination. Invoking "the fugitive slave" as a prototype, Jarvis R. Givens describes "fugitive pedagogy" as a metanarrative of Black teaching and learning practices that date back to enslavement. Fugitive pedagogy is part of the protracted Black freedom struggle, involving physical and intellectual acts of teachers and students that critique, invalidate, or subvert White supremacist and anti-Black, hegemonic educational beliefs and practices. Focusing on US history at the end of the Jim Crow era, Givens describes maroon societies as archetypical instances of Black fugitivity in general and points out alternative curricula as specific examples of fugitive pedagogy. Rickford, *We Are an African People*, 219; Scot Brown, *Fighting for US*, 129; Davis, *From Head Shops to Whole Foods*, 20–21; Givens, *Fugitive Pedagogy*, 5, 10, 17, 27.

5   Thomas, interview; Jones and Chimurenga, *What We Stood For*, 98. Confessing his own patriarchal tendencies, Amiri Baraka also indicated that excessive male chauvinism was prevalent in CFUN under his leadership during the Kawaida phases, and that the philosophy was particularly flawed in its legitimization of male dominance as "revolutionary." Amiri Baraka, *Autobiography*, 298–300; Rickford, *We Are an African People*, 123. Scot Brown wrote that South African associate Letta Mbulu indicated that Us men had a "naïve or distorted view" of "African" gender relations and wanted to obtain "total control." Scot Brown, *Fighting for US*, 57. Floyd W. Hayes III and Judson L. Jeffries also pointed out that Us's institutionalization of female subservience in ritual set it apart from other Black liberation movement organizations with records of marginalizing female members, such as the BPP and the SCLC. Hayes and Jeffries, "*US* Does Not Stand for United Slaves!," 83. Ashley Farmer wrote that certain Us catechisms articulated some of the most extreme perspectives on circumscribing women's roles in the Black freedom struggle, but the author carefully parsed through ways female advocates were central to developing early organizational infrastructure in *Remaking Black Power*, 98–100.

6   Scot Brown, *Fighting for US*, 40–41, 56; Farmer, *Remaking Black Power*, 98–99. Also see Jones and Chimurenga, *What We Stood For*, 51, for reflections on how Maulana Karenga's first wife, Haiba, was instrumental in laying the organization's foundation. The phrase quoted in the section title, "Knowledge is the prime need of the hour," is from Mary McLeod Bethune, "Last Will and Testament," *Ebony*, August 1995, 105–10, quoted by Kifano in her explanation of how Kawaida recognized the urgency of emancipatory education in the Black freedom struggle as well as in the larger effort to positively transform society and the world. Kifano, "Promise and Possibilities," 54–55.

7  Thomas, interview. Imani Omotayo also stated that mostly women directed and taught in the school. Omotayo, interview. Naima Olugbala also observed early Us masculinism and women's resulting resistance, stating that eventually, women like Subira Kifano and Tiamoyo Karenga held important leadership and administrative positions. Olugbala, interview. Farmer points out that the Us School of Afroamerican Culture was the most visible expression of Us women's activism in *Remaking Black Power*, 98–99.

8  Omotayo, interview.

9  Kifano, "Afrocentric Education."

10  Omotayo, interview. Scot Brown cited 1967–1969 as the apex of the Us Organization's potency and influence. Scot Brown, *Fighting for US*, 132.

11  Rickford, *We Are an African People*, 12; Farmer, "Renegotiating the 'African Woman,'" 97.

12  Farmer, "Renegotiating the 'African Woman,'" 86; Farmer, *Remaking Black Power*, 99.

13  Omotayo, interview.

14  The word "boot" in the name of the dance referred to the rubber footwear that South Africans wore in the wet Johannesburg gold mines. Performers vigorously slapped and stomped their boots as they danced and sang. Us Organization members performed the boot dance steps, lyrics, and music in an adapted Pan-African style. Scot Brown, *Fighting for US*, 133–34; Mason, "Diversity of African Musics." Omotayo indicated that Simba were teens. Omotayo, interview.

15  *Life*, July 15, 1966, cover, 62–63; Karenga, interview, 75–76. Deborah Jones recalled that the Simba Wachanga were between twelve and twenty-five years old in Jones and Chimurenga, *What We Stood For*, 53.

16  Omotayo, interview.

17  According to Rickford, Black independent institutions had a long history of reinforcing "essentialist and hierarchical notions of 'manhood' and 'womanhood'" in pupils. Rickford, *We Are an African People*, 250.

18  Omotayo, interview; Jones and Chimurenga, *What We Stood For*, 53–54.

19  Scot Brown, *Fighting for US*, 56.

20  Omotayo, interview; Thomas, interview; "Us: A History of Service"; Scot Brown, *Fighting for US*, 56; Farmer, *Remaking Black Power*, 100–104. Debora Jones said that the Matamba formed in 1966, citing Simba leader Amiri Jomo as the women's first trainer and discussing her short time as Nzinga, or head, of the Matamba in Jones and Chimurenga, *What We Stood For*, 54–59.

21  Thomas, interview; Omotayo, interview; Kifano, interview, December 30, 2010; Jones and Chimurenga, *What We Stood For*, 67–115.

22  Kifano, interview, December 30, 2010.

23  Kifano, interview, December 30, 2010; Kifano, "Promise and Possibilities," 52.

24  Kifano, "Promise and Possibilities," 51–52; Kifano, "Afrocentric Education," 210–11.

25  Kurashige, "Crenshaw," 41–42.

26  Kifano, "Promise and Possibilities," 53, 59.

27 Kifano, "Promise and Possibilities," 54, 65.

28 Kifano, interview, December 30, 2010.

29 Maulana Karenga, interview, 192, 281. In this interview, Maulana Karenga charts the Us Organization's educational influence through men.

30 Kifano, "Promise and Possibilities," 56.

31 Kifano, "Promise and Possibilities," 68. Historian Tsekani Browne asserted that Anna Julia Cooper was both radical and conservative within her context, a description that fits the overall ideology of Kawaida womanism, which drew upon Cooper's thinking. Kawaida womanism represents an improvement of earlier gender roles within the philosophy, but still suggests that women have a restricted "place." Browne, "Anna Julia Cooper's Radical Uses of History."

32 Kifano, "Promise and Possibilities," 71.

33 *The Liner* (yearbook), 1969, 190, Hamline University Catalogues and Yearbooks; Alethia [Aleathia] Parker, "Black Sketches: 'Oh, Save the Babies,'" *Oracle* (Hamline University), November 5, 1971, 3; "PRIDE Plans Art Shows," *Oracle*, October 13, 1972, 4; Community Calendar, *Los Angeles Sentinel*, May 28, 1981, June 25, 1981, and October 20, 1983; "Black Agenda Tells of Upcoming Kwanzaa Fete"; Murray, "Black Agenda Installs Officers." The Grenada takeover deposed prime minister Maurice Bishop, leader of the Marxist-Leninist New JEWEL Movement.

34 Kifano, interview, December 30, 2010; "Us: A History of Service."

35 Burns, "Jersey Public School"; Butterfield, "Experimental Class."

36 For a discussion of the idea that 1960s "radical chic" representations focused on revolutionary men, see Tillet, "Panthers' Revolutionary Feminism." For more on the claim that Black Power-era cultural nationalism is often viewed as rhetorical, but Pan-African nationalist schools were a concrete manifestation of such ideology, see Rickford, *We Are an African People.* The phrase quoted in the section title, "education is the root of development [and] defense," is from Amina Baraka, interview, July 17, 2012.

37 Amiri Baraka, *New Nationalism*, 51.

38 Rickford, *We Are an African People*, 138–39; Simanga, *Amiri Baraka*, 55; Woodard, *Nation within a Nation*, 2, 135; "African Free School Structure," paper, Series V: Congress of African People, 1960–1976: Congress of African People, Organizing Manual, 1972, Komozi Woodard Amiri Baraka Collection.

39 Amiri Baraka, *Autobiography*, 299; Rickford, *We Are an African People*, 139.

40 Rickford, *We Are an African People*, 139; Simanga, *Amiri Baraka*, 82; Omotayo, interview; Amina Baraka, interview, July 13, 2012.

41 Amiri Baraka, *Autobiography*, 299; Rickford, *We Are an African People*, 135, 138.

42 Amiri Baraka, *Autobiography*, 299; Rickford, *We Are an African People*, 138; "African Free School Structure"; "African Free School," *Black New Ark*, September 1972, 4 .

43 Amina Baraka, interview, July 13, 2012.

44 Amiri Baraka, *Autobiography*, 299–300; Rickford, *We Are an African People*, 138; Amina Baraka, interview, July 17, 2012; Mumininas, *Mwanamke Mwananchi*, 12; "Thirteenth Avenue School."

45  Kifano quoting Carol Lee in "Promise and Possibilities," 46. Rickford also pointed out that, "though Pan African nationalists touted institution building as a viable frontier for mass actions, the vast majority of African-American school children remained in public institutions." Rickford, *We Are an African People*, 5, 7.

46  "African Free School in Newark"; "African Free School Structure"; Amina Baraka, interviews, July 13, 2012, July 17, 2012; Burns, "Jersey Public School"; Rickford, *We Are an African People*, 138, 141, 142.

47  Amina Baraka, interview, July 17, 2012; Burns, "Jersey Public School."

48  The quoted phrase is taken from a longer statement in which Amiri Baraka stressed that one of the African Free School's goals was to teach students cooperation in the process of constructing community within their ravaged neighborhood. Burns, "Jersey Public School." Michael Simanga emphasized women's importance in building CAP's many programs in Simanga, *Amiri Baraka*, 82.

49  Amina Baraka, interview, July 17, 2012.

50  Teule, "Why Is Marcus Garvey Closed?"; "Thirteenth Avenue School," 1–2.

51  "Thirteenth Avenue School," 15; Rickford, *We Are an African People*, 140; Burns, "Jersey Public School."

52  Rickford, *We Are an African People*, 140; Burns, "Jersey Public School"; "African Free School," paper; "Positive Votes for New School Names"; Curvin, *Inside Newark*, 145, 160.

53  Several affiliates became full-time cadres and changed their names when United Brothers came under the CFUN umbrella. According to Woodard, the United Brothers would prove important in Campbell's ascent as a local educational administrator. Woodard listed a number of them in *A Nation within a Nation*. Amina Baraka added the additional information in her self-narrative that Campbell was known as Mkuu in his work with CFUN. Woodard, *Nation within a Nation*, 89; Amina Baraka, interview, July 17, 2012; "Parents Get Their Principal"; Johnston, "Committee to Carry On." Eugene Campbell is noted as Mkuu in "Education for Liberation Conference Held Here."

54  Amina Baraka, interview, July 17, 2012.

55  Burns, "Jersey Public School."

56  The FBI's covert Counterintelligence Program operated from 1956 until 1971. Amina Baraka, interview, July 13, 2012; Federal Bureau of Investigation, "FBI Records: The Vault."

57  Burns, "Jersey Public School."

58  Rickford, *We Are an African People*, 139.

59  Amina Baraka, interview, July 17, 2012.

60  "African Free School in Newark."

61  "NJ School Endorsed"; Amiri Baraka, *Autobiography*, 300.

62  Rickford, *We Are an African People*, 140–41. *Compradors* are defined as relatively wealthy, educated, elite native residents of a colony who are considered to be bought off by the colonizers and therefore less willing to struggle for local independence. Woodard explains that the ultimate critique of many Black officials

who came to power through the modern Black convention movement as "agents for white racism" developed from Amiri Baraka's growing socialist theorizing of Newark as a case of internal colonialism turned neocolonialism. Woodard, *Nation within a Nation*, 251, 254.

63 Rickford, *We Are an African People*, 140.

64 Rickford, *We Are an African People*, 140; Amiri Baraka, *Autobiography*, 243–44, 247, 300.

65 Amina Baraka, interview, July 17, 2012.

66 Amiri Baraka, *Autobiography*, 247, 300; Mumford, *Newark*, 188.

67 Amiri Baraka, *Autobiography*, 300; Rickford, *We Are an African People*, 139.

68 Amina Baraka, interview, July 17, 2012.

69 Amina Baraka, interview, July 17, 2012.

70 "African Free School Structure."

71 Woodard, *Nation within a Nation*, 259.

72 Amina Baraka, interview, July 17, 2012.

73 Amina Baraka, interview, July 17, 2012.

74 The term "cultural archive" is from Farmer, "Renegotiating the 'African Woman,'" 86. Farmer indicates that the term refers to historical media, oral traditions, activities, and educational materials that provide information about Kawaida-influenced practices and ideas. When conducting research for this manuscript, I observed Subira Kifano, prior to her 2016 death, teaching youth and training educators by drawing from the Kawaida-influenced cultural archive during Kwanzaa celebrations. Additionally, I observed the imprint of both women and men affiliated with The East organization in works meant for popular consumption, like Angaza, *Kwanzaa*, ii, 129–30.

75 Farmer, "Renegotiating the 'African Woman,'" 86.

76 Amina Baraka, interview, July 13, 2012.

77 Amina Baraka, interview, July 17, 2012. Amina Baraka recounted that the Simbas in the story were given the names and attributes of certain male advocates.

78 Jaime J. Weinman described filmmaker Bob Clampett's 1943 animated piece *Coal Black and the Sebben Dwarfs* as "a catalogue of every racial stereotype in 1940s cinema." The film appeared on the "Censored Eleven," a list of offensive cartoons that broadcasters would not televise by the 1960s. Weinman argued that audiences should have been able to access the film and laugh at the stereotypes while considering historical context, but the film and the subsequent debate over its appropriateness provide further confirmation of how important a holistic approach to the Black freedom struggle was, including cultural work. Weinman claimed that the film was "good-natured," particularly in its use of Black actors for the voice-overs. While Black actors might have found rare acting jobs via the film, they were unable to control the way their culture was depicted on-screen. Negative on-screen stereotypes were not only reflections of prevalent values within the dominant culture, they influenced how Black people were perceived and treated as well as how they saw themselves, and each other,

in the real world. Consumption of popular culture shapes viewers' understanding of individuals' places in society. Although it never reached as broad an audience as Clampett's cartoon, cultural nationalists' work sought to counter such dynamics, and the AFS women's story represented a small-scale disruption of practices that usurped African-descended people's ability to control their own cultural images. Weinman, "Best Cartoon You've Never Seen"; Crews, "What Will it Take?"

79  Amina Baraka, interview, July 17, 2012.
80  Amina Baraka, interview, July 17, 2012.
81  Farmer, "Renegotiating the 'African Woman,'" 90, 97; Amina Baraka, interview, July 12, 2012; Woodard, *Nation within a Nation*, 126; Congress of African People, "Woman Question," n.p.; Woman Question Commission-Sum Up, notes, Series X: Revolutionary Communist League, 1974–1982: Revolutionary Communist League, Women Question and Other Position Papers, 1977, Komozi Woodard Amiri Baraka Collection; "CAP General Assembly," *Unity and Struggle*, November 1974, 10; Hill, interview. Hill pointed out that the African Women's Conference was Amina Baraka's brainchild, and Simanga confirmed this claim. Simanga went a step further, noting that Amina took no leadership role in the conference or the Black Women's United Front, but trained and supported other women like Hill in directing both programs. Simanga, *Amiri Baraka*, 84.
82  Photograph, *Black New Ark*, October 1973, 2; *Bullet Holes* (photograph), *New Pittsburgh Courier*, August 11, 1973, 2; Jalia, "Monthly Kiswahili Lesson."
83  Jalia, "Monthly Kiswahili Lesson."
84  Woodard, interview.
85  Amina Baraka, interviews, July 12, 2012, July 17, 2012.
86  Woodard, *Nation within a Nation*, 133.
87  Amina Baraka, interview, July 17, 2012.
88  Amina Baraka, interview, July 17, 2012.
89  Amiri Baraka, *Autobiography*, 300.
90  Woodard, *Nation within a Nation*, 135; Simanga, *Amiri Baraka*, 82; Amiri Baraka, *Autobiography*, 300.
91  Woodard, *Nation within a Nation*, 135; "African Free School," paper; Simanga, *Amiri Baraka*, 55; Jamala Rogers, interview.
92  Jamala Rogers, interview. Rogers is a leader of the Organization for Black Struggle, which she cofounded in 1980. A longtime St. Louis community organizer, she served as an adviser to local Ferguson protestors in the aftermath of the police slaying of unarmed Black teen Michael Brown in August 2014. Deere, "Ferguson Protesters Disagree"; Jamala Rogers, *Ferguson Is America*, ix–xiv.
93  Burns, "Jersey Public School."
94  Rickford, *We Are an African People*, 142.
95  Amina Baraka, interview, July 17, 2012; Burns, "Jersey Public School." During my research for this book, I heard various individuals in Newark refer to Amina and Amiri Baraka as "mama" and "pops" with affection and reverence.

96  Kifano, "Promise and Possibilities," 44; Rickford, *We Are an African People*, 12. I added the phrase "in which Black children's lives mattered."

97  "African Free School Has Own Methodology."

98  "African Free School Structure"; "African Free School Has Own Methodology." Rickford opined that "independent institutions demanded of their staff nothing less than missionary zeal." Rickford, *We Are an African People*, 243.

99  Rickford, *We Are an African People*, 141–42.

100  "African Free School Has Own Methodology"; "African Free School in Newark"; "NJ School Endorsed."

101  Woodard, *Nation within a Nation*, 88.

102  Rickford also pointed out that the gender roles within Kawaida, which specified that women should perform the essential tasks of African womanhood, ironically enabled activists such as Amina Baraka (CFUN) and Tayari kwa Salaam (Ahidiana) to step into leadership positions as top administrators and curriculum developers. Rickford, *We Are an African People*, 155, 191.

103  Woodard, *Nation within a Nation*, 253–54.

104  Hill, interview.

105  Mumford, *Newark*, 119–12.

106  Rickford, *We Are an African People*, 20, 244–45; Konadu, *View from The East*, 107–8, 112. For more on the definition of Black nationalism, see Ogbar, "Black Nationalism," 90.

107  Campbell, interview.

108  In 1972 the preschool was at 10 Claver Place. The high school was on Bedford Avenue until 1974. The middle school was around the corner on Fulton Street near the Mavazi shop. Another school location opened in the Gowanus Projects on Bond Street. It later moved to a storefront on Rockaway Boulevard across from housing projects in Brownsville. Martha Bright in Angela Weusi et al., "Memories of The East"; Bright, interview; Walker and Felton, *Turn the Horns On*, 15; Konadu, *View from The East*, 107–8.

109  Adeyemi Bandele, interview. Bright remembered that Ayanna Johnson left Uhuru Sasa to find employment at Weusi Shule (later Johnson Preparatory School), a fact that was confirmed in the "Family Schools Newsletter" in *Black News*. Kina Joshua-Jasmine of New Orleans also mentioned Ayanna Johnson as a woman who headed independent Black institutions in New York City, possibly because Johnson traveled across the nation and abroad as an organizer of IBIs in her capacity as business meetings chair of the New York Family Schools, the Council of Independent Black Institutions (CIBI) New York regional chapter. Bright, interview; Kalamu ya Salaam, interview; "Family Schools Newsletter," 15. Mama Lubaba Ahmed was headmistress of Brooklyn's Uhuru Sasa in 1980. Rashida Kierstedt succeeded Lubaba in 1983. Rickford, *We Are an African People*, 251, 256; Konadu, *View from The East*, 111.

110  Akili Walker, interview; Walker and Felton, *Turn the Horns On*, 15–16.

111 Akili Walker, interview; Walker and Felton, *Turn the Horns On*, 15–16; Jones, "Uhuru Sasa Shule." The Uhuru Sasa Shule's curriculum is also listed in Konadu, *View from The East*, 165.

112 Biondi, *Black Revolution on Campus*, 117.

113 Scholars do not agree about the exact reason or date the teaching field came to be considered women's work in America; however, it is clear that the feminization of the field occurred sometime in the nineteenth century. According to some accounts, women began to outnumber men in the profession by 1860. Black female teachers did not gain status in the profession until the latter part of the century, as African American males dominated the field until they were able to pursue careers in professions like medicine, journalism, law and government, and religion. The teaching field became ever more feminized within both racial groups over the course of the twentieth century. Montgomery, "Why Men Left," 219; Rich, "Why Don't More Men Go into Teaching?"; Collier-Thomas, "Impact of Black Women in Education."

114 See Mayer, "Full and Sometimes Very Surprising Story" for information about the key roles that mothers played in the Ocean Hill-Brownsville experimental district. Adeyemi Bandele, interview; Bright in Angela Weusi et al., "Memories of The East"; Les Campbell, interview by Blackside, Inc., November 3, 1988, *Eyes on the Prize* Interview Transcripts.

115 Peterson in Angela Weusi et al., "Memories of The East." Both Martha Bright and Kwasi Konadu reported that Uhuru Sasa teachers' stipend was $200 a month (about $10,937 in 2016). Konadu, *View from The East*, 76; Bright in Angela Weusi et al., "Memories of The East." Rickford noted that six full-time faculty at Brooklyn's Uhuru Sasa made $8,500 each in 1975, which was equivalent to $36,000 in 2013 (or $38,737 in 2016). Rickford, *We Are an African People*, 243.

116 Adeyemi Bandele, interview. Martha Bright also noted the work that New York City school teachers performed at Uhuru Sasa. Bright, interview; Angela Weusi et al., "Memories of The East." Lady Byrd is listed as Imani Day Care staff along with Tamisha, Khadijah, Muslimah, Naima, Aminisha, Afua, Taifa, Nayo (Evelyn Clarke), Waridi, Mtamanika, Oseye, Wambui, Nassoma, Darra Iman, Ieola, Olabisi, and Ramona in the "East Time-Line," 3. Note that the East Timeline includes more details, in *Voices of The EAST*, 143. For a description of the child development center's offerings, see "Imani." For more information on the Imani Center, see Konadu, *View from The East*, 91–96. Lady Byrd is referred to as Lady Esther Byrd in Petri Byrd, "Petri Byrd and Family," and Nayo is listed as Evelyn Nayo Clark in *Voices of The EAST*, 39–40, 46.

117 Bright's quotes are from Bright, interview; and Angela Weusi et al., "Memories of The East." The papers of Harvey Scribner, first chancellor of the newly decentralized public school system, contain the 1970–1973 Model Cities files. Central Brooklyn housed a Model Cities experiment. These antipoverty projects existed from 1966 to 1974 and were initiated by the Lyndon Johnson

presidential administration. The program was initially designed to encourage members of economically disadvantaged groups to become more involved in municipal politics. Central Brooklyn's Model Cities education-related plans focused on dropout prevention and featured winter and summer academies. Uhuru Sasa's specific role in the program requires further research, particularly in the area of women's participation and leadership. See Finding Aid for Board of Education; and Weber and Wallace, "Revealing the Empowerment Revolution," 173. Konadu estimated that three hundred junior high school students from Brooklyn spent the summer of 1972 at Shaw University in Raleigh, North Carolina, although the origin of the number is unclear. Konadu, *View from The East*, 74. Bright indicated that her trip to Shaw was in 1971. Bright, interview. The Uhuru Sasa Freedom Now summer day camps were advertised in *Black News*. For examples, see *Black News* 2, no. 4 (June 2, 1973): 31, and *Black News* 3, no. 1 (May 31, 1975): n.p.

118 Rhody McCoy, interview by Louis Massiah, October 12, 1988, *Eyes on the Prize Interview Transcripts*.

119 Angela Weusi et al., "Memories of The East"; Bright, interview.

120 Akili Walker, interview; Walker and Felton, *Turn the Horns On*, 16. Bright also asserted that Uhuru Sasa served students who had left the public school system. She emphasized the important role that the professionally trained educators who worked with Uhuru Sasa played in assisting students with earning their high school diplomas. Bright, interview. For an example of a document reflecting the importance of discipline and order at Uhuru Sasa, see the "Uhuru Sasa Shule Protocol" as transcribed in Konadu, *View from The East*, 161–62.

121 The "600" Schools were New York City public day schools and long-term confinement facilities, which were possibly named for the fact that educators received an additional $600 as a form of hazard pay. The schools were intended to educate and rehabilitate special needs students who were withdrawn from mainstream schools due to behavior problems. New York City Board of Education, "'600' Schools"; "Guard against Dumping-Ground Schools." For an anecdote of an instance where a child services investigator insisted on placing a young girl from an abusive home with East advocates, see Arnie Goldwag, *Brooklyn CORE, on Jitu Weusi*; Peterson, interview.

122 Peterson, interview.

123 Walker and Felton, *Turn the Horns On*, 17; Bright, interview.

124 Walker and Felton, *Turn the Horns On*, 17; Angela Weusi et al., "Memories of The East"; Peterson, interview.

125 Peterson, interview.

126 Peterson, interview.

127 Peterson, interview. For a discussion on activist teaching at The East's Uhuru Sasa Shule, how certain programs were designed to reach parents, and how the school's instructors were educated to deliver a Pan-Africanist curriculum, see Abena Moto Branch, "Aluta Continua (The Struggle Continues)," in *Voices of The EAST*, 36–37.

128 Jones, "Uhuru Sasa Shule"; Uhuru Sasa Evening School fall session advertisement, *Black News* 2, no. 10 (October 22, 1973): 27.

129 Jones, "Uhuru Sasa Shule"; Surfaro, "The East."

130 Shukuru Sanders in Angela Weusi et al., "Memories of The East."

131 Rickford, *We Are an African People*, 244–45, 247; Konadu, *View from The East*, 111.

132 Walker and Felton, *Turn the Horns On*, 17.

133 The phrase quoted in the section title, "Our people's future is dependent on our children's vital education," is from "Ahidiana Work/Study Center: A Black Independent and Affirmative Institution of Vital Education," brochure, n.d., Tayari kwa Salaam Papers.

134 Kwesi Nantambu, interview; Joshua-Jasmine, interview, May 28, 2013; Tayari kwa Salaam, "So-Journeying," 2–3, 13; Camara, "'There Are Some Bad Brothers and Sisters,'" 183; Madzimoyo, "Afrikan-Americans Educate Their Own." Tayari kwa Salaam defined Dokpwe as an "independent Black institution"; however, I chose the language "Black independent school" based on Andrews's terminology, which differentiates education in early learning centers and elementary, middle, and high schools that developed as alternatives to mainstream state and private schooling from extra-schooling or supplementary programs such as Saturday and evening courses and summer camps, which were meant to overcome the inequalities and gaps in mainstream state or private programs. Andrews, "Toward a Black Radical Independent Education," 11–12.

135 Kiini Ibura Salaam, interview. The word "lifestyle" is Nilima Mwendo's; Camara, "'There Are Some Bad Brothers and Sisters,'" 183–84. In "Practice the Values," 40, Tayari kwa Salaam stated, "The Nguzo Saba, Seven Principles, are the values we live and believe in Ahidiana." She specifically pointed out that the Black value system to which Ahidiana adhered was initiated by Karenga and further developed by Amiri Baraka. Ahidiana members worked on transforming their entire community and themselves as individuals. Their Sunday meetings involved exercise, study, planning and implementation of projects and programs, school maintenance, and food preparation. Collective food buying was done on Saturdays along with communal childcare. Tayari kwa Salaam, "So-Journeying," 98. Williettatta Ferdinand was mentioned in Joshua-Jasmine, interview, May 28, 2013.

136 Camara, "'There Are Some Bad Brothers and Sisters,'" 183–84. The term "organization of organizers" was quoted in Rickford, *We Are an African People*, 10. Cadre is defined as "a closely knit and disciplined group of persons who share similar views, values, and commitment to make change" in St. Julien, *Upon the Shoulders of Elephants*, 61. The estimate of sixteen to seventeen members is from Kalamu ya Salaam, interview. The number of twenty-two members is from St. Julien, *Upon the Shoulders of Elephants*, n.p. The plan to develop Ahidiana as a cadre organization with mass-based programming is taken from St. Julien, 12; the brochure "Ahidiana Work/Study Center: A Black Independent and Affirmative Institution of Vital Education" has information on the founding of the Work/Study Center.

137 Tayari kwa Salaam, "Ahidiana"; "Ahidiana Work/Study Center: A Black Independent and Affirmative Institution of Vital Education." Amina Baraka also noted
that funding sources were a marker of institutional independence. For an assessment of issues linked to maintaining independence, avoiding state funding, and
resisting what was viewed as co-optation by outside forces, see Andrews, "Toward
a Black Radical Independent Education," 11–12.

138 Rickford, *We Are an African People*, 19.

139 Tayari kwa Salaam, "Ahidiana"; "The Work Study Center [Teaching Philosophy,
Method, and Technique]," 1; Kalamu ya Salaam, interview. Tayari kwa Salaam
referred to the Work/Study Center "prepared environment" as "purposeful."
Tayari kwa Salaam, "Practice the Values," 43; Warren-Williams, interview. During
its second year, the school had ten students. In 1980 the school served twenty-
four children. Tayari kwa Salaam, "Ahidiana," 45; Camara, "'There Are Some Bad
Brothers and Sisters,'" 201.

140 Tayari kwa Salaam, "So-Journeying," 107–8.

141 Tayari kwa Salaam, "Practice the Values," 42. Also see "Family Schools Newsletter," 15–17, for examples of female teachers referred to as *mwalimu*. Former
students and childhood community members referred to their elders as "mama"
and "baba" in their self-narratives for this study. Joshua-Jasmine, interview, May
28, 2013; Kiini Ibura Salaam, interview.

142 Kiini Ibura Salaam, interview.

143 The term "'dreaming' . . . a world" is a reference to the Langston Hughes poem "I
Dream a World," which is the author's reverie about a more loving and peaceful
world. Ahidiana members connected to others with similar views in various ways.
Kiini Ibura Salaam, interview.

144 Kwesi Nantambu, interview.

145 Joshua-Jasmine, interview, May 28, 2013. Kalamu ya Salaam indicated that men
were required to help support the school; however, according to his explanations,
men mainly made financial contributions as well as cleaned and maintained the
physical plant. Kalamu ya Salaam, interview.

146 Kwesi Nantambu, interview; Joshua-Jasmine, interview, May 28, 2013. An example of
Tayari kwa Salaam's organizing efforts can be seen in her service as a de facto fundraiser for programs. "KWANZAA News," brochure, 1985, Tayari kwa Salaam Papers.

147 Rickford, *We Are an African People*, 16.

148 Tayari kwa Salaam, "So-Journeying," 104. For an example of how each of the
Nguzo Saba was taught at the Work/Study Center, see Tayari kwa Salaam, "Practice the Values," 40–46.

149 "Work Study Center [Teaching Philosophy, Method, and Technique]," 2.

150 Tayari kwa Salaam, "So-Journeying," 2, 103.

151 Joshua-Jasmine, interview, May 28, 2013.

152 Majority-Black city centers, which liberationists treated as "liberated zones," were
referred to as "key sites for reimagining community" in Rickford, *We Are an
African People*, 12.

153 Kiini Ibura Salaam, interview.

154 Kiini Ibura Salaam, interview.

155 Warren-Williams, interview. The language for comparing independent Black institutions and mainstream schools is from Rickford, *We Are an African People*, 2. Kwesi Nantambu also praised Ahidiana's focus on academic excellence. Kwesi Nantambu, interview.

156 "Work/Study Center Ninth Annual Graduation Celebration."

157 St. Julien, *Upon the Shoulders of Elephants*, 61.

158 Tayari kwa Salaam quoting Shujaa's Education and Schooling in "So-Journeying," 111.

159 Rickford, *We Are an African People*, 144, 2.

160 Ahidiana Work/Study Center's teaching techniques were aimed at "bring[ing] the school to the home and the home to the school." "The Work Study Center [Teaching Philosophy, Method, and Technique]"; Joshua-Jasmine, interview, May 28, 2013.

161 "Work Study Center [Teaching Philosophy, Method, and Technique]," 2–3; "Ahidiana Work/Study Center: A Black Independent and Affirmative Institution of Vital Education." Syncretism refers to the combining of different religions, cultures, or schools of thought.

162 Tayari kwa Salaam, "Practice the Values," 43.

163 Tayari kwa Salaam, "Practice the Values," 44–45.

164 "Ahidiana Work/Study Center: A Black Independent and Affirmative Institution of Vital Education."

165 Kifano, *Promises and Possibilities*, 44.

166 Warren-Williams, interview.

167 "Young Soldiers and Warriors/Raising Emotionally Committed Black Leaders," revised paper, n.d., Tayari kwa Salaam Papers. In some pieces of literature and internal papers, the statement reads, "Raise soldiers and warriors, future revolutionaries, leaders, and workers." Kalamu ya Salaam with Tayari kwa Salaam and Kuishi kwa Taraji, *Herufi*. Notes written on a paper draft reflected that someone grappled with the language. "Young Soldiers and Warriors/Raising Emotionally Committed Black Leaders," paper draft, n.d., Tayari kwa Salaam Papers.

168 Rickford, *We Are an African People*, 136, 154.

169 Salaam and Salaam, *Who Will Speak for Us?*, n.p.

170 Rickford, *We Are an African People*, 142; Konadu, *View from The East*, 152; Mtume, "Baraka." The Work/Study Center chant is in "Young Soldiers and Warriors." The phrase is "Sifa zote ziende kwa mtu weusi" in "Sifas (Praise)," *Voices of The EAST*, 129.

171 The assertion that CAP affiliates "modernized" cultural nationalism can be found in Woodard, *Nation within a Nation*, 114.

172 Kifano, "Promise and Possibilities," 49; Tayari kwa Salaam, "So-Journeying," 98; Warren-Williams, interview; "Ahidiana Work/Study Center: A Black Independent and Affirmative Institution of Vital Education"; Camara, "'There Are Some Bad

Brothers and Sisters,'" 203; Dreier, "Reagan's Legacy"; Center on Budget and Policy Priorities, "Falling Behind," 149.

173 Kiini Ibura Salaam, interview.

174 Tayari kwa Salaam, "So-Journeying," 115–16; Camara, "'There Are Some Bad Brothers and Sisters,'" 203–4. Quotes are from Rickford, *We Are an African People*, 5, and generally referred to Pan-Africanist IBIs. Nantambu questioned Ahidiana advocates' lack of verve, stating that members were not very spiritual. Moreover, she believed, longtime friends in the organization, who had become like family members, declined invitations to her farewell celebration because they eschewed parties as decadent. Nantambu left the organization in 1980 to live and work in Nigeria. Nana Anoa Nantambu, interview.

175 Tayari kwa Salaam, "So-Journeying," 4; Kalamu ya Salaam, "Wounded"; Nana Anoa Nantambu, interview; Joshua-Jasmine, interview, May 28, 2013. Ahidiana advocates particularly used the word "struggle" to mean the freedom movement in general, more isolated instances of activism, vigorous resistance to domination, and armed resistance, as well as hard work.

176 Kalamu ya Salaam, interview.

EPILOGUE

1 I approached the early stages of my research for this book with a goal of thwarting framings of Black Power as an era of decline. Additionally, both my upbringing in a Deep South, African American family and my Pan-African nationalist leanings shaped my perspectives. I sometimes found myself falling back on an ingrained belief that I should not air Black folks' "dirty laundry." For a discussion of historiography and declension narratives centering Black Power, see Joseph, "Black Power Movement: A State of the Field," 751–52. Guy-Sheftall and Cole write about "airing dirty laundry," warning against the avoidance of grappling with multiple oppressions within African American communities in Guy-Sheftall and Cole, *Gender Talk*, xxi, 73. The phrase quoted in the subhead title, "Kazi like you mean it," was a subheading in Black and Angaza, *EAST Sisterhood*, 7.

2 Stiner, interview.

3 Bloom and Martin, *Black against Empire*, 142–43.

4 Konadu, *View from The East*, 126–27.

5 M. Ron Karenga, "Response to Muhammad Ahmad"; Stiner, interview; Scot Brown, *Fighting for US*, 117–19; Scot Ngozi Brown, "US Organization," 158. For an example of the FBI's plans for causing disruption between the Us Organization and the Black Panther Party, see Memorandum, FBI Director to Los Angeles Special Agent in Charge, June 3, 1968, FBI, COINTELPRO Surveillance Files, Black Extremists and Investigation of the Deacons for Defense and Justice, Part 1.

6 Scot Brown, *Fighting for US*, 112, 120, 122–25; Omotayo, interview; Jones and Chimurenga, *What We Stood For*, 61–112; Amiri Baraka, *Autobiography*, 278–80.

7 Scot Brown, *Fighting for US*, 126; "Prison Notes"; Halisi, "Maulana Ron Karenga," 27.

8 Scot Brown, *Fighting for US*, 129; Kabaila, "On Dr. Maulana Karenga."

9  Scot Brown, *Fighting for US*, 120; Thomas, interview.

10  Karenga and Tembo, "Kawaida Womanism."

11  Scot Brown, *Fighting for US*, 123–24, 129. For a snapshot of opinions about the Us Organization in 1969, see Cleaver, "Karenga, Black Panthers Speak Out."

12  Woodard, *Nation within a Nation*, 219.

13  Scot Brown, *Fighting for US*, 126–29; Amiri Baraka, *Autobiography*, 289–92; Woodard, *Nation within a Nation*, 219; Simanga, *Amiri Baraka*, 82–83; "Political Prisoners"; "Maulana Karenga Benefit."

14  Woodard, *Nation within a Nation*, 219, 222–23.

15  Woodard, *Nation within a Nation*, 224, 253–54. Newark mayor Ras J. Baraka is overseeing the planning of a 100 percent affordable housing unit named Kawaida Towers. Wiedmann, "Historic Kawaida Towers Project."

16  Moore, *Defeat of Black Power*, 11; Woodard, *Nation within a Nation*, 254; Rickford, *We Are an African People*, 225–26.

17  Konadu, *View from The East*, xxxiii, 62–65. Rickford critiques the cadre approach in *We Are an African People*, 133. Ahidiana's demise is addressed in the epilogue.

18  Konadu, *View from The East*, 66; Baillou, "Block Groups Want Armory." For more information on the International African Arts Festival, see its website, http://iaafestival.org.

19  Konadu, *View from The East*, 126.

20  Rickford, *We Are an African People*, 15.

21  Rickford, *We Are an African People*, 74, 133.

22  Kwesi Ayo Nantambu, interview. Kweli Campbell (Weusi) also described feeling as if he lived a "dual identity" growing up in The East organization while also residing and socializing in his Brooklyn neighborhood in *Voices of The EAST*, 40–41.

23  Kwesi Ayo Nantambu, interview. Kina B. Joshua-Jasmine also observed this occurrence. She speculated that emotional challenges, possibly related to the shock of growing up in a nationalist environment, impacted more of the second-generation males in their community than the female advocates. Joshua-Jasmine, interview, May 28, 2013. Scot Brown, *Fighting for US*, 121–22; and Rickford, *We Are an African People*, 247, both discuss how fatigue and paranoia caused mental distress and breakdowns in adult activists, but Kwesi Nantambu and Joshua-Jasmine pointed out a similar issue among the offspring of Pan-African nationalists.

24  Amina Baraka, interview, July 12, 2012.

25  Wanda Wilson-Pasha had filed at least twelve domestic violence complaints against her estranged husband. "Man Surrenders"; State of New Jersey v. Ibn El-Amin Pasha, No. A-1590–05T4 (N.J. Super. 2008), LexisNexis 1564.

26  Amina Baraka, interview, July 12, 2012.

27  Jamie Walker, "Home-Going Celebration."

28  Amiri Baraka, *Autobiography*, 298.

29  Tayari kwa Salaam, "So-Journeying," 115–16.

30  Simanga, *Amiri Baraka*, 82.

31 Amina Baraka, interview, July 12, 2012. SOBU was an acronym for Student Organization for Black Unity or Students Organized for Black Unity. SOBU was founded in 1969 and became Youth Organization for Black Unity (YOBU) approximately a year later. For more information on SOBU/YOBU, see Biondi, *Black Revolution on Campus*, 234; Ibram H. Rogers, *Black Campus Movement*, 108, 111; Rickford, *We Are an African People*, 166; and Woodard, *Nation within a Nation*, 127, 181.

32 Amina Baraka, interview, July 12, 2012.

33 Some of the women reported feelings of being watched and subverted, exhaustion, and a general loss of interest in activism, particularly due to extraordinary expectations related to *kazi* as well as the sense that the state was surveilling and disrupting their activities; Amina Baraka, interview, July 17, 2012; Rickford, *We Are an African People*, 247; Konadu, *View from The East*, 127.

34 Rickford, *We Are an African People*, 124; Amiri Baraka, *Autobiography*, 253, 276; Tayari kwa Salaam, "So-Journeying," 144–15.

35 Amina Baraka, interview, July 13, 2012.

36 Tayari kwa Salaam, "So-Journeying," 115.

37 "The East . . . Remembering a Wellspring."

38 Martha Bright in Angela Weusi et al., "Memories of The East."

39 Hill, interview.

40 Simanga, *Amiri Baraka*, 82.

41 This quote is from Martha Bright, who said that the high point of being in The East was the women's "irreplaceable East sisterhood." Angela Weusi et al., "Memories of The East."

42 Abimbola Wali in Angela Weusi et al., "Memories of The East"; Bright, interview; "The East . . . Remembering a Wellspring."

43 Herro, "Representation of African American Women"; Allison, *Black Women's Portrayals*, xxi, 83, 127.

44 Joshua-Jasmine, interview, May 28, 2013.

45 Rickford, *We Are an African People*, 235.

46 Hill, interview; Woodard, *Nation within a Nation*, 123–24; Simanga, *Amiri Baraka*, 82–84. Farmer asserts that women not only participated in CAP's theoretical life but also altered it. Farmer, "Renegotiating the 'African Woman,'" 76.

47 Hill, interview.

48 Ngoma Hill and Jaribu Hill, *For Your Consideration!*, liner notes.

49 Boyd, "Jaribu Hill"; Mississippi Workers' Center for Human Rights website, accessed October 8, 2016, http://themississippiproject.weebly.com. Amina Baraka discussed her desire to support other women through work such as developing the Black Women's United Front and supporting the leadership of women like Akiba and Jaribu, who served as second chair of the CFUN Women's Division, and Malaika Ibura, who was a leader in the African Free School. Amina Baraka, interview, July 12, 2012; "Education for Liberation Conference Held Here," 1; photograph, *Black New Ark*, October 1973, 2.

50 Staff Development Workshops website, accessed July 16, 2016, www.sdworkshops. org.

51 "The East . . . Remembering a Wellspring"; Fela Barclift in *Voices of The EAST*, 26–28.

52 Angela Weusi et al., "Memories of The East."

53 Rickford, *We Are an African People*, 4.

54 Rickford, *We Are an African People*, 21. Amina Baraka believed that Black nationalist IBIs were precursors to charter schools but expressed concern over government corruption and interference with the IBIs' curricula and spending in Amina Baraka, interviews, July 12, 2012, July 17, 2012.

55 "Community Organizing," in Congress of African People, Organizing Manual; Amina Baraka, interview, July 13, 2012; Rickford, *We Are an African People*, 73; Davis, *From Head Shops to Whole Foods*, 22.

56 Hill, interview.

57 Henderson, *Revolution Will Not Be Theorized*, 386; Eligon, "Poor Scores"; Rickford, *We Are an African People*, 144. Simanga also notes Safisha Madhubuti as a female leader but frames her work within the legacy of CAP programmatic expressions of self-determination and self-sufficiency. Simanga, *Amiri Baraka*, 82, 107; "CPS Applied Charter Heat"; "CPS Shake-Ups"; Ahmed-Ullah, "Charters That Don't Make Grade."

58 Howze, "Freedom Summer School"; Toler, "Malcolm's Legacy"; Tamara Hall, "Freedom School Teaches Self Pride"; Kurutz, "Summer Program."

59 Toler, "Malcolm's Legacy."

60 Kingsley Freedom School newsletter; Charles N. Brown, "Supporters Get on the Bus"; Wade, "Paintball Event"; Nuttall, "Hill District Education Council"; Aldrich, "'Cost of War.'"

61 Nuttall, "Kids Rally."

62 Marcella Lee, "Community Update."

63 "Others Who Were Nominated."

64 Webb, "Economic Independence."

65 Konadu cited the following offshoot institutions of The East: Ujamaa Institute, Little Sun People, Weusi Shule (Johnson Preparatory), Zidi Kuwa, Shule ya Mapenduzi, Imani Day School Computer Campus, and Black Veterans for Social Justice. Konadu, *View from The East*, 133; Rickford, *We Are an African People*, 262. Many of the institutions that Konadu cited are also mentioned in *Voices of The EAST*, 46, 60.

66 Tayari kwa Salaam, "So-Journeying," 116–17.

67 "Lock-In Draws over 250 Youth"; "NCNW Honor Nation's Finest Educators"; "Black Agenda Tells of Upcoming Kwanzaa Fete"; Conner, "Kwanzaa!"; "Millions Celebrated Kwanzaa."

68 "The East . . . Remembering a Wellspring"; Committee for Unified Newark, "Ritual Celebrating the Birth of Our Children," n.d., Komozi Woodard Amiri Baraka collection, reel 1, slide 824. The CFUN Muminina emphasized the importance of

children as constituents of the nation becoming, which might partially explain their emphasis on children as an outcome of their activism. Emphasis on nurturing a second generation and the legacy work that young advocates undertook was not just evident in women's stories; the theme also surfaced in the narratives of cultural nationalist men. Shabaka, interview; Akili Walker, interview.

69  Afrocentric schools flourished in the 1990s. Kifano, "Promise and Possibilities," 49. For more information on youth experiences in Pan-African nationalism, see Sunni-Ali, "Performing New African Childhood."

70  Thomas, interview; Nana Anoa Nantambu, interview; Safiya Bandele, interview.

71  Asare, "Combating Misogynoir."

# BIBLIOGRAPHY

PRIMARY SOURCE MATERIALS

*Author Interviews, Correspondence, Published Oral Histories, and Talks*
Akili, Sababa. Interview by author. Atlanta, GA. June 22, 2013.
Bandele, Adeyemi. Telephone interview by author. July 25, 2013.
Bandele, Safiya. "Retirement Ceremony for Renowned Medgar Evers College Professor." Interview. *New York Amsterdam News*, October 13–19, 2011, 31, 39.
———. Telephone interview by author. August 23, 2013.
Baraka, Amina. Interview by author. Newark, NJ. July 12, 2012.
———. Interview by author. Newark, NJ. July 13, 2012.
———. Interview by author. Newark, NJ. July 17, 2012.
———. Interview by Kim Brown. "Kim's Korner," May 28, 2013. YouTube. https://www.youtube.com/watch?v=QgcZjQ6vfBw.
Beatty, Mtamanika (Charlene). Interview by author. Atlanta, GA. July 23, 2013.
Bebelle, Carol. Telephone interview by author. July 3, 2013.
Bright, Martha. Interview by author. Warner Robins, GA. June 24, 2013.
Davis, Kicheko. Interview by Karen Stanford and Keith Rice. "Black Power Archives: Kicheko Davis on the Founding of Kwanzaa." YouTube. Tom and Ethel Bradley Center, November 15, 2021.
Goldwag, Arnie. *Brooklyn CORE, on Jitu Weusi*, n.d. Sheila Michaels Oral History Collection, Columbia University Library. www.corenyc.org.
Heru, Nzinga Ratibisha. Interview by author. Atlanta, GA. September 17, 2010.
———. Interview by author. Atlanta, GA. November 29, 2010.
Hill, Jaribu Sandra. Telephone interview by author. June 28, 2013.
Howze, Tamanika. Telephone interview by author. January 19, 2014.
Joshua-Jasmine, Kina. Interview by author. New Orleans, LA. April 13, 2013.
———. Interview by author. New Orleans, LA. May 28, 2013.
Karenga, Maulana. Interview by Elston Carr. 2002. Transcript. Center for Oral History Research, University of California, Los Angeles.
Karenga, Tiamoyo. Email message to author. October 12, 2012.
Kifano, Subira. Interview by author. Atlanta, GA. December 30, 2010.
———. Interview by author. Atlanta, GA. January 7, 2011.
Mashariki, Akilah. Panel discussion, International African Arts Festival Symposium, New York, July 6, 2019.
Mwendo, Nilima. Interview by author. New Orleans, LA. May 28, 2013.

Nantambu, Kwesi. Telephone interview by author. July 5, 2013.

Nantambu, Nana Anoa. Interview by author. New Orleans, LA. April 9, 2013.

Olugbala, Naima. Telephone interview by author. July 1, 2013.

Omotayo, Imani [pseud.]. Interview by author. February 11, 2013.

Ongoza, Maisha (Maxine) Sullivan. Email message to author, January 17, 2014.

———. Telephone interview by author. January 13, 2014.

Peterson, Tamisha Wendie. Interview by author. Atlanta, GA. January 25, 2013.

Powell, Azizi (Deborah Manning). Email correspondence with author. October 26, 2014.

———. Telephone interview by author. September 8, 2013.

Rogers, Jamala. Interview by author. Atlanta, GA. October 5, 2012.

Salaam, Asante. Interview by author. New Orleans, LA. May 27, 2013.

Salaam, Kalamu ya. Email message to author. September 28, 2012.

———. Interview by author. New Orleans, LA. April 6, 2013.

———. Interview by Kim Lacy Rogers. May 18, 1979. Transcript. Kim Lacy Rogers Collection, Amistad Research Center, Tulane University, New Orleans.

Salaam, Kiini Ibura. Interview by author. Brooklyn, NY. July 16, 2012.

Salaam, Tayari kwa. Interview by author. New Orleans, LA. April 6, 2013.

Sanders, Shukuru. Telephone interview by author. January 8, 2014.

Shabaka, Segun. Email correspondence with author. March 13, 2015.

———. Email correspondence with author. September 8, 2016.

———. Email message to author. June 30, 2012.

———. Email message to author. March 6, 2015.

———. Telephone interview by author. July 29, 2013.

Simanga, Michael. Interview by author. Atlanta, GA. June 25, 2013.

Stiner, Watani. Interview by Karen Stanford and Keith Rice. "Black Power Hour: Watani Stiner Interview 2022." YouTube. Tom and Ethel Bradley Center, June 30, 2022.

Thomas, Amina. Telephone interview by author. July 31, 2013.

Umoja, Akinyele. Interview. In *COINTELPRO 101*. DVD. Produced by Andres Algeria, Prentis Hemphill, Anita Johnson, and Claude Marks. San Francisco: Freedom Archives, 2011.

Walker, Akili. Telephone interview by author. August 27, 2013.

Warren-Williams, Vera. Interview by author. New Orleans, LA. May 27, 2013.

Weusi, Angela, Aminisha Black, Abimbola Wali, Martha Bright, Tamisha Peterson, Akilah Mashariki, and Shukuru Copeland Sanders. "Memories of The East." Interview by Dwight Brewster. OJBK Radio, Central Brooklyn Jazz Consortium. Podcast audio. October 11 and 12, 2014. www.centralbrooklynjazzconsortium.org.

Woodard, Komozi. Email message to author. December 16, 2012.

———. Telephone interview by author. July 24, 2013.

*Manuscript and Archival Collections*

Baraka, Amina. Papers. Private collection, Newark, NJ.

Bright, Martha. Papers. Private collection, Warner Robins, GA.

Chandler, Osei T. Papers. Private collection, Charleston, SC.

Constitution of Auset, an African Sisterhood, Inc. Article I, Section 2: Purpose. N.d. In the author's possession.

*Eyes on the Prize: America at the Racial Crossroads, 1965–1985* Interview Transcripts. Henry Hampton Collection, Washington University Libraries Film and Media Archive. St. Louis, MO.

FamilySearch. www.familysearch.org.

FBI. COINTELPRO Surveillance Files. ProQuest History Vault.

Hamline University. Catalogues and Yearbooks. Hamline University Archives, Saint Paul, MN.

Harris, Charles "Teenie." Archive. Carnegie Museum of Art. http://teenie.cmoa.org.

King, Martin Luther, Jr. Papers, 1950–1968. Martin Luther King, Jr., Center for Nonviolent Social Change, Atlanta, GA.

Nkombo Publications Records. Amistad Research Center, Tulane University, New Orleans, LA.

Salaam, Tayari kwa. Papers. Private collection, New Orleans, LA.

Warren-Williams, Vera. Papers. Private collection, New Orleans, LA.

Woodard, Komozi. Komozi Woodard Amiri Baraka Collection. Auburn Avenue Research Library on African American Culture and History, Archives Division, Atlanta, GA.


SECONDARY SOURCE MATERIALS

Abioye, Akin. "Vanguards in the Classroom: History and Lessons from the Black Panther Party's Oakland Community School." *Journal of African American Studies* 25, no. 4 (December 2021): 559–75.

"Action of Assembly Widens Gap between Local Udin, Carter Factions." *New Pittsburgh Courier*, May 3, 1975, 1.

"African Free School." *Black New Ark*, September 1972, 4.

"African Free School Has Own Methodology." *New York Amsterdam News*, June 26, 1971, D1.

"African Free School in Newark." *New York Amsterdam News*, July 24, 1971, D3.

"Africans to Meet." *New Pittsburgh Courier*, August 5, 1972, 20.

"Afrikan Women Unite." *Black News* 2, no. 16 (April 1974): 11.

Ahmed-Ullah, Noreen S. "Charters That Don't Make Grade Face CPS Crackdown." *Chicago Tribune*, February 28, 2013, 4.

Aiello, Thomas, ed. *The Artistic Activism of Elombe Brath*. Jackson: University Press of Mississippi, 2021.

Aldrich, Renee P. "'Cost of War' in the Black Community." *New Pittsburgh Courier*, February 6–12, 2013, A1, A3.

Alexander-Floyd, Nikol G., and Evelyn M. Simien. "Revisiting 'What's in a Name?': Exploring the Contours of African Womanist Thought." *Frontiers: A Journal of Women Studies* 27, no. 1 (2006): 67–89.

"The Alfred and Bernice Ligon Aquarian Collection at CSU Dominguez Hills." *Africology: The Journal of Pan African Studies* 9, no. 7 (September 2016): 204–5.

Allegheny County Department of Human Services. *Homewood: A Community Profile*. 2010. www.alleghenycountyanalytics.us.

Allison, Donnetrice C. *Black Women's Portrayals on Reality Television: The New Sapphire*. Lanham, MD: Lexington Books, 2016.

Andrews, Kehinde. "Toward a Black Radical Independent Education: Black Radicalism, Independence and Supplementary School Movement." *Journal of Negro Education* 83, no. 1 (Winter 2014): 5–14.

Angaza, Maitefa. *Kwanzaa: From Holiday to Everyday*. New York: Kensington, 2007.

Asante, Molefi Kete. *Afrocentricity: The Theory of Social Change*. 1980; reprint, Chicago: African American Images, 2003.

———. *Maulana Karenga: An Intellectual Portrait*. Cambridge: Polity, 2009.

Asare, Janice Gassam. "Combating Misogynoir This Election Season and Beyond." *Forbes*, November 11, 2024. www.forbes.com.

Asbury, Edith Evans. "16 Black Panthers Go on Trial Tomorrow in State Court Here." *New York Times*, February 1, 1970, 55.

"Ashé Cultural Arts Center." Accessed November 26, 2015. www.ashecac.org.

Asukile, Thabiti. "Joel Augustus Rogers' Race Vindication: A Chicago Pullman Porter and the Making of *From Superman to Man* (1917)." *Western Journal of Black Studies* 35, no. 4 (2011).

"Awakening of the Harambee Legacy." *New Pittsburgh Courier*, August 17, 2011, B5.

Baillou, Charles. "Block Groups Want Armory for Community." *New York Amsterdam News*, September 20, 1986, 11.

Baraka, Amina (Sylvia Jones). "For the Lady in Color." *Black Scholar* 12, no. 4 (July–August 1981): 54–55.

———. "Looking for the Lyrics (For Jayne Cortez)." *Black Scholar* 12, no. 4 (July–August 1981): 54.

———. "Sometime Woman." *Black American Literature Forum* 16, no. 3 (Autumn 1982): 105. http://www.jstor.org/stable/2904346.

———. "Sortin' Out." *Black American Literature Forum* 16, no. 3 (Autumn 1982): 106. http://www.jstor.org/stable/2904346.

Baraka, Amina, and Amiri Baraka. *5 Boptrees*. Newark, 1992.

Baraka, Amiri (LeRoi Jones), ed. *African Congress: A Documentary of the First Modern Pan-African Congress*. New York: William Morrow, 1972.

———. *The Autobiography of LeRoi Jones*. New York: Freundlich, 1984.

———. *Daggers and Javelins: Essays of Amiri Baraka (LeRoi Jones)*. New York: Quill, 1984.

———. *It's Nation Time*. Chicago: Third World Press, 1970.

———. *Kawaida, National Liberation and Socialism*. 1974. Stuart A. Rose Manuscript, Archives, and Rare Book Library, Emory University, Atlanta, GA.

———. *The Meaning and Development of Revolutionary Kawaida*. 1974. Raymond Danowski Poetry Collection, Stuart A. Rose Manuscript, Archives, and Rare Book Library, Emory University, Atlanta, GA.

———. *The Music: Reflections of Jazz and Blues*. New York: Quill, 1983.

———. *The New Nationalism: Kawaida Studies.* Chicago: Third World Press, 1972. Stuart A. Rose Manuscript, Archives, and Rare Book Library, Emory University, Atlanta, GA.

Baraka, Amiri (LeRoi Jones), and Amina Baraka. *Confirmation: An Anthology of African American Women.* New York: Quill, 1983.

Baraka, Bibi Amina. "Social Organization: Education as a Social Tool." *Black NewArk,* September 1972, 7. In *The Black Power Movement,* part 1, *Amiri Baraka, from Black Arts to Black Radicalism.* Bethesda, MD: University Publications of America, 2001. Microfilm.

———. "Social Organization: The Work of a Society." *Black NewArk,* October 1972. In *The Black Power Movement,* part 1, *Amiri Baraka, from Black Arts to Black Radicalism.* Bethesda, MD: University Publications of America, 2001. Microfilm.

"BAS Sponsors Report on Pan-African Meet." *New Pittsburgh Courier,* November 16, 1974, 28.

Baxandall, Rosalyn. "Re-Visioning the Women's Liberation Movement's Narrative: Early Second Wave African American Feminists." *Feminist Studies* 27, no. 1 (April 2001): 225–45.

Beaulac, Julie, Elizabeth Kristjansson, and Steven Cummins. "A Systematic Review of Food Deserts, 1966–2007." *Preventing Chronic Disease: Public Health Research, Practice, and Policy* 6, no. 3, A105 (July 2009): 1–10. Accessed April 1, 2016. www.cdc.gov.

Bebelle, Carol, and Charles Henry Rowell. "Carol Bebelle with Charles Henry Rowell." *Callaloo* 29, no. 4 (Autumn 2006): 1210–14.

"Bed-Stuy Is Looking Better These Days." *New York Amsterdam News,* October 11, 1980, 36.

Benson, Richard D., II. "A Learning Laboratory for Liberation: Black Power and the Communiversity of Chicago, 1969–78." In *Ideas in Unexpected Places: Reimagining Black Intellectual History,* edited by Brandon R. Byrd, Leslie M. Alexander, and Russell Rickford, 191–209. Chicago: University of Chicago Press, 2022.

Biondi, Martha. *The Black Revolution on Campus.* Berkeley: University of California Press, 2012.

Black, Aminisha, and Maitefa Angaza. *The EAST Sisterhood: An Institution beyond Walls.* Report to the Council of Independent Black Institutions, November 14, 2002. Martha Bright Papers.

Black, Big. "Around Our Way." *Black News* 1, no. 28 (February 7, 1971): 10.

———. "Around Our Way." *Black News* 1, no. 33 (July 17, 1974): 18.

Black, Mittie. "Dialogue with a 'Coloured' Beauty." *Black News* 3, no. 5 (December 1975): 25.

"Black Agenda Tells of Upcoming Kwanzaa Fete." *Los Angeles Sentinel,* December 2, 1993, C2.

"Black Arts Festival Scheduled." *New Pittsburgh Courier,* July 10, 1971, 2.

"Black Liberation Movement and the Role of Women." Conference paper. In *The Black Power Movement,* part 1, *Amiri Baraka, from Black Arts to Black Radicalism.* Bethesda, MD: University Publications of America, 2001. Microfilm.

Black Lives Matter. "All #BlackLivesMatter. This Is Not a Moment, but a Movement." N.d. Accessed June 23, 2015. http://blacklivesmatter.com.

"'Black News' of Bedford Stuyvesant." *Black News* 1, no. 1 (October 1969): cover.

"Blacks Demonstrate against Gulf Policy." *New Pittsburgh Courier*, February 3, 1973, 1, 5.

"Blacks Observe Kwanza [*sic*] to Cite Achievements." *New Pittsburgh Courier*, December 23, 1972, 2.

"Black Women Slate Forum." *New Pittsburgh Courier*, September 6, 1975, 8.

"Black Women's United Front Forms Feb. 29." *New Pittsburgh Courier*, February 28, 1976, 10.

"Black Women's United Front Plans Conference." *New Pittsburgh Courier*, February 28, 1976, 25.

Blain, Keisha N. *Set the World on Fire: Black Nationalist Women and the Global Struggle for Freedom*. Philadelphia: University of Pennsylvania Press, 2018.

———. *Until I Am Free: Fannie Lou Hamer's Enduring Message to America*. Boston: Beacon, 2021.

———. "'We Want to Set the World on Fire': Black Nationalist Women and Diasporic Politics in the *New Negro World*, 1940–1944." *Journal of Social History* 49, no. 1 (2015): 194–212.

Bloom, Joshua, and Waldo E. Martin Jr. *Black against Empire: The History and Politics of the Black Panther Party*. Oakland: University of California Press, 2016.

Blumenthal, Bob. "More Jazz and Sex." *JazzTimes*, April 2002. http://jazztimes.com.

Boyd, Herb. "Jaribu Hill: Working for Workers." *New York Amsterdam News*, October 22–28, 2009, 5.

Brathwaite, Kwame, with Tanisha C. Ford. *Kwame Brathwaite: Black Is Beautiful*. New York: Aperture, 2019.

"Breadbasket Maps A&P Confrontation." *New York Amsterdam News*, November 28, 1970, 3.

Brock, Lisa. "Selected Projects in Labor Education: The Chicago CommUniversity." *Radical History Review* 72 (1998): 78.

Brown, Charles N. "Pittsburgh Establishes Freedom Schools." *New Pittsburgh Courier*, February 9, 2002, A1.

Brown, Elaine. *A Taste of Power: A Black Woman's Story*. New York: Doubleday, 1992.

Brown, Marc D. "Building an Alternative: People's Food Cooperative in Southeast Portland." *Oregon Historical Quarterly* 112, no. 3 (Fall 2011): 298–321.

Brown, Scot. *Fighting for US: Maulana Karenga, the US Organization, and Black Cultural Nationalism*. New York: New York University Press, 2003.

———. "The US Organization, Black Power Vanguard Politics, and the United Front Ideal: Los Angeles and Beyond." *Black Scholar* 31 (Fall–Winter 2001): 21.

Brown, Scot Ngozi. "The US Organization, Maulana Karenga, and Conflict with the Black Panther Party: A Critique of Sectarian Influences on Historical Discourse." *Journal of Black Studies* 28 (November 1997): 157–70.

Browne, Tsekani. "Anna Julia Cooper's Radical Uses of History and Geography, 1892–1925." Paper presented at the Association for the Study of the Worldwide African Diaspora 8th Biennial Conference, Charleston, SC, 2015.

Burns, Ronald. "Jersey Public School Teaches Class in African Culture." *Chicago Daily Defender*, January 23, 1971, 18.

Butterfield, Fox. "Experimental Class in Newark School Is Indoctrinated in Black Subjects." *New York Times*, April 10, 1971, 42.

Byron, Jerry, and Jitu Weusi, eds. *Black United Front: Defend or Die!* New York: Black United Front, 1979.

"California State University, Long Beach, CSULB History." CSULB Historical Site, n.d. Accessed May 3, 2014. www.csulb.edu.

Camara, Samori Sekou. "'There Are Some Bad Brothers and Sisters in New Orleans': The Black Power Movement in the Crescent City from 1964–1977." PhD diss., University of Texas at Austin, 2011.

Campbell, Trevor A. "The Making of an Organic Intellectual: Walter Rodney (1942–1980)." *Latin American Perspectives* 8, no. 1 (Winter 1981): 49–63.

Carmichael, Stokely, with Ekwueme Michael Thelwell. *Ready for Revolution.* New York: Scribner, 2003.

"Carol Bebelle." Tulane University Center for Public Service. Accessed November 26, 2015. https://tulane.edu.

Center on Budget and Policy Priorities. "Falling Behind: A Report on How Blacks Have Fared under Reagan." *Journal of Black Studies* 17, no. 2 (December 1986): 148–71.

Cha-Jua, Sundiata, and Clarence Lang. "The 'Long Movement' as Vampire: Temporal and Spatial Fallacies in Recent Black Freedom Studies." *Journal of African American History* 92 (Spring 2007): 265–88.

Cleaver, Jim. "Karenga, Black Panthers Speak Out." *Los Angeles Sentinel*, March 6, 1969, A1, D2, D6.

Coates, Ta-Nahisi. *Between the World and Me.* New York: Spiegel and Grau, 2015.

Cole, Johnnetta Betsch, and Beverly Guy-Sheftall. *Gender Talk: The Struggle for Women's Equality in African American Communities.* New York: One World Ballantine Books, 2003.

Collier-Thomas, Bettye. "The Impact of Black Women in Education: An Historical Overview." *Journal of Negro Education* 51, no. 3 (Summer 1982): 173–80.

Collier-Thomas, Bettye, and V. P. Franklin, eds. *Sisters in the Struggle: African American Women in the Civil Rights-Black Power Movement.* New York: New York University Press, 2001.

"Community Book Center." Media NOLA: A Project of Tulane University, n.d. http://medianola.org.

Community Calendar. *Los Angeles Sentinel*, May 28, 1981, June 25, 1981, and October 20, 1983, A4.

Congress of African People. "The Woman Question: Black Women and the Struggle." In *The Black Power Movement*, part 1, *Amiri Baraka, from Black Arts to Black*

*Radicalism*. Series V: Congress of African People, 1960–1976: Congress of African People, 1975. Komozi Woodard Amiri Baraka Collection. Auburn Avenue Research Library on African American Culture and History, Atlanta, GA.

Conner, Tracy. "Kwanzaa! Celebrating Seven Principles of Self-Help." *Atlanta Daily World*, December 14, 1993, 1.

Conyers, James L., Jr. "Maulana Karenga, Kawaida, and Phenomenology: An Intellectual Study." In *Black Lives: Essays in African American Biography*, edited by James L. Conyers Jr., 3–18. Armonk, NY: M. E. Sharpe, 1999.

Cook, Ann F. (Tchaiko Kwayana). "Guyana as Seen by an African-American." *Black News* 1, no. 11 (March 21, 1970): 1–9.

"CPS Applied Charter Heat." *Chicago Tribune*, March 4, 2013, 14.

"CPS Shake-Ups Bounce Bronzeville Students from School to School." *Chicago Tribune*, January 9, 2012, 8.

Crews, Erin. "What Will It Take to Fix Hollywood's Race Problem?" Georgia State University, n.d. www.gsu.edu.

Cummins, Steven, and Sally Macintyre. "'Food Deserts': Evidence and Assumption in Health Policy Making." *BMJ: British Medical Journal* 325, no. 7361 (August 24, 2002): 436–38.

Curvin, Robert. *Inside Newark: Decline, Rebellion, and the Search for Transformation*. New Brunswick: Rutgers University Press, 2014.

Daniels, Ron. "Toward a Congress of African People." *New Pittsburgh Courier*, October 30, 1999, 5.

Davis, Joshua Clark. "Consumer Liberation: Baby Boomers, Hip Businesses, and the Challenge to Mass Consumption, 1968–1983." PhD diss., University of North Carolina at Chapel Hill, 2010.

———. *From Head Shops to Whole Foods*. New York: Columbia University Press, 2017.

Deere, Stephen. "Ferguson Protesters Disagree over Who Should Receive Donations." *St. Louis Post-Dispatch*, June 4, 2015, Newspaper Source Database.

Dixon-Spear, Patricia. *We Want for Our Sisters What We Want for Ourselves: African American Women Who Practice Polygyny by Consent*. Baltimore: Black Classic Press, 2009.

Dorestal, Philipp. *Style Politics: Mode, Geschlecht und Schwarzsein in den USA, 1943–1975*. Bielefeld, Germany: Transcript Verlag, 2012.

Dreier, Peter. "Reagan's Legacy: Homelessness in America." National Housing Institute. *Shelterforce Online* 35 (May–June 2004).www.nhi.org.

Duncan, Natanya. *An Efficient Womanhood: Women and the Making of the Universal Negro Improvement Association*. Chapel Hill: University of North Carolina Press, 2025.

———. "The 'Efficient Womanhood' of the Universal Negro Improvement Association, 1919–1930." PhD diss., University of Florida, 2009.

Dyer, Ervin. "Udin Talks about Slain Son at Neighborhood Forum." *Pittsburgh Post-Gazette*, November 4, 2005.

East Avenue High School Yearbook. 1967. www.donslist.net.

"The East . . . Remembering a Wellspring." *Our Time Press*, November 11, 2003. www.ourtimepress.com.

"Education for Liberation Conference Held Here." *Black New Ark*, November 1972, 1, 4.

Edwin, Andre. "Harambee Arts Festival Returns." *New Pittsburgh Courier*, July 27, 1985, 3.

Eligon, John. "Poor Scores Leave an Afrocentric School in Chicago Vulnerable." *New York Times*, February 28, 2016.

Emery, Kathy, Sylvia Braselmann, and Linda Gold, eds. "Freedom School Curriculum: Mississippi Freedom Summer, 1964." 2004. www.educationanddemocracy.org.

Espinal, Juan, Cyril Josh Barker, and Curtis Simmons. "The Legacy of Medgar Evers College." *New York Amsterdam News*, April 21, 2011, 5.

Essien-Udom, E. U. *Black Nationalism: A Search for an Identity in America*. Chicago: University of Chicago Press, 1962.

"Family Schools Newsletter." *Black News* 3, no. 23 (May 1978): 15.

Farmer, Ashley. *Remaking Black Power: How Black Women Transformed an Era*. Chapel Hill: University of North Carolina Press, 2017.

———. "Renegotiating the 'African Woman': Women's Cultural Nationalist Theorizing in the Us Organization and the Congress of African People, 1965–1975." *Black Diaspora Review* 4, no. 1 (Winter 2014): 76–112.

"F.A.T. Honors Guardians, Together." *New Pittsburgh Courier*, March 15, 1969, 3.

Federal Bureau of Investigation. "FBI Records: The Vault: COINTELPRO." Accessed February 21, 2017. https://vault.fbi.gov.

Felber, Garrett. "'Harlem Is the Black World': The Organization of Afro-American Unity at the Grassroots." *Journal of African American History* 100, no. 2 (April 2015): 199–225.

Ferguson, Iyaluua, and Herman Ferguson. *An Unlikely Warrior, Herman Ferguson: Evolution of a Black Nationalist Revolutionary*. Holly Springs, NC: Ferguson-Swan, 2011.

Finding Aid for Board of Education. Series 1101, Chancellor Harvey Scribner files, 1970–1973. Subseries IV: Model Cities Program. New York City Department of Records. Accessed June 21, 2015. www.nyc.gov.

Fisher, Maisha T. *Black Literate Lives*. New York: Routledge, 2009.

———. "'Earning Dual Degrees': Black Bookstores as Alternative Knowledge Spaces." *Anthropology and Education Quarterly* 37 (2006): 83–99.

Focht, Adam, and Michael Ponton. "Identifying Primary Characteristics of Servant Leadership: Delphi Study." *International Journal of Leadership Studies* 9, no. 1 (2015): 44–61.

Fonville, Althea. "Are Black Women for or against Women's Lib?" *New Pittsburgh Courier*, January 18, 1975, 5.

———. "Black Women's UF to Aid the Community." *New Pittsburgh Courier*, September 20, 1975, 1.

———. "Blacks Need Third Party." *New Pittsburgh Courier*, March 19, 1975, 1.

———. "Groundwork Laid for a Black Women's UF." *New Pittsburgh Courier*, February 22, 1975, 4.

———. "Pittsburghers Rally Support for North Carolina Woman." *New Pittsburgh Courier*, February 8, 1975, A1.

Ford, Tanisha C. *Liberated Threads: Black Women, Style, and the Global Politics of Soul*. Chapel Hill: University of North Carolina Press, 2015.

———. "Soul Generation: Radical Fashion, Beauty, and the Transnational Black Liberation Movement, 1954–1980." PhD diss., Indiana University, 2011.

Freeland, Gregory K. "'We're a Winner': Popular Music and the Black Power Movement." *Social Movement Studies* 8 (August 2009): 261–88.

"Free School." *New Pittsburgh Courier*, November, 3, 1973, 28.

Fried, Joseph P. "Bedford-Stuyvesant Has Bright Side, Too: Neat Blocks of Houses Attest to 'Other' Bedford-Stuyvesant." *New York Times*, February 1, 1969, 31.

*Fundisha* 1, no. 6. Published in *Black News* 2, no. 11 (December 11, 1973): 10.

"The Game of Politics Is Work." Politi Go Round (column). *New Pittsburgh Courier*, March 10, 1973, 1, 4.

Garland, Phyl. "Is the Afro on Its Way Out? Ancient African Hairstyles Win New Converts." *Ebony*, February 1973.

Gehman, Mary. "Toward an Understanding of the Quadroon Society of New Orleans, 1780–1860." In *Southern Women*, edited by Caroline Matheny Dillman, 47–55. New York: Routledge, 1988.

"General Statement." *Black News* 3, no. 23 (May 1978): 2.

Gershenhorn, Jerry. *Louis Austin and the Carolina Times: A Life in the Long Black Freedom Struggle*. Chapel Hill: University of North Carolina Press, 2018.

Gill, Tiffany. *Beauty Shop Politics: African American Women's Activism in the Beauty Industry*. Urbana: University of Illinois Press, 2010.

Givens, Jarvis R. *Fugitive Pedagogy: Carter G. Woodson and the Art of Black Teaching*. Cambridge: Harvard University Press, 2021.

Giwa, Tayo, and Cynthia Gordy Giwa. *The Sun Rises in the East*. YouTube. Indie Rights Movies, July 24, 2023. https://www.youtube.com/watch?v=rzYo5OyFGBQ.

Glaude, Eddie S., Jr., ed. *Is It Nation Time? Contemporary Essays on Black Power and Black Nationalism*. Chicago: University of Chicago Press, 2002.

Gore, Dayo, Jeanne Theoharis, and Komozi Woodard, eds. *Want to Start a Revolution? Radical Women in the Black Freedom Struggle*. New York: New York University Press, 2009.

Greene, Christina. *Free Joan Little: The Politics of Race, Sexual Violence, and Imprisonment*. Chapel Hill: University of North Carolina Press, 2022.

Greenleaf, Robert K. *Servant Leadership: A Journey into the Nature of Legitimate Power and Greatness*. New York: Paulist Press, 1977.

Griffin, Farah Jasmine. "'Ironies of the Saint': Malcolm X, Black Women, and the Price of Protection." In *Sisters in the Struggle: African American Women in the Civil Rights-Black Power Movement*, edited by Bettye Collier-Thomas and V. P. Franklin, 214–29. New York: New York University Press, 2001.

"Guard against Dumping-Ground Schools." *New York Times*, September 4, 1992, A20.

Halisi, Imamu [Clyde], ed. *Kitabu: Beginning Concepts in Kawaida*. Los Angeles: US Organization, 1971. Stuart A. Rose Manuscript, Archives, and Rare Book Library, Emory University, Atlanta, GA.

———. "Maulana Ron Karenga: Black Leader in Captivity." *Black Scholar* 3, no. 9 (May 1972): 27–31.

Halisi, Clyde, and James Mtume, eds. *The Quotable Karenga*. Los Angeles: US, 1967.

Hall, Jacquelyn Dowd. "The Long Civil Rights Movement as the Political Uses of the Past." *Journal of American History* 91 (March 2005): 1233–63.

Hall, Tamara. "Freedom School Teaches Self Pride for Brighter Futures." *New Pittsburgh Courier*, December 21, 2003, KA10.

Hayden, Tom. *Rebellion in Newark: Official Violence and Ghetto Response*. New York: Vintage, 1967.

Hayes, Floyd W., III, and Judson L. Jeffries. "*US* Does Not Stand for United Slaves!" In *Black Power in the Belly of the Beast*, edited by Judson L. Jeffries, 95–133. Urbana: University of Illinois Press, 2006.

Hayes, Robin J. *Love for Liberation: African Independence, Black Power, and a Diaspora Underground*. Seattle: University of Washington Press, 2021.

Haynes, Sonya M. "Hill House Program Stresses Education: At Kaufman Center." *New Pittsburgh Courier*, October 8, 1994, A1.

Heard, Nathan C. *Howard Street*. New York: Dial, 1968.

Heitner, Devorah. "The Good Side of the Ghetto: Visualizing Black Brooklyn: 1968–1971." *Velvet Light Trap* 62 (Fall 2008): 48–61.

Henderson, Errol A. *The Revolution Will Not Be Theorized: Cultural Revolution in the Black Power Era*. Albany: State University of New York Press, 2019.

Herro, Steven. "Representation of African American Women on Reality Television after the Great Recession." PhD diss., Georgia State University, 2015.

Hill, Jaribu. "Excerpts from a Life Standing at the Well." *Black Scholar* 36, no. 1 (Spring 2006): 31–36.

Hill, Ngoma, and Jaribu Hill. *For Your Consideration!* Serious Bizness. 1982. Folkways Records FW05520. Liner notes.

"Hill Mental Health Team Created to Serve Blacks." *New Pittsburgh Courier*, July 28, 1973, 2.

Hochschild, Jennifer L., and Vesla Weaver. "The Skin Color Paradox and the American Racial Order." *Social Forces* 86, no. 2 (December 2007): 643–70.

"How to Tie a Lapa." *Black News* 3, no. 5 (December 1975): 31.

Howze, Tamanikah [*sic*]. "Freedom Summer School: The Freedom Summer Died with the 1960s While Poverty and Illiteracy Remained. Now the Program Has Been Retooled and Resurrected." *Pittsburgh City Paper*, July 31, 2003. www.pghcitypaper.com.

Hudson-Weems, Clenora. "Africana Womanism." In *Sisterhood, Feminisms and Power: From Africa to the Diaspora*, edited by Obioma Nnaemeka, 149–61. Trenton, NJ: AfricaWorld Press, 1998.

———. *Africana Womanism: Reclaiming Ourselves.* Troy: Bedford, 2004.

"Imani." *Black News* 2, no. 11 (December 11, 1973): 19.

"Inmate Sets Record Straight on Black Mood Article about Pen." Reader's Forum. *New Pittsburgh Courier,* January 17, 1970, 9.

Isaac, Charles S. *Inside Ocean Hill-Brownsville: A Teacher's Education, 1968–69.* Albany: State University of New York Press, 2014.

Jalia, M. Monthly Kiswahili Lesson. Column. *Black New Ark,* January 1973, 2.

Johnson, Toki Schalk. "Black Group Holds Feast of Kwanza [*sic*]." *New Pittsburgh Courier,* January 9, 1971, 24.

Johnston, Ernie. "Committee to Carry on Newark Leader's Goals." *New York Amsterdam News,* August 30, 1980, 3.

Jones, Deborah, with Thandisizwe Chimurenga. *What We Stood For: The Story of a Revolutionary Black Woman.* New York: Diasporic Africa Press, 2023.

Jones, Lesly. "Uhuru Sasa Shule Says Family Must Re-Educate." *New York Amsterdam News,* January 15, 1972, B1.

Joseph, Peniel. "Black Liberation without Apology: Reconceptualizing the Black Movement." *Black Scholar* 31 (Fall–Winter 2001): 2–19.

———, ed. *The Black Power Movement: Rethinking the Civil Rights-Black Power Era.* New York: Routledge, 2006.

———. "The Black Power Movement: A State of the Field." *Journal of American History* 96, no. 3 (December 2009): 751–76.

———. *Stokely: A Life.* New York: Basic Civitas, 2014.

———. *Waiting 'til the Midnight Hour: A Narrative History of Black Power in America.* New York: Henry Holt, 2006.

Kabaila, Wesley. "On Dr. Maulana Karenga: An Open Letter by Wesley Kabaila." *Assata Shakur Blogspot,* July 9, 2010. http://assata-shakur.blogspot.com.

Karenga, Maulana Ron. "Black Alternative Educators Tour the People's Republic of China." *Black Scholar* 19 (September 1977): 55.

———. *Essays on Struggle: Position and Analysis.* San Diego: Kawaida Publications, 1978.

———. "In Defense of Sis. Joanne: For Ourselves and History." *Black Scholar* 6, no. 10 (July–August 1975): 37–42.

———. *In Love and Struggle: Poems for Bold Hearts.* San Diego: Kawaida Publications, 1978.

———. "Kawaida and Its Critics: A Sociohistorical Analysis." *Journal of Black Studies* 8, no. 2 (December 1977): 125–48.

———. "Kawaida Philosophy and Practice: Questions of Life and Struggle." *Los Angeles Sentinel,* August 2, 2007.

———. *Kawaida Theory: An Introductory Outline for Ourselves and History.* Inglewood, CA: Kawaida Publications, 1980.

———. *Kwanzaa: A Celebration of Family, Community and Culture.* Los Angeles: University of Sankore Press, 1998.

———. *Kwanzaa: Origin, Concepts, Practice*. Inglewood, CA: Kawaida Publications, 1977.

———. "A Response to Muhammad Ahmad." *Black Scholar* 9, no. 10 (July–August 1978): 55–57.

———. "US, Kawaida and the Black Liberation Movement in the 1960s: Culture, Knowledge and Struggle." In *Engines of the Black Power Movement: Essays on the Influence of Civil Rights Actions, Arts, and Islam*, edited by James L. Conyers Jr., 95–133. Jefferson: McFarland, 2007.

Karenga, Tiamoyo, and Chimbuko Tembo. "Kawaida Womanism: African Ways of Being Woman in the World." *Western Journal of Black Studies* 36, no. 1 (2012): 33–47.

Kelley, Robin D. G., and Betsy Esch. "Black Like Mao: Red China and Black Revolution." *Souls* 6 (Fall 1999): 6–41.

Kendrick, Louis. "To Tell the Truth Frogs Financial Support Must Be Duplicated." *New Pittsburgh Courier*, July 25, 2004, A7.

Kerber, Linda K. *Toward an Intellectual History of Women*. Chapel Hill: University of North Carolina Press, 1997.

Kifano, Subira. "Afrocentric Education in Supplementary Schools: Paradigm and Practice at the Mary McLeod Bethune Institute." *Journal of Negro Education* 65 (Spring 1996): 209–18.

———. "Promise and Possibilities in the Education of African American Children as Exemplified in the Mary McLeod Bethune Institute, an Afro-Centric Supplementary School." PhD diss., Claremont Graduate University and San Diego State University, 2010.

Kifner, John. "Rights Leaders Plan to Take Up Meredith's March in Mississippi." *New York Times*, June 7, 1966, 28.

Killens, John Oliver. "Black Man in the New China." *Black World*, November 1975, 41.

Kinchen, Shirletta J. *Black Power in the Bluff City: African American Youth and Student Activism in Memphis, 1965–1975*. Knoxville: University of Tennessee Press, 2016.

Kingsley Freedom School Newsletter. June 24–June 28, 2013. http://kingsleyassociation.org.

Konadu, Kwasi. *A View from The East: Black Cultural Nationalism and Education in New York City*. 2nd ed. Syracuse: Syracuse University Press, 2009.

Kong, Xurong. "Military Uniform as a Fashion during the Cultural Revolution." *Intercultural Communication Studies* 17 (2008): 287–303.

Kurashige, Scott. "Crenshaw and the Rise of Multiethnic Los Angeles." *Afro-Hispanic Review* 27 (Spring 2008): 41–58.

Kurutz, Daveen Rae. "Summer Program at Kingsley Lincoln Freedom School Adds African Culture." *Pittsburgh Tribune Review*, July 9, 2009. http://triblive.com.

"Kwanza [*sic*], a Tradition." *Black News* 3, no. 5 (December 1975): 17.

"Kwanza [*sic*], a Tradition." *Black News* 3, no. 13 (October 1976): 12.

Kwayana, Eusi. "Burnhamism, Jaganism and the People of Guyana." *Black Scholar* 4, nos. 8–9 (May–June 1973): 40–46.

Lee, Chana Kai. *For Freedom's Sake: The Life of Fannie Lou Hamer*. Urbana: University of Illinois Press, 2000.

Lee, Marcella. "Community Update, NAACP: Here and Now, Music Videos Outrageous." *New Pittsburgh Courier*, January 11, 2004, A7.

Lee, Trymaine. "Fulton Street Journal: A Merchant Watches as Bed-Stuy Gentrifies." *New York Times*, May 9, 2009, A15.

"Legal Updates." *Off Our Backs: A Women's News Journal* 8, no. 10 (November 1978): 3.

Lewis, John, with Michael D'Orso. *Walking with the Wind: A Memoir of the Movement*. New York: Simon and Schuster, 1998.

Li, Yan, Hui Chun, Neal Ashkanasy, and David Ahlstrom. "A Multi-Level Study of Emergent Group Leadership: Effects of Emotional Stability and Group Conflict." *Asia Pacific Journal of Management* 29, no. 2 (June 2012): 351–66.

Lindsey, Treva B. "Post-Ferguson: A 'Herstorical' Approach to Black Violability." *Feminist Studies* 41, no. 1 (2015): 232-237.

"Lock-In Draws Over 250 Youth." *Los Angeles Sentinel*, March 9, 1989, C12.

Macleod, David I. "Food Prices, Politics, and Policy in the Progressive Era." *Journal of the Gilded Age and Progressive Era* 8, no. 4 (July 2009): 365–406.

Madzimoyo, Wakesa. "Afrikan-Americans Educate Their Own." *Southern Exposure* 8, no. 3 (Fall 1980): 45.

Magaziner, Daniel R. "Pieces of a (Wo)man: Feminism, Gender and Adulthood in Black Consciousness, 1968–1977." *Journal of Southern African Studies* 37 (March 2011): 45–61.

Mandela, Winnie. *Part of My Soul Went with Him*. New York: Norton, 1985.

Manoni, Mary H. *Bedford-Stuyvesant: The Anatomy of a Central City Community*. New York: Quadrangle/*New York Times* Book Co., 1973.

"Man Surrenders in Deaths of Poet's Daughter and Her Friend." *New York Times*, August 18, 2003, B10.

Martin, Michel. "The #BlackLivesMatterMovement: Marches and Tweets for Healing." *Michel Martin Going There*. NPR, June 9, 2015. www.npr.org.

Martin, Tony. *Race First: The Ideological and Organizational Struggles of Marcus Garvey and the Universal Negro Improvement Association*. Westport, CT: Greenwood, 1976.

Maslin, Janet. "'Portrait of Teresa' at the Modern." *New York Times*, April 27, 1981, 51.

Mason, Nicola F. "The Diversity of African Musics: Zulu Kings, Xhosa Clicks, and Gumboot Dancing in South Africa." *General Music Today* 27 (January 2014): 30–35.

"Maulana Karenga Benefit: Parole Denied for Another Year!" *Black New Ark*, Septemba [*sic*] 1972, 1, 2.

Mayer, Martin. "The Full and Sometimes Very Surprising Story of Ocean Hill, the Teachers' Union and the Teacher Strikes of 1968: The Story of Ocean Hill." *New York Times*, February 2, 1969, SM18.

Mayes, Keith A. *Kwanzaa: Black Power and the Making of the African-American Holiday Tradition*. New York: Routledge, 2009.

McDonald, John F. *Urban America: Growth, Crisis, and Rebirth*. Armonk, NY: M. E. Sharpe, 2008.

McDuffie, Erik S. *Sojourning for Freedom: Black Women, American Communism, and the Making of Black Left Feminism*. Durham: Duke University Press, 2011.

McDuffie, Erik S., and Komozi Woodard. "'If You're in a Country That's Progressive, the Woman Is Progressive': Black Women Radicals and the Making of the Politics and Legacy of Malcolm X." *Biography* 36, no. 3 (Summer 2013): 507–39.

McGuire, Danielle L. *At the Dark End of the Street: Black Women, Rape and Resistance—A New History of the Civil Rights Movement from Rosa Parks to the Rise of Black Power*. New York: Knopf, 2010.

Mchawi, Basir. "Victor Rhodes: Another Case of Injustice." *Black News* 3 (special ed., c. Fall 1978): 2.

———. "Which Way Kwanza [*sic*]." *Black News* 3, no. 5 (December 1975): 8.

McNeil, Genna Rae. "'Joanne Is You and Joanne Is Me.'" In *Sisters in the Struggle: African American Women in the Civil Rights-Black Power Movement*, edited by Betty Collier-Thomas and V. P. Franklin. New York: New York University Press, 2001.

"Mental Health Team Conducts Drug Seminars to Better Understand Addicts." *New Pittsburgh Courier*, July 29, 1972.

Michna, Catherine. "Performance and Cross-Racial Storytelling in Post-Katrina New Orleans: Interviews with John O'Neal, Carol Bebelle, and Nicholas Slie." *Drama Review* 57, no. 1 (Spring 2013): 48–69.

*Military Support of Law Enforcement during Civil Disturbances*. August 1965. California State Military Museum. www.militarymuseum.org.

"Millions Celebrated Kwanzaa This Year." *Philadelphia Tribune*, January 6, 1995, 3D.

Mississippi Workers' Center for Human Rights. The Mississippi Project. Accessed October 8, 2016. http://themississippiproject.weebly.com/.

"A Mobile Clinic for Our Community." *Black News* 1, no. 39 (April 1972): 12–14.

Montgomery, Sarah E. "Why Men Left: Reconsidering the Feminization of Teaching in the Nineteenth Century." *American Educational History Journal* 36, no. 1 (2009): 219–36.

Moore, Leonard M. *The Defeat of Black Power: Civil Rights and the National Black Political Convention of 1972*. Baton Rouge: Louisiana State University Press, 2018.

Moses, Wilson Jeremiah. *Afrotopia: The Roots of African American Popular History*. Cambridge: Cambridge University Press, 1998.

———, ed. *Classical Black Nationalism: From the American Revolution to Marcus Garvey*. New York: New York University Press, 1996.

Mtume, James. "Baraka." *Kawaida*. Recorded December 11, 1969. O'Be Records OB-301, 33 1/3 rpm.

Mumford, Kevin J. *Newark: A History of Race, Rights, and Riots in America*. New York: New York University Press, 2007.

Mumininas of Committee for Unified Newark. *Mwanamke Mwananchi (The Nationalist Woman)*. 1971. Pamphlet. Komozi Woodard Amiri Baraka Collection, Auburn Avenue Research Library on African American Culture and History, Archives Division, Atlanta, GA.

Murray, Virgie. "Black Agenda Installs Officers." *Los Angeles Sentinel*, December 23, 1982, C11.

"Mwanamke Weusi (Black Woman)." *Black News* 2, no. 14 (February 1974): n.p.

"NCNW Honor Nation's Finest Educators." *New Journal and Guide* (Norfolk), November 7, 2001, 14.

"NCNW Opens Inner Cities Food Cooperative Sept. 3." *Los Angeles Sentinel*, September 1, 1983, C10.

Nembhard, Jessica Gordon. *Collective Courage: A History of African American Cooperative Economic Thought and Practice*. University Park: Pennsylvania State University Press, 2014.

"New Date Set for Parley." *New Pittsburgh Courier*, February 22, 1975, 1.

New Jersey Department of Labor and Workforce Development. Table 6, New Jersey Population by Municipality: 1930–1990. Census Data for New Jersey, 1990. Accessed August 15, 2014. lwd.dol.state.nj.us.

New York City Board of Education, Brooklyn, NY. "'600' Schools, Yesterday, Today, and Tomorrow." N.d. ERIC, EBSCOhost. Accessed March 4, 2016.

"NJ School Endorsed by Solon." *New York Amsterdam News*, July 24, 1971, D1.

Nuttall, Rebecca. "Hill District Education Council Empowers Parents." *New Pittsburgh Courier*, November 16–22, 2011, A1, A4.

———. "Kids Rally for National Health Care." *New Pittsburgh Courier*, July 22–28, 2009, A5.

Nyerere, Julius K. *Ujamaa: Essays on Socialism*. London: Oxford University Press, 1968.

Ogbar, Jeffrey O. G. "Black Nationalism." In *Routledge Handbook of Pan-Africanism*, edited by Reiland Rabaka, 89–99. London: Routledge, 2020.

———. *Black Power: Radical Politics and African American Identity*. Baltimore: Johns Hopkins University Press, 2004.

Omolade, Barbara. "Sisterhood in Black and White." In *The Feminist Memoir Project: Voices from Women's Liberation*, edited by Rachel Blau DuPlessis and Ann Snitow, 377–408. New York: Three Rivers Press, 1998.

Onaci, Edward. *Free the Land: The Republic of New Afrika and the Pursuit of a Black Nation-State*. Chapel Hill: University of North Carolina Press, 2020.

"Organizers Schedule Black Political Action Forum." *New Pittsburgh Courier*, August 27, 1983, A3.

"Others Who Were Nominated." *Pittsburgh Post-Gazette*, October 20, 2004. www.post-gazette.com.

"Overdue Victory." *Harvard Crimson*, March 26, 1968. www.thecrimson.com.

Panzer, Michael G. "The Pedagogy of Revolution: Youth, Generational Conflict, and Education in the Development of Mozambican Nationalism and the State, 1962–1970." *Journal of Southern African Studies* 35 (December 2009): 803–20.

"Parents Get Their Principal." *New York Amsterdam News*, January 17, 1970, 31.

"Parents of Young Offenders Meet and Ask, 'What Went Wrong?'" *New York Times*, February 25, 1975, 40.

Pellegrinelli, Lara. "The Women Jacketed by Records." *JazzTimes*, December 2001. http://jazztimes.com.

Perkins, Margo V. *Autobiography as Activism: Three Black Women of the Sixties*. Jackson: University Press of Mississippi, 2000.

Peter, Noel. "4 Evers Faculty Lose Jobs." *New York Amsterdam News*, October 23, 1982, 18.

Philip, Dawad Wayne. "Is the Black Bookstore an Endangered Species? Prospects for Black Literature Appear Bleak." *New York Amsterdam News*, January 8, 1977, B2.

"Political Prisoners." *Black New Ark*, November 1972, 4.

Pope, John. "Virginia Evalena Young Collins, Teacher, Nurse, and Activist, Dies at Age 96." *Times-Picayune*, July 28, 2011.

Posey, Sean. "Will Black Nationalism Reemerge?" *Truthout*, September 21, 2013. www.truth-out.org.

"Positive Votes for New School Names." *New York Amsterdam News*, October 16, 1971, C6.

Pride, Armistead S., and Clint C. Wilson II. *A History of the Black Press*. Washington, DC: Howard University Press, 1997.

"Prison Notes." *Black Scholar* 6, no. 5 (January–February 1975): 31.

"Public Auditorium Authority Members Sworn in Tuesday." *Pittsburgh Courier*, April 10, 1954, 13.

"Queen Crowns Queen." *Chicago Defender*, November 12, 1966, 5.

"Queen Mother Moore." *Black Scholar* 1, no. 8 (June 1970): 50–52.

Quest, Matthew. "Sister Tchaiko Kwayana: An Original Educator of the African World." *Black Agenda Report*, May 30, 2017. www.blackagendareport.com.

Ransby, Barbara. *Ella Baker and the Black Freedom Movement: A Radical Democratic Vision*. Chapel Hill: University of North Carolina Press, 2003.

"The Relationship between the Sexes." In *The Black Power Movement*, part 1, *Amiri Baraka, from Black Arts to Black Radicalism*. Bethesda, MD: University Publications of America, 2001. Microfilm.

Rich, Motoko. "Why Don't More Men Go into Teaching?" *New York Times*, September 7, 2015, SR 3.

Rickford, Russell. "'Kazi Is the Blackest of All': Pan-African Nationalism and the Making of the 'New Man,' 1969–1975." *Journal of African American History* 101, nos. 1–2 (Winter–Spring 2016): 97–125.

———. *We Are an African People: Independent Education, Black Power, and the Radical Imagination*. Oxford: Oxford University Press, 2016.

———. "We Can't Grow Food on All This Concrete: The Land Question, Agrarianism, and Black Nationalist Thought in the Late 1960s and 1970s." *Journal of American History* 103, no. 4 (March 2017): 956–80.

Robnett, Belinda. *How Long? How Long? African-American Women in the Struggle for Civil Rights*. Oxford: Oxford University Press, 1997.

Rogers, Ibram H. *The Black Campus Movement: Black Studies and the Racial Reconstitution of Higher Education, 1965–1972*. New York: Palgrave Macmillan, 2012.

Rogers, Jamala. *Ferguson Is America: Roots of Rebellion*. St. Louis: Mira Digital Publishing, 2015.

Rooks, Noliwe. *Hair Raising: Beauty, Culture, and African American Women*. New Brunswick: Rutgers University Press, 1996.

Ross, Loretta J. "A Personal Journey from Women's Rights to Civil Rights to Human Rights." *Black Scholar* 36, no. 1 (March 2006): 45–53.

Salaam, Kalamu ya. "Hofu Ni Kwenu (My Fear Is for You)." 1973. In *Art for Life: My Story, My Song*, Published in *Chicken Bones: A Journal for Literary and Artistic African-American Themes*, n.d. www.nathanielturner.com.

———. *Ibura*. New Orleans: Ahidiana, 1976.

———. *Our Women Keep Our Skies from Falling: Six Essays in Support of the Struggle to Smash Sexism/Develop Women*. New Orleans: Nkombo, 1980.

———. *Pamoja Tutashinda: Together We Will Win*. New Orleans: Ahidiana, 1974.

———. "Wounded." *Neo-Griot: Kalamu ya Salaam's Information Blog*, April 24, 2013. http://kalamu.com.

Salaam, Kalamu ya, with Tayari kwa Salaam and Kuishi kwa Taraji. *Herufi: An Alphabet Reader*. New Orleans: Ahidiana, 1978.

Salaam, Sala Udin Saif. Afrikan View. Column. *New Pittsburgh Courier*, January 9, 1971–February 22, 1975.

Salaam, Tayari kwa. "Ahidiana." *Southern Exposure* 8, no. 3 (Fall 1980): 45.

———. "Practice the Values and Love Revolution." *Black Books Bulletin* 2 (Winter 1974): 40–49.

———. "So-Journeying: Creating Sacred Space in Education." PhD diss., Louisiana State University, 2003.

———. *Working Together, We Can Make a Change: Towards Sisterhoods of Struggle*. New Orleans: Nkombo, 1981.

Salaam, Tayari kwa, and Kalamu ya Salaam. *Who Will Speak for Us? New Afrikan Folktales*. New Orleans: Ahidiana, 1974.

Simanga, Michael. *Amiri Baraka and the Congress of African People: History and Memory*. New York: Palgrave Macmillan, 2015.

———. "The Congress of African People (1970–1980): History and Memory of an Ideological Journey." PhD diss., Union Institute and University, 2008.

Simmons, Lakisha Michelle. *Crescent City Girls: The Lives of Young Women in Segregated New Orleans*. Chapel Hill: University of North Carolina Press, 2015.

"'Spiritual Revolution of the Mind' Launched." *New Pittsburgh Courier*, May 27, 1972, 10.

Stanford, Karin L. "Reverend Jesse and the Rainbow/PUSH Coalition: Institutionalizing Economic Opportunity." In *Black Political Organizations in the Post–Civil Rights Era*, edited by Ollie Johnson III and Karin L. Stanford, 150–69. New Brunswick: Rutgers University Press, 2002.

State of New Jersey v. Ibn El-Amin Pasha. No. A-1590-05T4 (N.J. Super. 2008). Lexis-Nexis 1564.

Stern, Nicholas C. "A Conversation with Arun Gandhi." *Frederick News Post*, June 9, 2012.

St. Julien, Mtumishi. *Upon the Shoulders of Elephants We Reach the Sky: A Parent's Farewell to a Collegian.* New Orleans: Rungate Press, 1995.

Stokes, Tom. "Arusi! East Afrikan Wedding Rites Vibrate to the Beat of Drums." Willa's Women's Whirl (column). *New Pittsburgh Courier*, July 21, 1973, 9.

———. "Black Politicos Adopt 12-Pt. Platform at Confab." *New Pittsburgh Courier*, February 5, 1972, 1.

"Storm over Teen Halfway House." *New York Amsterdam News*, January 13, 1979, B1.

Strauss, Greg. "Is Polygamy Inherently Unequal?" *Ethics* 122 (April 2012): 516–44.

Sunni-Ali, Asantewa. "Performing New African Childhood: Agency, Conformity, and the Spaces in Between." PhD diss., Arizona State University, 2014.

Surfaro, Monica. "The East, a Black Culture and Education Center, Brings Bit of Africa to Brooklyn." *New York Times*, August 17, 1975, 87.

Tager, Florence, and Zala Highsmith-Taylor. *Medgar Evers College: The Pursuit of a Community's Dream.* New York: Caribbean Diaspora Press, 2008. In The Founding of Medgar Evers College collection, CUNY Digital History Archive. https://cdha.cuny.edu.

Taylor, Jeffrey. "'Live from The East': Pharoah Sanders in Brooklyn." *American Music Review* 62, no. 2 (Spring 2013). www.brooklyn.cuny.edu.

Taylor, Ula. *The Promise of Patriarchy: Women and the Nation of Islam.* Chapel Hill: University of North Carolina Press, 2017.

———. *The Veiled Garvey: The Life and Times of Amy Jacques Garvey.* Chapel Hill: University of North Carolina Press, 2002.

Teule, Cheo. "Why Is Marcus Garvey Closed?" *Black New Ark*, February 1973, 5.

Theoharis, Jeanne. "Black Freedom Studies: Re-Imagining and Redefining the Fundamentals." *History Compass* 4, no. 2 (2006): 348–67.

"Thirteenth Avenue School." Historic American Buildings Survey, National Park Service. 2003. HABS no. NJ-1246, 2 and 15. Accessed July 9, 2016. http://cdn.loc.gov.

"The Three Homes Are Saved." *Black News* 1, no. 36 (December 1971): 16.

Tillet, Salamishah. "The Panthers' Revolutionary Feminism." *New York Times*, October 2, 2015. www.nytimes.com.

Tinson, Christopher M. *Radical Intellect: Liberator Magazine and Black Activism in the 1960s.* Chapel Hill: University of North Carolina Press, 2017.

Toler, Sonya M. "Malcolm's Legacy Still Lives On." *New Pittsburgh Courier*, February 16, 2005, A1.

Trent, Mattie. "East Area Chatter." *New Pittsburgh Courier*, August 14, 1971, 21.

Ture, Kwame, and Charles V. Hamilton. *Black Power: The Politics of Liberation.* Rev. ed. New York: Vintage, 1992.

Udin, Sala. "Black Women's United Front." Serve the People (column). *New Pittsburgh Courier*, January 25, 1975, 20.

Ukombozi, Amani na Uwezo ya (Michael McMillan). "Reparation for the Descendants of Enslaved Africans: What's Psychology Got to Do with It?" *Race, Gender, and Class* 18, nos. 1–2 (2011): 111–24.

Umoja, Akinyele K. "From Malcolm X to Omowale Malik Shabazz: The Transformation and Its Impact on the Black Liberation Struggle." In *Malcolm X: A Historical*

*Reader*, edited by James L. Conyers Jr. and Andrew P. Smallwood, 31–53. Durham: Carolina Academic Press, 2008.

Umoja, Akinyele, and Charles Jones. "Black Power Rivals." Unpublished manuscript, 2012. In author's possession.

"Us: A History of Service, Struggle, and Institution Building." *Harambee Notes* 2.8–2.9 (August–September 1996). www.us-organization.org.

US Department of Labor Statistics. "National Survey of Professional, Administrative, Technical, and Clerical Pay, June 1969." February 1970.

Van Deburg, William L., ed. *Modern Black Nationalism: From Marcus Garvey to Louis Farrakhan*. New York: New York University Press, 1997.

———. *New Day in Babylon: The Black Power Movement and American Culture, 1965–1975*. Chicago: University of Chicago Press, 1992.

*Voices of The EAST: A Collection of Reflections*. New York: EAST 50th Anniversary Committee, 2019.

Wade, Treshea N. "Paintball Event to Raise Funds for Hill Playground." *Pittsburgh Tribune-Review*, May 17, 2000, A1.

Walker, Alice. *In Search of Our Mothers' Gardens*. 1983; San Diego: Harcourt Brace Jovanovich, 2011.

Walker, Jamie. "Home-Going Celebration for Daughter of Amina and Amiri Baraka Touches Many." *New York Amsterdam News*, August 21–27, 2003, 5, 30.

Walker, Steven Akili, with ElizaBeth Felton. *Turn the Horns On*. New York: Wynter-Lynn, 2011.

Wallach, Jennifer Jensen. *Every Nation Has Its Dish: Black Bodies and Black Food in Twentieth-Century America*. Chapel Hill: University of North Carolina Press, 2019.

———. "How to Eat to Live: Black Nationalism and the Post-1964 Culinary Turn." *Study the South*, July 2, 2014. https://southernstudies.olemiss.edu.

Webb, Genea L. "Economic Independence: The 21st Century Struggle, Activist Nkomo Says South Africa, US Should Partner." *New Pittsburgh Courier*, September 22, 2001, B2.

Weber, Bret A., and Amanda Wallace. "Revealing the Empowerment Revolution: A Literature Review of the Model Cities Program." *Journal of Urban History* 38, no. 1 (2012): 173–92.

Weinman, Jaime J. "The Best Cartoon You've Never Seen." *Maclean's* 119, no. 13 (March 27, 2006): 57.

Westmaas, Nigel. "An Organic Activist: Eusi Kwayana, Guyana, and Global Pan-Africanism." In *Black Power in the Caribbean*, edited by Kate Quinn, 159–78. Gainesville: University Press of Florida, 2014.

Weusi, Aminisha. "Arthur Eve Speaks at Forum." *New York Amsterdam News*, August 5, 1978, A-4.

———. "Assemblyman Arthur Eve Speaks at B.C.C. Forum." *Black News* 3, no. 24 (August 1978): 20, 26.

———. "Bklyn Tenants Fight to Save Their Homes." *New York Amsterdam News*, April 27, 1985, 9.

Weusi, Jitu. "The Re-Emergence of B'klyn Grassroots Politics." *New York Amsterdam News*, December 31, 1977, B1.

———. "Why Was Arthur Miller Murdered." *Black News* 3 (special ed., c. Fall 1978): 2.

Weusi, Kasisi Jitu. "Around Our Way." *Black News* 2, no. 12 (December 26, 1973): 12–13.

———. "Around Our Way." *Black News* 2, no. 18 (June 1974): 12.

———. "Around Our Way." *Black News* 2, no. 19 (July 1974): 14.

White, Deborah Gray. *Too Heavy a Load: Black Women in Defense of Themselves, 1894–1994*. New York: Norton, 1999.

White, E. Frances. "Africa on My Mind: Gender, Counter Discourse and African-American Nationalism." *Journal of Women's History* 2 (Spring 1999): 73–97.

"White Merchants and Black Power." *Black News* 1, no. 39 (April 1972): 25.

Wiedmann, Thom. "Historic Kawaida Towers Project to Come before Planning Board Next Week." *Tap into Newark*, September 24, 2021. www.tapinto.net.

Williams, Rhonda Y. *Concrete Demands: The Search for Black Power in the 20th Century*. New York: Routledge, 2015.

Woodard, Komozi. *A Nation within a Nation: Amiri Baraka (LeRoi Jones) and Black Power Politics*. Chapel Hill: University of North Carolina Press, 1999.

"Workshop on Women in the Struggle." *African World*, July 1975, 5. In *The Black Power Movement*, part 1, *Amiri Baraka, from Black Arts to Black Radicalism*. Bethesda, MD: University Publications of America, 2001. Microfilm.

X, Malcolm. "Message to the Grass Roots." In *Malcolm X Speaks: Selected Speeches and Statements*, edited by George Breitman, 3–17. New York: Merit, 1965.

Yee, Herbert S. "The Three World Theory and Post-Mao China's Global Strategy." *International Affairs* 59, no. 2 (Spring 1983): 239–49.

Yerkey, Gary G. *He's Coming to Start Riots: On the Road to Black Power with 'The Reverend' Willie Ricks*. Washington, DC: GK Press, 2016.

"A Yoruban Wedding at The East." *Black News* 1, no. 33 (July 17, 1971): 10.

# INDEX

Page numbers in italics indicate Tables

# ABOUT THE AUTHOR

KENJA MCCRAY is Assistant Professor of History in Clayton State University's Department of Humanities. She writes about twentieth-century US history, focusing on African Americans, leadership, transnationalism, and women. She is the coauthor of *Atlanta Metropolitan State College*, a campus history commemorating the school's fiftieth anniversary.